영어 원서로 읽는 고전 Frankenstein
메리 셸리 Mary Shelley

펴낸곳: 북스트릿
원작: 메리 셸리 Mary Shelley
편집 및 주석: 신찬범
북커버 및 내지 디자인: 북스트릿
E-mail: invino70@gmail.com
Homepage: https://bookstreetpress.modoo.at
Blog: blog.naver.com/invino70
Fax: 0504-405-6711
초판 2022년 3월 26일

© 2022 북스트릿 BookStreet
북스트릿의 허락없는 이 책의 일부 또는 전부의 무단 복제, 전재, 발췌를 금합니다

ISBN: 979-11-90536-24-0

영어 원서로 읽는 고전

Frankenstein

영어 원서로 읽는 고전

Frankenstein

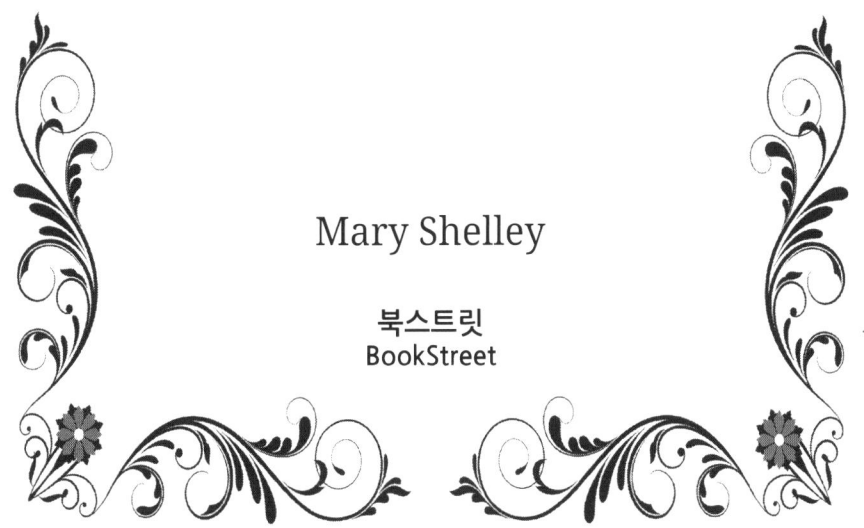

Mary Shelley

북스트릿
BookStreet

머리말

　이 책은 영문 고전을 깊이 있게 이해하고 감상하기 위해 기획되었습니다.

　영어 원서를 읽는 데에 있어서 가장 큰 어려움 중 하나는 생소한 단어와 구 등을 매번 영어사전에서 찾아봐야 하는 번거로움입니다. 이러한 이유로 영어 원서의 독해가 쉽지 않은 것으로 인식되고 있으며, 특히 영어가 모국어가 아닌 분이나 영어를 공부하시는 분에게 어려움이 있습니다.

　이 책은 이러한 어려움을 고려하여 영어 원서를 읽는 도중에 빈번하게 영어사전을 찾아봐야 하는 번거로움을 대폭 줄였으며, 영어사전을 될 수 있는 대로 적게 참조하면서 더 수월하게 영어 원서를 읽을 수 있게 했습니다.

　이 책에는 영문 고전의 원본 텍스트가 수록되어 있습니다. 문장 해석에 중요한 숙어, 구동사, 그 외 어려운 단어와 구 들을 선택하고 강조했습니다. 이들 단어와 구를 각 페이지 왼쪽에 단락별로 정의하고 설명했습니다. 각 단어의 발음기호를 기재하여, 어휘력을 높이는 데 도움이 되게 했습니다.

　이 책이 독자분이 영문 고전을 읽는 데 의미 있는 도움이 되기를 바랍니다.

신찬범

Frankenstein

Letter 1	11
Letter 2	17
Letter 3	24
Letter 4	26
Chapter 1	39
Chapter 2	48
Chapter 3	59
Chapter 4	72
Chapter 5	84
Chapter 6	95
Chapter 7	108
Chapter 8	125
Chapter 9	140
Chapter 10	151

Chapter 11	162
Chapter 12	175
Chapter 13	185
Chapter 14	195
Chapter 15	204
Chapter 16	218
Chapter 17	233
Chapter 18	242
Chapter 19	256
Chapter 20	269
Chapter 21	285
Chapter 22	302
Chapter 23	318
Chapter 24	330

Frankenstein

Letter 1

*T*o *Mrs. Saville, England._*

St. Petersburgh, Dec. 11th, 17—.

You will **rejoice** to hear that no **disaster** has accompanied the **commencement** of an enterprise which you have regarded with such evil **forebodings**. I arrived here yesterday, and my first **task** is to assure my dear sister of my welfare and increasing confidence in the success of my **undertaking**.

I am already far north of London, and as I walk in the streets of Petersburgh, I feel a cold northern breeze play upon my cheeks, which **braces** my nerves and fills me with delight. Do you understand this feeling? This breeze, which

---

rejoice [ridʒɔ́is] v.
기뻐하다
disaster [dizǽstər, -zάːs-] n.
재해, 참사, 큰 불운
commencement [kəménsmənt] n. 시작, 개시, 착수
foreboding [fɔːrbóudiŋ] n.
(불길한) 예감, 전조, 조짐
task [tæsk, tɑːsk] n.
일, 임무
undertaking [Àndərtéikiŋ] n.
일, 사업
brace [breis] v.
긴장하다, 대비하다, 마음을 다잡다

foretaste [fɔ́:rtèist] n. 미리 맛봄, 예기, 전조
clime [klaim] n. 나라, 지방; 풍토
fervent [fə́:rvənt] adj. 열의 있는
desolation [dèsəléiʃən] n. 황무지
skirt [skə:rt] v. ~의 가장자리를 지나다, ~와 접경하다
diffuse [difjú:z] v. 흩뜨리다, 발산하다
perpetual [pərpétʃuəl] adj. 부단한, 끊임없는
splendor [spléndə:r] n. 빛남, 호화, 화려함
surpass [sərpǽs, -pá:s] v. ~보다 낫다, 능가하다, 뛰어나다
habitable [hǽbətəbəl] adj. 거주할 수 있는, 살기에 적당한
render [réndə:r] v. ~이 되게 하다
satiate [séiʃièit] v. 물리게 하다, 충분히 만족시키다
ardent:[á:rdənt] adj. 열렬한, 정열적인

has travelled from the regions towards which I am advancing, gives me a **foretaste** of those icy **climes**. Inspirited by this wind of promise, my daydreams become more **fervent** and vivid. I try in vain to be persuaded that the pole is the seat of frost and **desolation**; it ever presents itself to my imagination as the region of beauty and delight. There, Margaret, the sun is for ever visible, its broad disk just **skirting** the horizon and **diffusing** a **perpetual splendour**. There — for with your leave, my sister, I will put some trust in preceding navigators — there snow and frost are banished; and, sailing over a calm sea, we may be wafted to a land **surpassing** in wonders and in beauty every region hitherto discovered on the **habitable** globe. Its productions and features may be without example, as the phenomena of the heavenly bodies undoubtedly are in those undiscovered solitudes. What may not be expected in a country of eternal light? I may there discover the wondrous power which attracts the needle and may regulate a thousand celestial observations that require only this voyage to **render** their seeming eccentricities consistent for ever. I shall **satiate** my **ardent** curiosity with the sight of a part of the world never before visited, and may tread a land never before imprinted by the foot of man. These are my enticements, and they are sufficient to conquer all fear of danger or death and to induce me to commence this laborious voyage with the joy a child feels when he embarks in a little boat, with his holiday mates, on an **expedition** of discovery up his native river. But supposing all these conjectures to be false, you cannot **contest** the **inestimable** benefit which I shall **confer** on all mankind, to the last generation, by discovering a passage near the pole to those countries, to reach which at present so many months are **requisite**; or by ascertaining the secret of the magnet, which, if at all possible, can only be effected by an undertaking such as mine.

These reflections have **dispelled** the agitation with which I began my letter, and I feel my heart glow with an enthusiasm which elevates me to heaven, for nothing contributes so much to **tranquillise** the mind as a steady purpose—a point on which the soul may fix its intellectual eye. This expedition has been the favourite dream of my early years. I have read with **ardour** the accounts of the various voyages which have been made in the **prospect** of arriving at the North Pacific Ocean through the seas which surround the pole. You may remember that a history of all the voyages made for purposes of discovery composed the

---

expedition [èkspədíʃən] n.
(집단, 단체의) 모험, 원정
contest [kəntést] v.
논쟁하다, 이의를 제기하다, 의문시하다
inestimable [inéstəməbəl] adj.
헤아릴 수 없는, 평가할 수 없을 만큼 귀중한
confer [kənfə́:r] v.
수여하다, 베풀다
requisite [rékwəzit] n.
필수품, 필요 조건

I shall satiate my ardent curiosity with the sight of a part of the world never before visited, and may tread a land never before imprinted by the foot of man.

dispel [dispél] v.
일소하다, 쫓아버리다, 없애다
tranquillize [trǽŋkwəlàiz] v.
잠잠하게 하다, 진정시키다
ardour [á:rdər] n.
열정, 열의
prospect [práspekt / prɔ́s-] n.
전망, 가능성, 예상, 기대

injunction [indʒʌ́ŋkʃən] n.
지시, 명령

peruse [pərúːz] v.
숙독하다, 음미하다
effusion [efjúːʒən] n.
감정, 말 등의 분출
entrance [entrǽns, -trάːns] v.
넋을 잃게 하다, 매혹하다
niche [nitʃ] n.
벽감, 한 구석, 적합한 지위
consecrate [kάnsəkrèit / kɔ́n-]
v. 신성하게 하다, 성화하다
be acquainted with:
~을 알고 있다, 정통하다
bent [bent] n.
경향, 성벽, 좋아함

resolve [rizάlv / -zɔ́lv] v.
결정하다, 결심하다
inure [injúər] v.
익숙케 하다, 단련하다, 공고히 하다
famine [fǽmin] n.
기근, 굶주림, 기아

whole of our good Uncle Thomas' library. My education was neglected, yet I was passionately fond of reading. These volumes were my study day and night, and my familiarity with them increased that regret which I had felt, as a child, on learning that my father's dying **injunction** had forbidden my uncle to allow me to embark in a seafaring life.

These visions faded when I **perused**, for the first time, those poets whose **effusions entranced** my soul and lifted it to heaven. I also became a poet and for one year lived in a paradise of my own creation; I imagined that I also might obtain a **niche** in the temple where the names of Homer and Shakespeare are **consecrated**. You **are** well **acquainted with** my failure and how heavily I bore the disappointment. But just at that time I inherited the fortune of my cousin, and my thoughts were turned into the channel of their earlier **bent**.

Six years have passed since I **resolved** on my present undertaking. I can, even now, remember the hour from which I dedicated myself to this great enterprise. I commenced by **inuring** my body to hardship. I accompanied the whale-fishers on several expeditions to the North Sea; I voluntarily endured cold, **famine**, thirst, and want of sleep; I often worked harder than the common sailors during the day and devoted my nights to the study of mathematics, the theory of medicine, and those branches of physical science from which a naval adventurer might **derive** the greatest practical advantage. Twice I actually hired myself as an under-mate in a Greenland whaler, and **acquitted** myself to admiration. I must **own** I felt a little proud when my captain offered me the second dignity in the vessel and **entreated** me to remain with the greatest earnestness, so valuable did he consider my services.

And now, dear Margaret, do I not deserve to accomplish some great purpose? My life might have been passed in ease and luxury, but I preferred glory to every enticement that wealth placed in my path. Oh, that some encouraging voice would answer in the **affirmative**! My courage and my **resolution** is firm; but my hopes **fluctuate**, and my spirits are often depressed. I am about to proceed on a long and difficult voyage, the emergencies of which will demand all my **fortitude**: I am required not only to raise the spirits of others, but sometimes to **sustain** my own, when theirs are failing.

This is the most favourable period for travelling in Russia. They fly quickly over the snow in their sledges; the motion is pleasant, and, in my opinion, far more agreeable than that

---

derive [diráiv] v.
끌어 내다, 손에 넣다
acquit [əkwít] v.
행동하다, 처신하다; 다하다
own [oun] v.
인정하다, 자인하다
entreat [entríːt] v.
원하다, 부탁하다

affirmative [əfə́ːrmətiv] n.
긍정, 확언
resolution [rèzəlúːʃ-ən] n.
결심, 결의
fluctuate [flʌ́ktʃuèit] v.
오르내리다, 변동하다
fortitude [fɔ́ːrtətjùːd] n.
용기, 불굴의 정신, 인내
sustain [səstéin] v.
지지하다, 격려하다, 기운내게 하다

stagecoach [stéidʒkòutʃ] n.
역마차
deck [dek] n.
갑판
post road:
(옛날의) 역로; 우편물 수송 도로

depart [dipá:rt] v.
출발하다, 떠나다
fortnight [fɔ́:rtnàit] n.
2주간
accustomed [əkʌ́stəmd] adj.
익숙한

shower [ʃáuə:r] v.
퍼붓다, 뿌리다, 쏟다
testify [téstəfài] v.
증언하다, 증명하다, 입증하다
gratitude [grǽtətjù:d] n.
감사, 사의

of an English **stagecoach**. The cold is not excessive, if you are wrapped in furs — a dress which I have already adopted, for there is a great difference between walking the **deck** and remaining seated motionless for hours, when no exercise prevents the blood from actually freezing in your veins. I have no ambition to lose my life on the **post-road** between St. Petersburgh and Archangel.

I shall **depart** for the latter town in a **fortnight** or three weeks; and my intention is to hire a ship there, which can easily be done by paying the insurance for the owner, and to engage as many sailors as I think necessary among those who are **accustomed** to the whale-fishing. I do not intend to sail until the month of June; and when shall I return? Ah, dear sister, how can I answer this question? If I succeed, many, many months, perhaps years, will pass before you and I may meet. If I fail, you will see me again soon, or never.

Farewell, my dear, excellent Margaret. Heaven **shower** down blessings on you, and save me, that I may again and again **testify** my **gratitude** for all your love and kindness.

Your affectionate brother,
R. Walton

Letter 2

*T*o Mrs. Saville, England._

Archangel, 28th March, 17—.

How slowly the time passes here, **encompassed** as I am by frost and snow! Yet a second step is taken towards my enterprise. I have hired a vessel and am occupied in collecting my sailors; those whom I have already engaged appear to be men on whom I can depend and are certainly possessed of **dauntless** courage.

But I have one **want** which I have never yet been able to satisfy, and the absence of the object of which I now feel as a most severe evil, I have no friend, Margaret: when I am glowing with the enthusiasm of success, there will be

encompass [inkʎmpəs] v.
둘러싸다, 에워싸다, 포위하다
dauntless [dɔ́:ntlis] adj.
두려움 없는, 용감한

want [wɔ(:)nt, wɑnt] n.
결핍, 부족

sustain [səstéin] v.
지지하다, 격려하다, 기운내게 하다
dejection [didʒékʃən] n.
의기소침, 낙담
deem [di:m] v.
생각하다, 판단하다
capacious [kəpéiʃəs] adj.
널찍한, 도량이 큰, 너그러운
celebrated [séləbrèitid] adj.
유명한, 고명한
derive [diráiv] v.
끌어 내다, 손에 넣다
conviction [kənvíkʃən] n.
신념, 확신
perceive [pərsí:v] v.
알아차리다, 이해하다
illiterate [ilítərit] adj.
무식한, 문맹의, 교양이 없는

none to participate my joy; if I am assailed by disappointment, no one will endeavour to **sustain** me in **dejection**. I shall commit my thoughts to paper, it is true; but that is a poor medium for the communication of feeling. I desire the company of a man who could sympathise with me, whose eyes would reply to mine. You may **deem** me romantic, my dear sister, but I bitterly feel the want of a friend. I have no one near me, gentle yet courageous, possessed of a cultivated as well as of a **capacious** mind, whose tastes are like my own, to approve or amend my plans. How would such a friend repair the faults of your poor brother! I am too ardent in execution and too impatient of difficulties. But it is a still greater evil to me that I am self-educated: for the first fourteen years of my life I ran wild on a common and read nothing but our Uncle Thomas' books of voyages. At that age I became acquainted with the **celebrated** poets of our own country; but it was only when it had ceased to be in my power to **derive** its most important benefits from such a **conviction** that I **perceived** the necessity of becoming acquainted with more languages than that of my native country. Now I am twenty-eight and am in reality more **illiterate** than many schoolboys of fifteen. It is true that I have thought more and that my daydreams are more extended and magnificent, but they want (as the painters call it) *keeping*; and I greatly need a friend who would have sense enough not to **despise** me as romantic, and affection enough for me to endeavour to regulate my mind.

Well, these are useless complaints; I shall certainly find no friend on the wide ocean, nor even here in Archangel, among merchants and seamen. Yet some feelings, unallied to the **dross** of human nature, beat even in these rugged bosoms. My lieutenant, for instance, is a man of wonderful courage and enterprise; he is madly desirous of glory, or rather, to **word** my phrase more characteristically, of advancement in his profession. He is an Englishman, and in the midst of national and professional **prejudices**, unsoftened by cultivation, **retains** some of the noblest **endowments** of humanity. I first became acquainted with him on board a whale vessel; finding that he was unemployed in this city, I easily engaged him to assist in my enterprise.

The master is a person of an excellent **disposition** and is remarkable in the ship for his gentleness and the mildness of his **discipline**. This circumstance, added to his well-known **integrity** and dauntless courage, made me very desirous to engage him. A youth passed in

despise [dispáiz] v.
경멸하다, 얕보다

dross [drɔːs, drɑs / drɔs] n.
불순물, 찌꺼기, 쓸모 없는 것
word [wəːrd] v.
말로 나타내다
prejudice [prédʒudis] n.
편견, 선입관
retain [ritéin] v.
보유하다, 유지하다
endowment [endáumənt] n.
자질, 재능, 소질

disposition [dìspəzíʃən] n.
기질, 성미, 성격, 취향
discipline [dísəplin] n.
훈련, 규율, 풍기
integrity [intégrəti] n.
성실, 정직, 고결

fosterage [fɔ́(:)stəridʒ, fɑ́s-] n.
양육, 육성
groundwork [´-wə̀:rk] n.
토대, 기초, 기반, 근거
amass [əmǽs] v.
모으다, 축적하다
consent [kənsént] v.
동의하다, 찬성하다, 승인하다
mistress [místris] n.
(고어) 사랑하는 여인, 연인
entreat [entrí:t] v.
원하다, 부탁하다
reassure [rì:əʃúə:r] v.
안심시키다, 장담하다, 기운을 돋우다
suppliant [sʌ́pliənt] n.
탄원자, 애원자
bestow [bistóu] v.
주다, 부여하다

solitude, my best years spent under your gentle and feminine **fosterage**, has so refined the **groundwork** of my character that I cannot overcome an intense distaste to the usual brutality exercised on board ship: I have never believed it to be necessary, and when I heard of a mariner equally noted for his kindliness of heart and the respect and obedience paid to him by his crew, I felt myself peculiarly fortunate in being able to secure his services. I heard of him first in rather a romantic manner, from a lady who owes to him the happiness of her life. This, briefly, is his story. Some years ago he loved a young Russian lady of moderate fortune, and having **amassed** a considerable sum in prize-money, the father of the girl **consented** to the match. He saw his **mistress** once before the destined ceremony; but she was bathed in tears, and throwing herself at his feet, **entreated** him to spare her, confessing at the same time that she loved another, but that he was poor, and that her father would never consent to the union. My generous friend **reassured** the **suppliant**, and on being informed of the name of her lover, instantly abandoned his pursuit. He had already bought a farm with his money, on which he had designed to pass the remainder of his life; but he **bestowed** the whole on his rival, together with

stock [stɑk / stɔk] n.
가축
solicit [səlísit] v.
간청하다
inexorable [inéksərəbəl] adj.
가차없는, 움직이지 않는
quit [kwit] v.
떠나다, 물러나다
inclination [ìnklənéiʃən] n.
좋아함, 기호, 의향
attend [əténd] v.
수반하다, 부수하다, 따르다
detract [ditrǽkt] v.
줄이다, 떨어뜨리다

consolation [kɑ̀nsəléiʃən / kɔ̀n-] n.
위로, 위안
toil [tɔil] n.
힘드는 일, 수고, 노고
waver [wéivəːr] v.
흔들리다, 망설이다, 주저하다
embarkation [èmbɑːrkéiʃən] n.
승선, 출항
confide [kənfáid] v.
믿다, 신뢰하다
prudence [prúːdəns] n.
신중, 세심, 분별

the remains of his prize-money to purchase **stock**, and then himself **solicited** the young woman's father to consent to her marriage with her lover. But the old man decidedly refused, thinking himself bound in honour to my friend, who, when he found the father **inexorable**, **quitted** his country, nor returned until he heard that his former mistress was married according to her **inclinations**. "What a noble fellow!" you will exclaim. He is so; but then he is wholly uneducated: he is as silent as a Turk, and a kind of ignorant carelessness **attends** him, which, while it renders his conduct the more astonishing, **detracts** from the interest and sympathy which otherwise he would command.

Yet do not suppose, because I complain a little or because I can conceive a **consolation** for my **toils** which I may never know, that I am **wavering** in my resolutions. Those are as fixed as fate, and my voyage is only now delayed until the weather shall permit my **embarkation**. The winter has been dreadfully severe, but the spring promises well, and it is considered as a remarkably early season, so that perhaps I may sail sooner than I expected. I shall do nothing rashly: you know me sufficiently to **confide** in my **prudence** and considerateness whenever the safety of others is committed to my care.

worn [wɔːrn] adj.
지친, 야윈, 초췌한
woeful [wóufəl] adj.
슬픈, 비참한, 애처로운
attribute [ətríbjuːt] v.
~에 기인한다고 생각하다, ~의 결과라고 생각하다
attachment [ətǽtʃmənt] n.
애정, 사모, 애착
industrious [indʌ́striəs] adj.
근면한, 부지런한
perseverance [pə̀ːrsəvíːrəns] n.
인내, 끈기, 버팀
intertwine [intərtwáin] v.
뒤얽히다, 한데 꼬이다

I cannot describe to you my sensations on the near prospect of my undertaking. It is impossible to communicate to you a conception of the trembling sensation, half pleasurable and half fearful, with which I am preparing to depart. I am going to unexplored regions, to "the land of mist and snow," but I shall kill no albatross; therefore do not be alarmed for my safety or if I should come back to you as **worn** and **woeful** as the "Ancient Mariner." You will smile at my allusion, but I will disclose a secret. I have often **attributed** my **attachment** to, my passionate enthusiasm for, the dangerous mysteries of ocean to that production of the most imaginative of modern poets. There is something at work in my soul which I do not understand. I am practically **industrious**—painstaking, a workman to execute with **perseverance** and labour—but besides this there is a love for the marvellous, a belief in the marvellous, **intertwined** in all my projects, which hurries me out of the common pathways of men, even to the wild sea and unvisited regions I am about to explore.

But to return to dearer considerations. Shall I meet you again, after having **traversed** immense seas, and returned by the most southern cape of Africa or America? I dare not expect such success, yet I cannot bear to look on the

traverse [trǽvəːrs, trəvə́ːrs] v.
가로지르다, 횡단하다

reverse of the picture. Continue for the present to write to me by every opportunity: I may receive your letters on some occasions when I need them most to support my spirits. I love you very tenderly. Remember me with affection, **should you never** hear from me again.

Your affectionate brother,
Robert Walton

---

should you never: if you should never

Letter 3

*T*o Mrs. Saville, England._

July 7th, 17—.

My dear Sister,

I write a few lines in haste to say that I am safe—and well advanced on my voyage. This letter will reach England by a merchantman now on its **homeward** voyage from Archangel; more fortunate than I, who may not see my native land, perhaps, for many years. I am, however, in good spirits: my men are bold and apparently firm of purpose, nor do the floating sheets of ice that continually pass us, indicating the dangers of the region towards which we are advancing, appear to **dismay** them. We

---

homeward [hóumwərd] adj.
귀로의, 집으로 향하는
dismay [disméi] v.
놀라게 하다, 불안하게 하다,
당황케 하다

have already reached a very high **latitude**; but it is the height of summer, and although not so warm as in England, the southern **gales**, which blow us speedily towards those shores which I so ardently desire to attain, breathe a degree of renovating warmth which I had not expected.

No **incidents** have **hitherto befallen** us that would make a figure in a letter. One or two stiff gales and the springing of a leak are accidents which experienced navigators scarcely remember to record, and I shall be well content if nothing worse happen to us during our voyage.

Adieu, my dear Margaret. Be assured that for my own sake, as well as yours, I will not rashly encounter danger. I will be cool, **persevering**, and **prudent**.

But success *shall* crown my endeavours. **Wherefore** not? Thus far I have gone, tracing a secure way over the pathless seas, the very stars themselves being witnesses and testimonies of my triumph. Why not still proceed over the untamed yet obedient **element**? What can stop the determined heart and resolved will of man?

My swelling heart involuntarily pours itself out thus. But I must finish. Heaven bless my beloved sister!

R.W.

---

latitude [lǽtətjùːd] n.
위도
gale [geil] n.
센바람, 강풍

incident [ínsədənt] n.
사건, 생긴 일
hitherto [hìðərtúː] adv.
지금까지
befall[bifɔ́ːl] v.
발생하다, 일어나다

persevering [pə̀ːrsəvíəriŋ] adj.
참을성 있는, 끈기 있는
prudent [prúːdənt] adj.
신중한, 조심성 있는, 세심한

wherefore [hwέərfɔːr] adv.
(의문사) 무엇 때문에, 왜
element [éləmənt] n.
(날씨나 대기의) 작용력, 자연력; 악천후

Letter 4

To Mrs. Saville, England._

August 5th, 17—.

So strange an accident has happened to us that I cannot **forbear** recording it, although it is very probable that you will see me before these papers can come into your possession.

Last Monday (July 31st) we were nearly surrounded by ice, which closed in the ship on all sides, scarcely leaving her the **sea-room** in which she floated. Our situation was somewhat dangerous, especially as we were compassed round by a very thick fog. We accordingly lay to, hoping that some change would **take place** in the atmosphere and weather.

---

forbear [fɔːrbέəːr] v.
삼가다, 그만두다, 억제하다
sea room:
배를 운용할 공간
take place:
발생하다, 일어나다

behold [bihóuld] v.
보다
comrade [kǽmræd, -rid / kɔ́m-] n. 동료, 동지, 친구
groan [groun] v.
신음하다, 끙끙거리다
divert [divə́:rt, dai-] v.
전환시키다, 돌리다
solicitude [səlísətjù:d] n.
근심, 우려, 염려
sledge [sledʒ] n.
썰매
inequality [ìnikwálətí / -kwɔ́l-] n.
(표면의) 거칢, 기복, 높낮이

unqualified [ʌnkwáləfàid / -kwɔ́l-] adj.
제한 없는, 무조건의; 순전한, 철저한
apparition [æ̀pəríʃən] n.
갑자기 나타나는 것, 유령, 귀신(과 같은 것)
denote [dinóut] v.
나타내다, 표시하다

ground sea:
(먼 곳의 폭풍·지진 등에 의한) 큰 놀, 큰 파도, 여파

About two o'clock the mist cleared away, and we **beheld**, stretched out in every direction, vast and irregular plains of ice, which seemed to have no end. Some of my **comrades groaned**, and my own mind began to grow watchful with anxious thoughts, when a strange sight suddenly attracted our attention and **diverted** our **solicitude** from our own situation. We perceived a low carriage, fixed on a **sledge** and drawn by dogs, pass on towards the north, at the distance of half a mile; a being which had the shape of a man, but apparently of gigantic stature, sat in the sledge and guided the dogs. We watched the rapid progress of the traveller with our telescopes until he was lost among the distant **inequalities** of the ice.

This appearance excited our **unqualified** wonder. We were, as we believed, many hundred miles from any land; but this **apparition** seemed to **denote** that it was not, in reality, so distant as we had supposed. Shut in, however, by ice, it was impossible to follow his track, which we had observed with the greatest attention.

About two hours after this occurrence we heard the **ground sea**, and before night the ice broke and freed our ship. We, however, lay to until the morning, fearing to encounter in the dark those large loose masses which float about

profit [práfit / prɔ́f-] v.
이익을 보다, 소득을 얻다, 덕을 입다
savage [sǽvidʒ] adj.
야만의, 미개한, 미개인의
inhabitant [inhǽbətənt] n.
주민, 거주자
undiscovered [ʌ̀ndiskʌ́vərd] adj. 발견되지 않은, 찾아내지 못한, 미지의
perish [périʃ] v.
죽다, 소멸하다
open sea:
공해(公海), 외해

whither [hwíðəːr] adv. conj.
어디로
bound [baund] adj.
~행의, ~로 가는 길인

conceive [kənsíːv] v.
(감정, 의견 따위를) 마음에 품다, 느끼다
on the brink of:
~의 직전에
resource [ríːsɔːrs, -zɔːrs] n.
수단, 방편, 방책

after the breaking up of the ice. I **profited** of this time to rest for a few hours.

In the morning, however, as soon as it was light, I went upon deck and found all the sailors busy on one side of the vessel, apparently talking to someone in the sea. It was, in fact, a sledge, like that we had seen before, which had drifted towards us in the night on a large fragment of ice. Only one dog remained alive; but there was a human being within it whom the sailors were persuading to enter the vessel. He was not, as the other traveller seemed to be, a **savage inhabitant** of some **undiscovered** island, but a European. When I appeared on deck the master said, "Here is our captain, and he will not allow you to **perish** on the **open sea**."

On perceiving me, the stranger addressed me in English, although with a foreign accent. "Before I come on board your vessel," said he, "will you have the kindness to inform me **whither** you are **bound**?"

You may **conceive** my astonishment on hearing such a question addressed to me from a man **on the brink of** destruction and to whom I should have supposed that my vessel would have been a **resource** which he would not have exchanged for the most precious wealth the earth can afford. I replied, however, that we were on a voyage of discovery towards the northern pole.

Upon hearing this he appeared satisfied and consented to come on board. Good God! Margaret, if you had seen the man who thus **capitulated** for his safety, your surprise would have been **boundless**. His limbs were nearly frozen, and his body dreadfully **emaciated** by fatigue and suffering. I never saw a man in so **wretched** a condition. We attempted to carry him into the cabin, but as soon as he had quitted the fresh air he fainted. We accordingly brought him back to the deck and restored him to animation by rubbing him with brandy and forcing him to swallow a small quantity. As soon as he showed signs of life we wrapped him up in blankets and placed him near the chimney of the kitchen stove. By slow degrees he recovered and ate a little soup, which restored him wonderfully.

Two days passed in this manner before he was able to speak, and I often feared that his sufferings had **deprived** him of understanding. When he had in some measure recovered, I removed him to my own cabin and attended on him as much as my duty would permit. I never saw a more interesting creature: his eyes have generally an expression of wildness, and even madness, but there are moments when, if anyone performs an act of kindness towards

---

capitulate [kəpítʃəlèit] v.
항복하다
boundless [báundlis] adj.
무한한, 끝없는
emaciate [iméiʃièit] v.
야위다
wretched [rétʃid] adj.
불행한, 비참한, 불쌍한

You may conceive my astonishment on hearing such a question addressed to me from a man on the brink of destruction...

deprive [dipráiv] v.
빼앗다

countenance [káuntənəns] n.
얼굴 표정, 안색
benevolence [bənévələns] n.
자비심, 박애
melancholy [mélənkɑ̀li / -kɔ̀li]
adj. 구슬픈, 울적한
despairing [dispéəriŋ] adj.
절망적인, 자포자기의
gnash [næʃ] v.
(이를) 갈다
woe [wou] n.
비애, 비통, 고뇌
torment [tɔːrmént] v.
괴롭히다, 고문하다
repose [ripóuz] n.
휴식, 고요함, 침착

gloom [gluːm] n.
어둠, 우울, 침울; 슬픔

..., and sometimes he gnashes his teeth, as if impatient of the weight of woes that oppresses him.

him or does him any the most trifling service, his whole **countenance** is lighted up, as it were, with a beam of **benevolence** and sweetness that I never saw equalled. But he is generally **melancholy** and **despairing**, and sometimes he **gnashes** his teeth, as if impatient of the weight of **woes** that oppresses him.

When my guest was a little recovered I had great trouble to keep off the men, who wished to ask him a thousand questions; but I would not allow him to be **tormented** by their idle curiosity, in a state of body and mind whose restoration evidently depended upon entire **repose**. Once, however, the lieutenant asked why he had come so far upon the ice in so strange a vehicle.

His countenance instantly assumed an aspect of the deepest **gloom**, and he replied, "To seek one who fled from me."

"And did the man whom you pursued travel in the same fashion?"

"Yes."

"Then I fancy we have seen him, for the day before we picked you up we saw some dogs drawing a sledge, with a man in it, across the ice."

This aroused the stranger's attention, and he asked a multitude of questions concerning the route which the daemon, as he called him,

considerate [kənsídərit] adj.
사려깊은, 이해심 많은, 동정심 많은
inquiry [inkwáiəri, ínkwəri] n.
질문, 심문, 의문

impertinent [impə́:rtənənt] adj. 무례한
inhuman [inhjú:mən] adj.
비인간적인, 냉혹한, 몰인정한
inquisitiveness [inkwízətivnis] n.
호기심
perilous [pérələs] adj.
위험한, 모험적인

manifest [mǽnəfèst] v.
명백히 하다, 명시하다, (감정을) 드러내다
eagerness [í:gərnis] n.
열심, 열망
rawness [rɔ́:nis] n.
미숙, 거칢, 냉습

had pursued. Soon after, when he was alone with me, he said, "I have, doubtless, excited your curiosity, as well as that of these good people; but you are too **considerate** to make **inquiries**."

"Certainly; it would indeed be very **impertinent** and **inhuman** in me to trouble you with any **inquisitiveness** of mine."

"And yet you rescued me from a strange and **perilous** situation; you have benevolently restored me to life."

Soon after this he inquired if I thought that the breaking up of the ice had destroyed the other sledge. I replied that I could not answer with any degree of certainty, for the ice had not broken until near midnight, and the traveller might have arrived at a place of safety before that time; but of this I could not judge.

From this time a new spirit of life animated the decaying frame of the stranger. He **manifested** the greatest **eagerness** to be upon deck to watch for the sledge which had before appeared; but I have persuaded him to remain in the cabin, for he is far too weak to sustain the **rawness** of the atmosphere. I have promised that someone should watch for him and give him instant notice if any new object should appear in sight.

Such is my journal of what relates to this

strange occurrence up to the present day. The stranger has gradually improved in health but is very silent and appears uneasy when anyone except myself enters his cabin. Yet his manners are so conciliating and gentle that the sailors are all interested in him, although they have had very little communication with him. For my own part, I begin to love him as a brother, and his constant and deep **grief** fills me with sympathy and **compassion**. He must have been a noble creature in his better days, being even now in wreck so attractive and **amiable**.

I said in one of my letters, my dear Margaret, that I should find no friend on the wide ocean; yet I have found a man who, before his spirit had been broken by misery, I should have been happy to have possessed as the brother of my heart.

I shall continue my journal concerning the stranger at intervals, **should I have** any fresh **incidents** to record.

August 13th, 17—.

My affection for my guest increases every day. He excites at once my admiration and my pity to an astonishing degree. How can I see so noble a creature destroyed by misery without feeling the most **poignant** grief? He is so gentle, yet so wise; his mind is so **cultivated**, and

cull [kʌl] v.
따다, 고르다, 발췌하다
unparalleled [ʌnpǽrəlèld] adj.
전대미문의, 비길 데 없는
eloquence [éləkwəns] n.
웅변, 능변
precede [prisíːd] v.
선행하다, 앞서다, 먼저 일어나다
converse [kənvə́ːrs] v.
대화하다
minute [mainjúːt, mi-] adj.
상세한, 정밀한, 세심한
measure [méʒəːr] n.
수단, 방책, 조처
evince [ivíns] v.
(감정 따위를) 분명히 나타내다, 명시하다; 증명하다
fervor / fervour [fə́ːrvər] n.
열렬함, 진지함
furtherance [fə́ːrðərəns] n.
조장, 촉진, 증진
acquirement [əkwáiərmənt] n.
취득, 습득
dominion [dəmínjən] n.
지배, 통치, 주권

when he speaks, although his words are **culled** with the choicest art, yet they flow with rapidity and **unparalleled eloquence**.

He is now much recovered from his illness and is continually on the deck, apparently watching for the sledge that **preceded** his own. Yet, although unhappy, he is not so utterly occupied by his own misery but that he interests himself deeply in the projects of others. He has frequently **conversed** with me on mine, which I have communicated to him without disguise. He entered attentively into all my arguments in favour of my eventual success and into every **minute** detail of the **measures** I had taken to secure it. I was easily led by the sympathy which he **evinced** to use the language of my heart, to give utterance to the burning ardour of my soul and to say, with all the **fervour** that warmed me, how gladly I would sacrifice my fortune, my existence, my every hope, to the **furtherance** of my enterprise. One man's life or death were but a small price to pay for the **acquirement** of the knowledge which I sought, for the **dominion** I should acquire and transmit over the elemental foes of our race. As I spoke, a dark gloom spread over my listener's countenance. At first I perceived that he tried to suppress his emotion; he placed his hands before his eyes, and my voice

quiver [kwívər] v.
떨리다
intoxicating [intáksikèitiŋ / -tɔ́ksi-] adj.
취하게 하는, 도취하게 하는
draught [dræft, drɑ:ft] n.
(한 모금) 마시기, 들이켜기
dash [dæʃ] v.
내던지다, 부딪뜨리다

paroxysm [pǽrəksìzəm] n.
발작, 격발
composure [kəmpóuʒər] n.
침착, 평정

quell [kwel] v.
억누르다, 가라앉히다, 끝나게 하다
tyranny [tírəni] n.
포학, 폭정, 전제 정치
train[trein] n.
연속, 과정, 맥락
lot [lɑt / lɔt] n.
운, 운명
conviction [kənvíkʃən] n.
신념, 확신
boast [boust] v.
자랑하다, 뽐내다

quivered and failed me as I beheld tears trickle fast from between his fingers; a groan burst from his heaving breast. I paused; at length he spoke, in broken accents: "Unhappy man! Do you share my madness? Have you drunk also of the **intoxicating draught**? Hear me; let me reveal my tale, and you will **dash** the cup from your lips!"

Such words, you may imagine, strongly excited my curiosity; but the **paroxysm** of grief that had seized the stranger overcame his weakened powers, and many hours of repose and tranquil conversation were necessary to restore his **composure**.

Having conquered the violence of his feelings, he appeared to despise himself for being the slave of passion; and **quelling** the dark **tyranny** of despair, he led me again to converse concerning myself personally. He asked me the history of my earlier years. The tale was quickly told, but it awakened various **trains** of reflection. I spoke of my desire of finding a friend, of my thirst for a more intimate sympathy with a fellow mind than had ever fallen to my **lot**, and expressed my **conviction** that a man could **boast** of little happiness who did not enjoy this blessing.

"I agree with you," replied the stranger; "we are unfashioned creatures, but half made up,

perfectionate [pəˈfɛkʃəˌneɪt] v. (고어) 완벽하게 하다, 완성하다
anew [ənjúː] adv. 다시, 새로이

"Unhappy man! Do you share my madness? Have you drunk also of the intoxicating draught? Hear me; let me reveal my tale, and you will dash the cup from your lips!"

if one wiser, better, dearer than ourselves— such a friend ought to be — do not lend his aid to **perfectionate** our weak and faulty natures. I once had a friend, the most noble of human creatures, and am entitled, therefore, to judge respecting friendship. You have hope, and the world before you, and have no cause for despair. But I — I have lost everything and cannot begin life **anew**."

As he said this his countenance became expressive of a calm, settled grief that touched me to the heart. But he was silent and presently retired to his cabin.

Even broken in spirit as he is, no one can feel more deeply than he does the beauties of nature. The starry sky, the sea, and every sight afforded by these wonderful regions seem still to have the power of elevating his soul from earth. Such a man has a double existence: he may suffer misery and be overwhelmed by disappointments, yet when he has retired into himself, he will be like a celestial spirit that has a halo around him, within whose circle no grief or folly ventures.

Will you smile at the enthusiasm I express concerning this divine wanderer? You would not if you saw him. You have been tutored and refined by books and retirement from the world, and you are therefore somewhat

fastidious [fæstídiəs, fəs-] adj. 까다로운, 세심한 주의가 필요한	
render [réndə:r] v. ~을 (~으로) 만들다, 되게 하다	
immeasurably [iméʒərəbəli] adv. 헤아릴 수 없이, 끝없이, 광대하게	
intuitive [intjú:itiv] adj. 직각적인, 직관적인	
discernment [disə́:rnmənt] n. 식별력, 통찰력	
penetration [pènətréiʃən] n. 꿰뚫고 들어감; 통찰력, 식견	

fastidious; but this only **renders** you the more fit to appreciate the extraordinary merits of this wonderful man. Sometimes I have endeavoured to discover what quality it is which he possesses that elevates him so **immeasurably** above any other person I ever knew. I believe it to be an **intuitive discernment**, a quick but never-failing power of judgment, a **penetration** into the causes of things, unequalled for clearness and precision; add to this a facility of expression and a voice whose varied intonations are soul-subduing music.

August 19th, 17—.

alter [ɔ́:ltər] v. 바꾸다, 변경하다	
ardently [ɑ́:rdəntli] adv. 열렬하게, 격렬하게	
gratification [græ̀təfikéiʃən] n. 만족, 큰 기쁨	
relation [riléiʃ-ən] n. 설화, 진술; 이야기	
deduce [didjú:s] v. 연역하다, 추론하다	
apt [æpt] adj. 적절한, 적당한	

Yesterday the stranger said to me, "You may easily perceive, Captain Walton, that I have suffered great and unparalleled misfortunes. I had determined at one time that the memory of these evils should die with me, but you have won me to **alter** my determination. You seek for knowledge and wisdom, as I once did; and I **ardently** hope that the **gratification** of your wishes may not be a serpent to sting you, as mine has been. I do not know that the **relation** of my disasters will be useful to you; yet, when I reflect that you are pursuing the same course, exposing yourself to the same dangers which have rendered me what I am, I imagine that you may **deduce** an **apt** moral from my tale, one that may direct you if you succeed in your undertaking and **console** you in case of failure. Prepare to hear of occurrences which are usually deemed marvellous. **Were we** among the tamer scenes of nature I might fear to encounter your **unbelief**, perhaps your ridicule; but many things will appear possible in these wild and mysterious regions which would provoke the laughter of those **unacquainted** with the ever-varied powers of nature; nor can I doubt but that my tale **conveys** in its series internal evidence of the truth of the events of which it is composed."

You may easily imagine that I was much gratified by the offered communication, yet I could not endure that he should renew his grief by a **recital** of his misfortunes. I felt the greatest eagerness to hear the promised narrative, partly from curiosity and partly from a strong desire to **ameliorate** his fate if it were in my power. I expressed these feelings in my answer.

"I thank you," he replied, "for your sympathy, but it is useless; my fate is nearly fulfilled. I wait but for one event, and then I shall repose in peace. I understand your feeling," continued he, perceiving that I wished to interrupt him; "but you are mistaken, my friend, if thus you will allow me to **name** you; nothing can alter

---

console [kənsóul] v. to allay t
위로하다, 위안하다
Were we:
If we were
unbelief [Ànbilíːf] n.
불신, 의혹, 회의
unacquainted [Ànəkwéintid] adj. 모르는, 낯선, 생소한
convey [kənvéi] v.
알리다, 나타내다, 표현하다

recital [risáitl] n.
이야기, 기술
ameliorate [əmíːljərèit, -liə-] v.
개선하다, 좋아지게 하다

name [neim] v.
이름을 붙이다, ~라고 부르다

irrevocably [irévəkəbəli] adv.
되돌릴 수 없게, 취소할 수 없게

resolve [rizálv / -zɔ́lv] v.
결정하다, 결심하다
imperatively [impérətivli] adv.
절박하게, 긴급하게
engaged [engéidʒd] adj.
바쁜, 작업 중인
lustrous [lʌ́strəs] adj.
빛나는, 찬란한, 훌륭한
animation [æ̀nəméiʃən] n.
생기, 활기, 쾌활, 기운
lineament [líniəmənt] n.
용모, 얼굴 생김새, 이목구비
irradiate [iréidièit] v.
비추다, 빛나게 하다, 빛나다
harrowing [hǽrouiŋ] adj.
마음 아픈, 비참한

my destiny; listen to my history, and you will perceive how **irrevocably** it is determined."

He then told me that he would commence his narrative the next day when I should be at leisure. This promise drew from me the warmest thanks. I have **resolved** every night, when I am not **imperatively** occupied by my duties, to record, as nearly as possible in his own words, what he has related during the day. If I should be **engaged**, I will at least make notes. This manuscript will doubtless afford you the greatest pleasure; but to me, who know him, and who hear it from his own lips — with what interest and sympathy shall I read it in some future day! Even now, as I commence my task, his full-toned voice swells in my ears; his **lustrous** eyes dwell on me with all their melancholy sweetness; I see his thin hand raised in **animation**, while the **lineaments** of his face are **irradiated** by the soul within. Strange and **harrowing** must be his story, frightful the storm which embraced the gallant vessel on its course and wrecked it — thus!

Chapter 1

distinguished [distíŋwiʃt] adj.
현저한, 출중한, 유명한
syndic [síndik] n.
지방 행정관
integrity [intégrəti] n.
성실, 정직, 고결
indefatigable [indifǽtigəbəl]
adj. 지칠 줄 모르는, 끈기있는
decline [dikláin] n.
만년, 말년

refrain [rifréin] v.
그만두다, 삼가다

I am by birth a Genevese, and my family is one of the most **distinguished** of that republic. My ancestors had been for many years counsellors and **syndics**, and my father had filled several public situations with honour and reputation. He was respected by all who knew him for his **integrity** and **indefatigable** attention to public business. He passed his younger days perpetually occupied by the affairs of his country; a variety of circumstances had prevented his marrying early, nor was it until the **decline** of life that he became a husband and the father of a family.

As the circumstances of his marriage illustrate his character, I cannot **refrain** from

mischance [mistʃǽns, -tʃɑ́:ns]
n. 불운, 불행, 재난
unbending [ʌnbéndiŋ] adj.
꺾이지 않는, 불굴의; 고집센
disposition [dìspəzíʃən] n.
기질, 성미, 성격
oblivion [əblíviən] n.
망각, 잊혀짐
magnificence [mægnífəsns] n.
장대, 장엄함, 훌륭함
deplore [diplɔ́:r] v.
한탄하다, 유감으로 여기다

relating them. One of his most intimate friends was a merchant who, from a flourishing state, fell, through numerous **mischances**, into poverty. This man, whose name was Beaufort, was of a proud and **unbending disposition** and could not bear to live in poverty and **oblivion** in the same country where he had formerly been distinguished for his rank and **magnificence**. Having paid his debts, therefore, in the most honourable manner, he retreated with his daughter to the town of Lucerne, where he lived unknown and in wretchedness. My father loved Beaufort with the truest friendship and was deeply grieved by his retreat in these unfortunate circumstances. He bitterly **deplored** the false pride which led his friend to a conduct so little worthy of the affection that united them. He lost no time in endeavouring to seek him out, with the hope of persuading him to begin the world again through his credit and assistance.

effectual [ifékt∫uəl] adj.
효과적인, 효험 있는, 유효한
abode [əbóud] n.
주거, 거처
mean street:
빈민가, 우범 지대

Beaufort had taken **effectual** measures to conceal himself, and it was ten months before my father discovered his **abode**. Overjoyed at this discovery, he hastened to the house, which was situated in a **mean street** near the Reuss. But when he entered, misery and despair alone welcomed him. Beaufort had saved but a very small sum of money from the wreck of his fortunes, but it was sufficient to provide him with **sustenance** for some months, and in the meantime he hoped to **procure** some respectable employment in a merchant's house. The interval was, consequently, spent in inaction; his grief only became more deep and rankling when he had leisure for reflection, and at length it took so fast hold of his mind that at the end of three months he lay on a bed of sickness, incapable of any **exertion**.

His daughter attended him with the greatest tenderness, but she saw with despair that their little fund was rapidly decreasing and that there was no other **prospect** of support. But Caroline Beaufort possessed a mind of an uncommon **mould**, and her courage rose to support her in her **adversity**. She **procured** plain work; she plaited straw and by various means **contrived** to earn a **pittance** scarcely sufficient to support life.

Several months passed in this manner. Her father grew worse; her time was more entirely occupied in attending him; her means of subsistence decreased; and in the tenth month her father died in her arms, leaving her an orphan and a beggar. This last blow overcame her, and she knelt by Beaufort's coffin weeping bitterly, when my father entered the chamber. He came like a protecting spirit to the poor girl, who

---

sustenance [sʌ́stənəns] n.
생계수단, 음식물
procure [proukjúər, prə-] v.
입수하다, 손에 넣다, 획득하다
exertion [igzə́:rʃən] n.
노력, 진력, 고된 일

prospect [práspekt / prɔ́s-] n.
전망, 가능성, 예상
mold [mould] n.
특성, 특질, 성격
adversity [ædvə́:rsəti, əd-] n.
역경, 불행, 불운
procure [proukjúər, prə-] v.
손에 넣다, 획득하다
contrive [kəntráiv] v.
궁리하다, 기도하다
pittance [pítəns] n.
적은 생활비(수입)

interment [intə́:rmənt] n.
매장, 장례

upright [ʌ́pràit] adj.
곧은, 청렴한, 정직한
doting [dóutiŋ] adj.
사랑에 빠진, 지나치게 사랑하는
reverence [rév-ərəns] n.
경의, 숭배
recompense [rékəmpèns] v.
보상하다, 치르다
inexpressible [iniksprésəbəl] adj. 형언할 수 없는
exotic [igzátik / -zɔ́t-] n.
이국적인 것; 외래품, 외래식물
tend [tend] v.
이바지하다, 공헌하다, 도움이 되다
tranquillity [træŋkwíləti] n.
평정, 평온, 침착

committed herself to his care; and after the **interment** of his friend he conducted her to Geneva and placed her under the protection of a relation. Two years after this event Caroline became his wife.

There was a considerable difference between the ages of my parents, but this circumstance seemed to unite them only closer in bonds of devoted affection. There was a sense of justice in my father's **upright** mind which rendered it necessary that he should approve highly to love strongly. Perhaps during former years he had suffered from the late-discovered unworthiness of one beloved and so was disposed to set a greater value on tried worth. There was a show of gratitude and worship in his attachment to my mother, differing wholly from the **doting** fondness of age, for it was inspired by **reverence** for her virtues and a desire to be the means of, in some degree, **recompensing** her for the sorrows she had endured, but which gave **inexpressible** grace to his behaviour to her. Everything was made to yield to her wishes and her convenience. He strove to shelter her, as a fair **exotic** is sheltered by the gardener, from every rougher wind and to surround her with all that could **tend** to excite pleasurable emotion in her soft and benevolent mind. Her health, and even the **tranquillity** of her

elapse [ilǽps] v.
지나다, 경과하다
relinquish [rilíŋkwiʃ] v.
포기하다, 그만두다
restorative [ristɔ́:rətiv] n.
건강 증진약, 강장제, 영양식

ramble [rǽmb-əl] n.
소요, 산책
inexhaustible [ìnigzɔ́:stəbəl] adj. 다할 줄 모르는, 무진장한
idol [áidl] n.
우상, 숭배의 대상

hitherto constant spirit, had been shaken by what she had gone through. During the two years that had **elapsed** previous to their marriage my father had gradually **relinquished** all his public functions; and immediately after their union they sought the pleasant climate of Italy, and the change of scene and interest attendant on a tour through that land of wonders, as a **restorative** for her weakened frame.

From Italy they visited Germany and France. I, their eldest child, was born at Naples, and as an infant accompanied them in their **rambles**. I remained for several years their only child. Much as they were attached to each other, they seemed to draw **inexhaustible** stores of affection from a very mine of love to bestow them upon me. My mother's tender caresses and my father's smile of benevolent pleasure while regarding me are my first recollections. I was their plaything and their **idol**, and something better—their child, the innocent and helpless creature bestowed on them by Heaven, whom to bring up to good, and whose future lot it was in their hands to direct to happiness or misery, according as they fulfilled their duties towards me. With this deep consciousness of what they owed towards the being to which they had given life, added to the active spirit of tenderness that animated both, it may be imagined that while during every hour of my infant life I received a lesson of patience, of charity, and of self-control, I was so guided by a silken cord that all seemed but one train of enjoyment to me.

For a long time I was their only care. My mother had much desired to have a daughter, but I continued their single **offspring**. When I was about five years old, while making an **excursion** beyond the frontiers of Italy, they passed a week on the shores of the Lake of Como. Their benevolent disposition often made them enter the cottages of the poor. This, to my mother, was more than a duty; it was a necessity, a passion — remembering what she had suffered, and how she had been relieved — for her to act in her turn the **guardian angel** to the afflicted. During one of their walks a poor **cot** in the foldings of a vale attracted their notice as being singularly **disconsolate**, while the number of half-clothed children gathered about it spoke of **penury** in its worst shape. One day, when my father had gone by himself to Milan, my mother, accompanied by me, visited this abode. She found a peasant and his wife, hard working, bent down by care and labour, distributing a **scanty** meal to five hungry babes. Among these there was one which attracted my mother far above all the rest. She

---

offspring [ɔ́:fsprìŋ] n.
자식, 자손, 후예
excursion [ikskə́:rʒən, -ʃən] n.
외출, 짧은 여행
guardian angel:
수호천사
cot [kɑt / kɔt] n.
시골집, 오두막집
disconsolate [diskɑ́nsəlit / -kɔ́n-] adj.
어두운, 우울한
penury [pénjəri] n.
빈곤, 궁핍
scanty [skǽnti] adj.
부족한, 불충분한

stock [stɑk / stɔk] n.
혈통, 가계(家系), 가문
despite [dispáit] prep.
~에도 불구하고
distinction [distíŋkʃən] n.
탁월함, 우수함, 고귀함
behold [bihóuld] v.
보다
celestial [səléstʃəl] adj.
하늘의, 천국의, 거룩한
stamp [stæmp] n.
흔적, 특징, 성격

perceive [pərsí:v] v.
알아차리다, 이해하다
better off:
상황이 더 나은, 보다 유리한, (금전적으로) 더 풍족한
exert [igzá:rt] v.
노력하다
dungeon [dʌ́ndʒən] n.
지하 감옥
confiscate [kɑ́nfiskèit, kənfís-/ kɔ́n-] v.
몰수하다, 압류하다

appeared of a different **stock**. The four others were dark-eyed, hardy little vagrants; this child was thin and very fair. Her hair was the brightest living gold, and **despite** the poverty of her clothing, seemed to set a crown of **distinction** on her head. Her brow was clear and ample, her blue eyes cloudless, and her lips and the moulding of her face so expressive of sensibility and sweetness that none could **behold** her without looking on her as of a distinct species, a being heaven-sent, and bearing a **celestial stamp** in all her features.

The peasant woman, **perceiving** that my mother fixed eyes of wonder and admiration on this lovely girl, eagerly communicated her history. She was not her child, but the daughter of a Milanese nobleman. Her mother was a German and had died on giving her birth. The infant had been placed with these good people to nurse: they were **better off** then. They had not been long married, and their eldest child was but just born. The father of their charge was one of those Italians nursed in the memory of the antique glory of Italy — one among the *schiavi ognor frementi*, who **exerted** himself to obtain the liberty of his country. He became the victim of its weakness. Whether he had died or still lingered in the **dungeons** of Austria was not known. His property was **confiscated**;

his child became an orphan and a beggar. She continued with her foster parents and bloomed in their rude abode, fairer than a garden rose among dark-leaved brambles.

When my father returned from Milan, he found playing with me in the hall of our villa a child fairer than pictured **cherub** — a creature who seemed to **shed** radiance from her looks and whose form and motions were lighter than the **chamois** of the hills. The apparition was soon explained. With his permission my mother **prevailed** on her rustic guardians to yield their charge to her. They were fond of the sweet orphan. Her presence had seemed a blessing to them, but it would be unfair to her to keep her in poverty and want when **Providence** afforded her such powerful protection. They consulted their village priest, and the result was that Elizabeth Lavenza became the **inmate** of my parents' house — my more than sister — the beautiful and adored companion of all my occupations and my pleasures.

Everyone loved Elizabeth. The passionate and almost **reverential attachment** with which all regarded her became, while I shared it, my pride and my delight. On the evening previous to her being brought to my home, my mother had said playfully, "I have a pretty present for

---

cherub [tʃérəb] n. (pl. cherubim) 케루빔, 지품 천사
shed [ʃed] v. (빛, 열, 소리, 향기 등을) 발산하다, 비추다
chamois [ʃǽmi / ʃǽmwɑ:] n. 샤무아(알프스 영양)
prevail [privéil] v. 설복하다, 설득하다
Providence [prάvədəns / prɔ́v-] n. God, 신
inmate [ínmèit] n. 주거인, 동거인

reverential [rèvərénʃ-əl] adj. 존경하는
attachment [ətǽtʃmənt] n. 애정, 사모, 애착

bestow [bistóu] v.
주다, 부여하다
body [bádi / bɔ́di] v.
구체화하다, 여실히 나타내다

my Victor — tomorrow he shall have it." And when, on the morrow, she presented Elizabeth to me as her promised gift, I, with childish seriousness, interpreted her words literally and looked upon Elizabeth as mine — mine to protect, love, and cherish. All praises **bestowed** on her I received as made to a possession of my own. We called each other familiarly by the name of cousin. No word, no expression could **body** forth the kind of relation in which she stood to me — my more than sister, since till death she was to be mine only.

Chapter 2

disunion [disjúːnjən] n.
분리, 분열, 불화, 알력
subsist [səbsíst] v.
존재하다, 존속하다
aerial [ɛ́əriəl, eiíər-] adj.
공기와 같은, 꿈 같은, 영묘한
sublime [səbláim] adj.
장대한, 웅대한, 장엄한

We were brought up together; there was not quite a year difference in our ages. I need not say that we were strangers to any species of **disunion** or dispute. Harmony was the soul of our companionship, and the diversity and contrast that **subsisted** in our characters drew us nearer together. Elizabeth was of a calmer and more concentrated disposition; but, with all my ardour, I was capable of a more intense application and was more deeply smitten with the thirst for knowledge. She busied herself with following the **aerial** creations of the poets; and in the majestic and wondrous scenes which surrounded our Swiss home — the **sublime** shapes of the mountains, the changes of the seasons, tempest and calm, the silence of winter, and the life and turbulence of our Alpine summers — she found **ample** scope for admiration and delight. While my companion **contemplated** with a serious and satisfied spirit the magnificent appearances of things, I delighted in investigating their causes. The world was to me a secret which I desired to **divine**. Curiosity, earnest research to learn the hidden laws of nature, gladness **akin** to rapture, as they were unfolded to me, are among the earliest sensations I can remember.

On the birth of a second son, my junior by seven years, my parents gave up entirely their wandering life and fixed themselves in their native country. We possessed a house in Geneva, and a *campagne* on Belrive, the eastern shore of the lake, at the distance of rather more than a league from the city. We **resided** principally in the latter, and the lives of my parents were passed in considerable **seclusion**. It was my temper to avoid a crowd and to attach myself fervently to a few. I was **indifferent**, therefore, to my school-fellows in general; but I united myself in the bonds of the closest friendship to one among them. Henry Clerval was the son of a merchant of Geneva. He was a boy of singular talent and fancy. He loved enterprise,

---

ample [ǽmpl] adj.
풍부한, 충분한
contemplate [kántəmplèit / kóntem-] v.
명상하다, 깊이 생각하다
divine [diváin] v.
발견하다, 간파하다
akin [əkín] adj.
가까운, 유사한

reside [rizáid] v.
살다, 주재하다
seclusion [siklú:ʒ-ən] n.
은둔, 격리
indifferent [indífərənt] adj.
무관심한, 개의치 않는

The world was to me a secret which I desired to divine.

redeem [ridí:m] v.
도로 찾다, 되찾다
sepulcher [sépəlkər] n.
묘, 무덤
infidel [ínfədl] n.
무신론자, 이교도

indulgence [indʌ́ldʒəns] n.
응석을 받음, 멋대로 하게 둠, 관대
tyrant [tái-ərənt] n.
폭군, 독재자
caprice [kəprí:s] n.
변덕, 종작 없음
discern [disə́:rn, -zə́:rn] v.
알아보다, 알아내다, 식별하다
filial [fíliəl] adj.
자식의, 자식다운

vehement [ví:əmənt] adj.
격렬한, 맹렬한
indiscriminately
[ìndiskrímənitli] adv.
무차별적으로, 닥치는 대로, 분별 없이

hardship, and even danger for its own sake. He was deeply read in books of chivalry and romance. He composed heroic songs and began to write many a tale of enchantment and knightly adventure. He tried to make us act plays and to enter into masquerades, in which the characters were drawn from the heroes of Roncesvalles, of the Round Table of King Arthur, and the chivalrous train who shed their blood to **redeem** the holy **sepulchre** from the hands of the **infidels**.

No human being could have passed a happier childhood than myself. My parents were possessed by the very spirit of kindness and **indulgence**. We felt that they were not the **tyrants** to rule our lot according to their **caprice**, but the agents and creators of all the many delights which we enjoyed. When I mingled with other families I distinctly **discerned** how peculiarly fortunate my lot was, and gratitude assisted the development of **filial** love.

My temper was sometimes violent, and my passions **vehement**; but by some law in my temperature they were turned not towards childish pursuits but to an eager desire to learn, and not to learn all things **indiscriminately**. I confess that neither the structure of languages, nor the code of governments, nor the politics of various states possessed attractions for me.

occupy [ákjəpài / ɔ́k-] v.
(마음을) 사로잡다
inquiry [inkwáiəri] n.
연구, 탐구

gallant [gǽlənt] adj.
씩씩한, 용감한, 당당한
benefactor [bénəfæ̀ktər] n.
은인, 후원자
sullen [sʌ́lən] adj.
시무룩한
subdue [səbdjú:] v.
억제하다, 가라앉히다, 경감하다
semblance [sémbləns] n.
유사, 닮음, 비슷한 것
aught [ɔ:t] pron.
어떤 일, 무언가
entrench [entréntʃ] v.
참호를 파다; 침해하다, 침범하다
had she not:
if she had not

It was the secrets of heaven and earth that I desired to learn; and whether it was the outward substance of things or the inner spirit of nature and the mysterious soul of man that **occupied** me, still my **inquiries** were directed to the metaphysical, or in its highest sense, the physical secrets of the world.

Meanwhile Clerval occupied himself, so to speak, with the moral relations of things. The busy stage of life, the virtues of heroes, and the actions of men were his theme; and his hope and his dream was to become one among those whose names are recorded in story as the **gallant** and adventurous **benefactors** of our species. The saintly soul of Elizabeth shone like a shrine-dedicated lamp in our peaceful home. Her sympathy was ours; her smile, her soft voice, the sweet glance of her celestial eyes, were ever there to bless and animate us. She was the living spirit of love to soften and attract; I might have become **sullen** in my study, rough through the ardour of my nature, but that she was there to **subdue** me to a **semblance** of her own gentleness. And Clerval — could **aught** ill **entrench** on the noble spirit of Clerval? Yet he might not have been so perfectly humane, so thoughtful in his generosity, so full of kindness and tenderness amidst his passion for adventurous exploit, **had she not** unfolded

beneficence [bənéfəsəns] n.
선행, 은혜, 자선

exquisite [ikskwízit, ékskwi-] adj. 절묘한, 세련된, 고상한
taint [teint] v.
더럽히다, 오염시키다, 부패시키다
ignoble [ignóubəl] adj.
비천한, 열등한
torrent [tɔ́:r-ənt, tár- / tɔ́r-] n.
급류, 분류

natural philosophy:
자연 철학 (natural science)
genius [dʒí:njəs, -niəs] n.
(시대, 사회, 국민 등의) 특질, 정신, 경향
predilection [prì:dəlékʃən, prèd-] n.
편애, 역성
inclemency [inklémənsi] n.
(날씨의) 험악; 무자비, 가혹
apathy [ǽpəθi] n.
냉담, 무관심, 무감동

to him the real loveliness of **beneficence** and made the doing good the end and aim of his soaring ambition.

I feel **exquisite** pleasure in dwelling on the recollections of childhood, before misfortune had **tainted** my mind and changed its bright visions of extensive usefulness into gloomy and narrow reflections upon self. Besides, in drawing the picture of my early days, I also record those events which led, by insensible steps, to my after tale of misery, for when I would account to myself for the birth of that passion which afterwards ruled my destiny I find it arise, like a mountain river, from **ignoble** and almost forgotten sources; but, swelling as it proceeded, it became the **torrent** which, in its course, has swept away all my hopes and joys.

Natural philosophy is the **genius** that has regulated my fate; I desire, therefore, in this narration, to state those facts which led to my **predilection** for that science. When I was thirteen years of age we all went on a party of pleasure to the baths near Thonon; the **inclemency** of the weather obliged us to remain a day confined to the inn. In this house I chanced to find a volume of the works of Cornelius Agrippa. I opened it with **apathy**; the theory which he attempts to demonstrate and the wonderful facts which he relates soon changed this feeling

dawn [dɔ:n] v.
(생각이) 떠오르다, 이해되기 시작하다
bound [baund] v.
뛰어가다, 뛰어오르다

chimerical [kimérikəl, kai-] adj. 비현실적인, 황당무계한
content [kəntént] v.
만족시키다, (~에) 만족하다
fatal [féitl] adj.
운명의, 파멸적인
impulse [ímpʌls] n.
충동, 일시적인 감정
cursory [kə́:rsəri] adj.
몹시 서두른, 엉성한
by no means:
절대 아닌
avidity [əvídəti] n.
탐욕, 갈망, 욕심

procure [proukjúər, prə-] v.
입수하다, 손에 넣다, 획득하다

into enthusiasm. A new light seemed to **dawn** upon my mind, and **bounding** with joy, I communicated my discovery to my father. My father looked carelessly at the title page of my book and said, "Ah! Cornelius Agrippa! My dear Victor, do not waste your time upon this; it is sad trash."

If, instead of this remark, my father had taken the pains to explain to me that the principles of Agrippa had been entirely exploded and that a modern system of science had been introduced which possessed much greater powers than the ancient, because the powers of the latter were **chimerical**, while those of the former were real and practical, under such circumstances I should certainly have thrown Agrippa aside and have **contented** my imagination, warmed as it was, by returning with greater ardour to my former studies. It is even possible that the train of my ideas would never have received the **fatal impulse** that led to my ruin. But the **cursory** glance my father had taken of my volume **by no means** assured me that he was acquainted with its contents, and I continued to read with the greatest **avidity**.

When I returned home my first care was to **procure** the whole works of this author, and afterwards of Paracelsus and Albertus Magnus. I read and studied the wild fancies of these

imbue [imbjú:] v.
감염시키다, 감화시키다, 불어넣다
discontented [dìskənténtid] adj. 불만스러운, 불평스러운
avow [əváu] v.
공언하다, 인정하다, 자백하다
tyro [táirou] n.
초학자, 초심자, 신참자

untaught [ʌntɔ́:t] adj.
교육을 받지 못한, 무식한
learned [lə́:rnid] adj.
학식이 있는, 박식한
lineament [líniəmənt] n.
특징, 성질, (얼굴 등의) 생김새
tertiary [tə́:rʃièri, -ʃəri] adj.
제3의, 세번째의
fortification [fɔ̀:rtəfikéiʃ-ne] n.
무장화, 요새화, 방어벽
impediment [impédəmənt] n.
방해, 장애물
citadel [sítədl] n.
성채, 요새
repine [ripáin] v.
불평하다, 투덜거리다

writers with delight; they appeared to me treasures known to few besides myself. I have described myself as always having been **imbued** with a fervent longing to penetrate the secrets of nature. In spite of the intense labour and wonderful discoveries of modern philosophers, I always came from my studies **discontented** and unsatisfied. Sir Isaac Newton is said to have **avowed** that he felt like a child picking up shells beside the great and unexplored ocean of truth. Those of his successors in each branch of natural philosophy with whom I was acquainted appeared even to my boy's apprehensions as **tyros** engaged in the same pursuit.

The **untaught** peasant beheld the elements around him and was acquainted with their practical uses. The most **learned** philosopher knew little more. He had partially unveiled the face of Nature, but her immortal **lineaments** were still a wonder and a mystery. He might dissect, anatomise, and give names; but, not to speak of a final cause, causes in their secondary and **tertiary** grades were utterly unknown to him. I had gazed upon the **fortifications** and **impediments** that seemed to keep human beings from entering the **citadel** of nature, and rashly and ignorantly I had **repined**.

But here were books, and here were men who had penetrated deeper and knew more. I took their word for all that they **averred**, and I became their **disciple**. It may appear strange that such should arise in the eighteenth century; but while I followed the routine of education in the schools of Geneva, I was, to a great degree, self-taught with regard to my favourite studies. My father was not scientific, and I was left to struggle with a child's blindness, added to a student's thirst for knowledge. Under the guidance of my new **preceptors** I entered with the greatest diligence into the search of the **philosopher's stone** and the **elixir** of life; but the latter soon obtained my **undivided** attention. Wealth was an inferior object, but what glory would **attend** the discovery if I could **banish** disease from the human frame and render man **invulnerable** to any but a violent death!

Nor were these my only visions. The raising of ghosts or devils was a promise liberally **accorded** by my favourite authors, the fulfilment of which I most eagerly sought; and if my **incantations** were always unsuccessful, I **attributed** the failure rather to my own inexperience and mistake than to a want of skill or fidelity in my instructors. And thus for a time I was occupied by exploded systems,

unadept [ǽdept] n.
문외한, 아마추어
flounder [fláundər] v.
버둥거리다, 허둥대다, 실수하다
slough [slau] n.
진창길, 구렁텅이
multifarious [mʌltəfɛ́-əriəs] adj. 가지가지의, 다방면의
dazzling [dǽzliŋ] adj.
눈부신, 빛나는
blasted [blǽstid, blɑ́:st-] adj.
시든, 무너진, 망가진
stump [stʌmp] n.
(나무의) 그루터기
singular [síŋgjələ:r] adj.
이상한, 희한한
splinter [splíntə:r] v.
쪼개지다, 찢어지다, 산산조각이 되다

mingling, like an **unadept**, a thousand contradictory theories and **floundering** desperately in a very **slough** of **multifarious** knowledge, guided by an ardent imagination and childish reasoning, till an accident again changed the current of my ideas.

When I was about fifteen years old we had retired to our house near Belrive, when we witnessed a most violent and terrible thunderstorm. It advanced from behind the mountains of Jura, and the thunder burst at once with frightful loudness from various quarters of the heavens. I remained, while the storm lasted, watching its progress with curiosity and delight. As I stood at the door, on a sudden I beheld a stream of fire issue from an old and beautiful oak which stood about twenty yards from our house; and so soon as the **dazzling** light vanished, the oak had disappeared, and nothing remained but a **blasted stump**. When we visited it the next morning, we found the tree shattered in a **singular** manner. It was not **splintered** by the shock, but entirely reduced to thin ribbons of wood. I never beheld anything so utterly destroyed.

unacquainted [ʌ̀nəkwéintid] adj. 모르는, 낯선, 생소한

Before this I was not **unacquainted** with the more obvious laws of electricity. On this occasion a man of great research in natural philosophy was with us, and excited by this

catastrophe [kətǽstrəfi] n.
대참사, 재앙, 불운
enter on:
시작하다, 착수하다
galvanism [gǽlvənìzəm] n.
직류 전기
put(throw, cast) ~ in(into) the shade:
~을 무색하게 하다, ~과 큰 차이가 나다
disincline [dìsinkláin] v.
마음이 내키지 않게 하다, 싫증을 일으키다
despicable [déspikəbəl, dispík-] adj.
천한, 비열한
progeny [prádʒəni / pródʒ-] n.
자손, 후계자, 결과, 소산
disdain [disdéin] n.
경멸, 모멸
would-be [wúdbì:] adj.
겉꾸민, 자칭의, 사이비의
appertain [æ̀pərtéin] v.
귀속하다, 관계하다

ligament [lígəmənt] n.
인대, 줄, 끈, 유대

catastrophe, he **entered on** the explanation of a theory which he had formed on the subject of electricity and **galvanism**, which was at once new and astonishing to me. All that he said **threw** greatly **into the shade** Cornelius Agrippa, Albertus Magnus, and Paracelsus, the lords of my imagination; but by some fatality the overthrow of these men **disinclined** me to pursue my accustomed studies. It seemed to me as if nothing would or could ever be known. All that had so long engaged my attention suddenly grew **despicable**. By one of those caprices of the mind which we are perhaps most subject to in early youth, I at once gave up my former occupations, set down natural history and all its **progeny** as a deformed and abortive creation, and entertained the greatest **disdain** for a **would-be** science which could never even step within the threshold of real knowledge. In this mood of mind I betook myself to the mathematics and the branches of study **appertaining** to that science as being built upon secure foundations, and so worthy of my consideration.

Thus strangely are our souls constructed, and by such slight **ligaments** are we bound to prosperity or ruin. When I look back, it seems to me as if this almost miraculous change of inclination and will was the immediate suggestion

envelop [envéləp] vt.
싸다, 봉하다, 포위하다
relinquish [rilíŋkwiʃ] v.
포기하다, 그만두다, 버리다, 철회하다

ineffectual [iniféktʃuəl] adj.
효과 없는, 헛된, 무력한
potent [póutənt] adj.
세력 있는, 유력한, 힘센
immutable [imjú:təbəl] adj.
변치 않는
utter [Átər] adj.
완전한, 절대적인

Destiny was too potent, and her immutable laws had decreed my utter and terrible destruction.

of the guardian angel of my life — the last effort made by the spirit of preservation to avert the storm that was even then hanging in the stars and ready to **envelop** me. Her victory was announced by an unusual tranquillity and gladness of soul which followed the **relinquishing** of my ancient and latterly tormenting studies. It was thus that I was to be taught to associate evil with their prosecution, happiness with their disregard.

It was a strong effort of the spirit of good, but it was **ineffectual**. Destiny was too **potent**, and her **immutable** laws had decreed my **utter** and terrible destruction.

Chapter 3

attain [ətéin] v.
이르다, 도달하다
hitherto [hìðərtú:] adv.
지금까지, 여기까지
omen [óumən] n.
전조, 징조, 조짐

When I had **attained** the age of seventeen my parents resolved that I should become a student at the university of Ingolstadt. I had **hitherto** attended the schools of Geneva, but my father thought it necessary for the completion of my education that I should be made acquainted with other customs than those of my native country. My departure was therefore fixed at an early date, but before the day resolved upon could arrive, the first misfortune of my life occurred — an **omen**, as it were, of my future misery.

scarlet fever:
성홍열

Elizabeth had caught the **scarlet fever**; her illness was severe, and she was in the greatest danger. During her illness many arguments

refrain [rifréin] v.
그만두다, 삼가다
entreaty [entríti] n.
간절한 부탁, 애원, 탄원
menace [ménəs] v.
위협하다, 위태롭게 하다
malignity [məlígnəti] n.
(병의) 악성, 불치
distemper [distémpər] n.
병, (심신의) 이상
imprudence [imprú:dəns] n.
경솔, 무분별
prognosticate [prɑgnástikèit / prɔgnɔ́sti-] v.
예언하다, 예측하다
fortitude [fɔ́:rtətjù:d] n.
용기, 불굴의 정신, 인내
benignity [binígnəti] n.
인자, 은혜, 자비
consolation [kɑ̀nsəléiʃən / kɔ̀n-] n.
위로, 위안
befit [bifít] v.
걸맞다, 어울리다
indulge [indʌ́ldʒ] v.
~에 빠지다, 탐닉하다

had been urged to persuade my mother to **refrain** from attending upon her. She had at first yielded to our **entreaties**, but when she heard that the life of her favourite was **menaced**, she could no longer control her anxiety. She attended her sickbed; her watchful attentions triumphed over the **malignity** of the **distemper** — Elizabeth was saved, but the consequences of this **imprudence** were fatal to her preserver. On the third day my mother sickened; her fever was accompanied by the most alarming symptoms, and the looks of her medical attendants **prognosticated** the worst event. On her deathbed the **fortitude** and **benignity** of this best of women did not desert her. She joined the hands of Elizabeth and myself. "My children," she said, "my firmest hopes of future happiness were placed on the prospect of your union. This expectation will now be the **consolation** of your father. Elizabeth, my love, you must supply my place to my younger children. Alas! I regret that I am taken from you; and, happy and beloved as I have been, is it not hard to quit you all? But these are not thoughts **befitting** me; I will endeavour to resign myself cheerfully to death and will **indulge** a hope of meeting you in another world."

She died calmly, and her countenance expressed affection even in death. I need not

rend [rend] v.
찢다, 떼어놓다, 강탈하다
irreparable [irépərəbəl] adj.
돌이킬 수 없는
void [vɔid] n.
허공, 진공, 공백 상태
lapse [læps] n.
(시간의) 경과, 흐름, 추이
sacrilege [sǽkrəlidʒ] n.
신성 모독, 벌받을 행위

defer [difə́ːr] v.
늦추다, 물리다, 연기하다

describe the feelings of those whose dearest ties are **rent** by that most **irreparable** evil, the **void** that presents itself to the soul, and the despair that is exhibited on the countenance. It is so long before the mind can persuade itself that she whom we saw every day and whose very existence appeared a part of our own can have departed for ever — that the brightness of a beloved eye can have been extinguished and the sound of a voice so familiar and dear to the ear can be hushed, never more to be heard. These are the reflections of the first days; but when the **lapse** of time proves the reality of the evil, then the actual bitterness of grief commences. Yet from whom has not that rude hand rent away some dear connection? And why should I describe a sorrow which all have felt, and must feel? The time at length arrives when grief is rather an indulgence than a necessity; and the smile that plays upon the lips, although it may be deemed a **sacrilege**, is not banished. My mother was dead, but we had still duties which we ought to perform; we must continue our course with the rest and learn to think ourselves fortunate whilst one remains whom the spoiler has not seized.

My departure for Ingolstadt, which had been **deferred** by these events, was now again determined upon. I obtained from my father a

respite [réspit] n.
연기, 유예, 휴식

enchanting [entʃǽntiŋ, -tʃɑ́:nt-] adj.
매혹적인, 황홀하게 하는

in vain:
효과 없이, 보람 없이, 헛되이
aspiration [æspəréiʃən] n.
강렬한 소망, 동경, 야심
debar [dibɑ́:r] v.
내쫓다, 제외하다, 금하다

respite of some weeks. It appeared to me sacrilege so soon to leave the repose, akin to death, of the house of mourning and to rush into the thick of life. I was new to sorrow, but it did not the less alarm me. I was unwilling to quit the sight of those that remained to me, and above all, I desired to see my sweet Elizabeth in some degree consoled.

She indeed veiled her grief and strove to act the comforter to us all. She looked steadily on life and assumed its duties with courage and zeal. She devoted herself to those whom she had been taught to call her uncle and cousins. Never was she so **enchanting** as at this time, when she recalled the sunshine of her smiles and spent them upon us. She forgot even her own regret in her endeavours to make us forget.

The day of my departure at length arrived. Clerval spent the last evening with us. He had endeavoured to persuade his father to permit him to accompany me and to become my fellow student, but **in vain**. His father was a narrow-minded trader and saw idleness and ruin in the **aspirations** and ambition of his son. Henry deeply felt the misfortune of being **debarred** from a liberal education. He said little, but when he spoke I read in his kindling eye and in his animated glance a restrained but

resolve [rizálv / -zólv] n.
결심, 결의
commerce [kámərs / kóm-] n.
상업, 무역, 거래
pretence [priténs] n.
구실, 핑계

firm **resolve** not to be chained to the miserable details of **commerce**.

We sat late. We could not tear ourselves away from each other nor persuade ourselves to say the word "Farewell!" It was said, and we retired under the **pretence** of seeking repose, each fancying that the other was deceived; but when at morning's dawn I descended to the carriage which was to convey me away, they were all there—my father again to bless me, Clerval to press my hand once more, my Elizabeth to renew her entreaties that I would write often and to bestow the last feminine attentions on her playmate and friend.

chaise [ʃeiz] n.
2륜 경마차
melancholy [mélənkàli / -kòli]
adj. 구슬픈, 울적한
whither [hwíðə:r] adv. conj.
어디로
invincible [invínsəbəl] adj.
정복할 수 없는, 무적의
repugnance [ripʌ́gnəns] n.
질색, 강한 반감

I threw myself into the **chaise** that was to convey me away and indulged in the most **melancholy** reflections. I, who had ever been surrounded by amiable companions, continually engaged in endeavouring to bestow mutual pleasure—I was now alone. In the university **whither** I was going I must form my own friends and be my own protector. My life had hitherto been remarkably secluded and domestic, and this had given me **invincible repugnance** to new countenances. I loved my brothers, Elizabeth, and Clerval; these were "old familiar faces," but I believed myself totally unfitted for the company of strangers. Such were my reflections as I commenced my journey; but as

acquisition [æ̀kwəzíʃən] n.
취득, 획득
cooped up :
~에 틀어박혀 있다

steeple [stí:p-əl] n.
(교회 따위의) 뾰족탑
alight [əláit] v.
내리다

omnipotent [ɑmnípətənt / ɔm-] adj. 전능의
sway [swei] n.
지배, 영향, 통치
uncouth [ʌnkú:θ] adj.
어색한, 괴상한
imbue [imbjú:] v.
감염시키다, 감화시키다, 불어넣다
appertain [æ̀pərtéin] v.
귀속하다, 관계하다

I proceeded, my spirits and hopes rose. I ardently desired the **acquisition** of knowledge. I had often, when at home, thought it hard to remain during my youth **cooped up** in one place and had longed to enter the world and take my station among other human beings. Now my desires were complied with, and it would, indeed, have been folly to repent.

I had sufficient leisure for these and many other reflections during my journey to Ingolstadt, which was long and fatiguing. At length the high white **steeple** of the town met my eyes. I **alighted** and was conducted to my solitary apartment to spend the evening as I pleased.

The next morning I delivered my letters of introduction and paid a visit to some of the principal professors. Chance—or rather the evil influence, the Angel of Destruction, which asserted **omnipotent sway** over me from the moment I turned my reluctant steps from my father's door—led me first to M. Krempe, professor of natural philosophy. He was an **uncouth** man, but deeply **imbued** in the secrets of his science. He asked me several questions concerning my progress in the different branches of science **appertaining** to natural philosophy. I replied carelessly, and partly in contempt, mentioned the names of my alchemists as the principal authors I had studied. The professor stared. "Have you," he said, "really spent your time in studying such nonsense?"

I replied in the **affirmative**. "Every minute," continued M. Krempe with warmth, "every instant that you have wasted on those books is **utterly** and entirely lost. You have burdened your memory with exploded systems and useless names. Good God! In what **desert** land have you lived, where no one was kind enough to inform you that these fancies which you have so greedily **imbibed** are a thousand years old and as **musty** as they are ancient? I little expected, in this enlightened and scientific age, to find a **disciple** of Albertus Magnus and Paracelsus. My dear sir, you must begin your studies entirely **anew**."

So saying, he stepped aside and wrote down a list of several books treating of natural philosophy which he desired me to procure, and dismissed me after mentioning that in the beginning of the following week he intended to commence a course of lectures upon natural philosophy in its general relations, and that M. Waldman, a fellow professor, would lecture upon chemistry the alternate days that he omitted.

I returned home not disappointed, for I have said that I had long considered those authors

---

affirmative [əfə́:rmətiv] n.
긍정, 확언
utterly [ʌ́tərli] adv.
아주, 완전히
desert [dézərt] adj.
사막의, 불모의, 황량한
imbibe [imbáib] v.
마시다, 흡수하다, 받아들이다
musty [mʌ́sti] adj.
곰팡내 나는
disciple [disáipəl] n.
제자, 문하생, 신봉자
anew [ənjú:] adv.
다시, 새로이

"... Good God! In what desert land have you lived, ..."

reprobate [réprəbèit] v.
책망하다, 비난하다, 배척하다
recur [rikə́:r] v.
되돌아가다
gruff [grʌf] adj.
거친, 걸걸한
prepossess [prì:pəzés] v.
호의를 품게 하다, 좋은 인상을 주다
strain [strein] n.
변설, 어조, 문체
retread [ri:tréd] v.
되걸어 가다, 다시 밟다
immortality [ìmɔ:rtǽləti] n.
불사, 불멸
futile [fjú:tl, -tail] adj.
쓸데 없는, 무익한, 하찮은
annihilation [ənàiəléiʃən] n.
멸망, 소멸
chimera [kimí:rə, kai-] n.
(그리스 신화의) 키메라, 괴물, 망상
grandeur [grǽndʒər, -dʒuər] n.
위대함, 위엄, 웅장함

useless whom the professor **reprobated**; but I returned not at all the more inclined to **recur** to these studies in any shape. M. Krempe was a little squat man with a **gruff** voice and a repulsive countenance; the teacher, therefore, did not **prepossess** me in favour of his pursuits. In rather a too philosophical and connected a **strain**, perhaps, I have given an account of the conclusions I had come to concerning them in my early years. As a child I had not been content with the results promised by the modern professors of natural science. With a confusion of ideas only to be accounted for by my extreme youth and my want of a guide on such matters, I had **retrod** the steps of knowledge along the paths of time and exchanged the discoveries of recent inquirers for the dreams of forgotten alchemists. Besides, I had a contempt for the uses of modern natural philosophy. It was very different when the masters of the science sought **immortality** and power; such views, although **futile**, were grand; but now the scene was changed. The ambition of the inquirer seemed to limit itself to the **annihilation** of those visions on which my interest in science was chiefly founded. I was required to exchange **chimeras** of boundless **grandeur** for realities of little worth.

Such were my reflections during the first

conceited [kənsíːtid] adj.
자만하는, 으스대는
recollect [rèkəlékt] v.
생각해 내다, 회상하다

recapitulation
[riːkəpitʃəleiʃən] n.
요점의 반복, 개괄, 요약
cursory [kə́ːrsəri] adj.
몹시 서두른, 엉성한, 피상적인

two or three days of my residence at Ingolstadt, which were chiefly spent in becoming acquainted with the localities and the principal residents in my new abode. But as the ensuing week commenced, I thought of the information which M. Krempe had given me concerning the lectures. And although I could not consent to go and hear that little **conceited** fellow deliver sentences out of a pulpit, I **recollected** what he had said of M. Waldman, whom I had never seen, as he had hitherto been out of town.

Partly from curiosity and partly from idleness, I went into the lecturing room, which M. Waldman entered shortly after. This professor was very unlike his colleague. He appeared about fifty years of age, but with an aspect expressive of the greatest benevolence; a few grey hairs covered his temples, but those at the back of his head were nearly black. His person was short but remarkably erect and his voice the sweetest I had ever heard. He began his lecture by a **recapitulation** of the history of chemistry and the various improvements made by different men of learning, pronouncing with fervour the names of the most distinguished discoverers. He then took a **cursory** view of the present state of the science and explained many of its elementary terms. After having made a few preparatory experiments,

panegyric [pæ̀nədʒírik, -dʒái-] n. 찬사, 칭찬의 말

transmute [trænsmjúːt, trænz-] v.
변형시키다, 바꾸다
elixir [ilíksər] n.
불로장생의 약, 만병 통치약
dabble [dǽbəl] v.
장난삼아 하다, 잠깐 손을 대다
crucible [krúːsəbl] n.
도가니
recess [ríːses, risés] n.
은거지, 구석진 곳, 벽의 움푹 들어간 곳
mimic [mímik] v.
흉내내다, 모사하다
mock [mɑk / mɔ(ː)k] v.
조롱하다, 놀리다

enounce [ináuns] v.
선언하다, 명쾌하게 말하다
palpable [pǽlpəbəl] adj.
뚜렷한, 명백한

he concluded with a **panegyric** upon modern chemistry, the terms of which I shall never forget: —

"The ancient teachers of this science," said he, "promised impossibilities and performed nothing. The modern masters promise very little; they know that metals cannot be **transmuted** and that the **elixir** of life is a chimera but these philosophers, whose hands seem only made to **dabble** in dirt, and their eyes to pore over the microscope or **crucible**, have indeed performed miracles. They penetrate into the **recesses** of nature and show how she works in her hiding-places. They ascend into the heavens; they have discovered how the blood circulates, and the nature of the air we breathe. They have acquired new and almost unlimited powers; they can command the thunders of heaven, **mimic** the earthquake, and even **mock** the invisible world with its own shadows."

Such were the professor's words — rather let me say such the words of the fate — **enounced** to destroy me. As he went on I felt as if my soul were grappling with a **palpable** enemy; one by one the various keys were touched which formed the mechanism of my being; chord after chord was sounded, and soon my mind was filled with one thought, one conception, one purpose. So much has been done, exclaimed the soul of Frankenstein—more, far more, will I achieve; treading in the steps already marked, I will **pioneer** a new way, explore unknown powers, and **unfold** to the world the deepest mysteries of creation.

I closed not my eyes that night. My internal being was in a state of **insurrection** and **turmoil**; I felt that order would thence arise, but I had no power to produce it. By degrees, after the morning's dawn, sleep came. I awoke, and my yesternight's thoughts were as a dream. There only remained a resolution to return to my ancient studies and to devote myself to a science for which I believed myself to possess a natural talent. On the same day I paid M. Waldman a visit. His manners in private were even more mild and attractive than in public, for there was a certain dignity in his **mien** during his lecture which in his own house was replaced by the greatest **affability** and kindness. I gave him pretty nearly the same account of my former pursuits as I had given to his fellow professor. He heard with attention the little narration concerning my studies and smiled at the names of Cornelius Agrippa and Paracelsus, but without the contempt that M. Krempe had exhibited. He said that "These were men to whose **indefatigable zeal** modern philosophers were **indebted** for most of the

---

pioneer [pàiəníər] v.
개척하다, 선도하다
unfold [ʌnfóuld] v.
펼치다, 나타내다

insurrection [ìnsərékʃən] n.
반란, 폭동
turmoil [tə́:rmɔil] n.
소동, 혼란, 불안, 동요
mien [mi:n] n.
풍채, 태도, 모습
affability [æ̀fəbíləti] n.
상냥함, 붙임성 있음
indefatigable [ìndifǽtigəbəl] adj. 지칠 줄 모르는, 끈기있는
zeal [zi:l] n.
열심, 열의
indebted [indétid] adj.
은혜를 입은, 신세진

... treading in the steps already marked, I will pioneer a new way, explore unknown powers, and unfold to the world the deepest mysteries of creation.

presumption [prizʌ́mpʃən] n. 주제넘음, 뻔뻔스러움
affectation [æ̀fektéiʃən] n. 가장, 허세
deference [défərəns] n. 존경, 경의

foundations of their knowledge. They had left to us, as an easier task, to give new names and arrange in connected classifications the facts which they in a great degree had been the instruments of bringing to light. The labours of men of genius, however erroneously directed, scarcely ever fail in ultimately turning to the solid advantage of mankind." I listened to his statement, which was delivered without any **presumption** or **affectation**, and then added that his lecture had removed my prejudices against modern chemists; I expressed myself in measured terms, with the modesty and **deference** due from a youth to his instructor, without letting escape (inexperience in life would have made me ashamed) any of the enthusiasm which stimulated my intended labours. I requested his advice concerning the books I ought to procure.

"I am happy," said M. Waldman, "to have gained a disciple; and if your application equals your ability, I have no doubt of your success. Chemistry is that branch of natural philosophy in which the greatest improvements have been and may be made; it is on that account that I have made it my peculiar study; but at the same time, I have not neglected the other branches of science. A man would make but a very sorry chemist if he attended to that department

petty [péti] adj.
이류의, 열등한, 종속의
experimentalist [ikspərə-mentəlist] n.
실험주의자

as to ~:
~에 관하여
derange [diréindʒ] v.
혼란시키다, 어지럽히다

of human knowledge alone. If your wish is to become really a man of science and not merely a **petty experimentalist**, I should advise you to apply to every branch of natural philosophy, including mathematics."

He then took me into his laboratory and explained to me the uses of his various machines, instructing me **as to** what I ought to procure and promising me the use of his own when I should have advanced far enough in the science not to **derange** their mechanism. He also gave me the list of books which I had requested, and I took my leave.

Thus ended a day memorable to me; it decided my future destiny.

Chapter 4

occupation [ɑ̀kjəpéiʃən / ɔ̀k-] n.
직업, 업무, 일과
cultivate [kʌ́ltəvèit] v.
(교제를) 구하다, 깊게 하다
physiognomy [fiziágnəmi / -ɔ́n-] n.
인상학, 인상, 형상
dogmatism [dɔ́(:)gmətìzəm, dɑ́g-] n.
독단주의, 교조주의

From this day natural philosophy, and particularly chemistry, in the most comprehensive sense of the term, became nearly my sole **occupation**. I read with ardour those works, so full of genius and discrimination, which modern inquirers have written on these subjects. I attended the lectures and **cultivated** the acquaintance of the men of science of the university, and I found even in M. Krempe a great deal of sound sense and real information, combined, it is true, with a repulsive **physiognomy** and manners, but not on that account the less valuable. In M. Waldman I found a true friend. His gentleness was never tinged by **dogmatism**, and his instructions were given

pedantry [pédəntri] n.
학자연함, 아는 체함, 현학
abstruse [æbstrú:s] adj.
난해한, 이해하기 어려운
facile [fǽsil / fǽsail] adj.
손쉬운, 용이한
apprehension [æ̀prihénʃən] n.
이해, 터득
fluctuate [flʌ́ktʃuèit] v.
오르내리다, 변동하다

conceive [kənsí:v] v.
마음속에 그리다, ~라고 생각하다
proficiency [prəfíʃənsi] n.
숙달, 능숙
exultation [èɡzʌltéiʃən, éksʌl-] n. 환희, 기쁨
heart and soul:
열심히, 전적으로
enticement [entáismənt] n.
유혹, 유인
infallibly [infǽləbəli] adv.
틀림없이, 확실히

with an air of frankness and good nature that banished every idea of **pedantry**. In a thousand ways he smoothed for me the path of knowledge and made the most **abstruse** inquiries clear and **facile** to my **apprehension**. My application was at first **fluctuating** and uncertain; it gained strength as I proceeded and soon became so ardent and eager that the stars often disappeared in the light of morning whilst I was yet engaged in my laboratory.

As I applied so closely, it may be easily **conceived** that my progress was rapid. My ardour was indeed the astonishment of the students, and my **proficiency** that of the masters. Professor Krempe often asked me, with a sly smile, how Cornelius Agrippa went on, whilst M. Waldman expressed the most heartfelt **exultation** in my progress. Two years passed in this manner, during which I paid no visit to Geneva, but was engaged, **heart and soul**, in the pursuit of some discoveries which I hoped to make. None but those who have experienced them can conceive of the **enticements** of science. In other studies you go as far as others have gone before you, and there is nothing more to know; but in a scientific pursuit there is continual food for discovery and wonder. A mind of moderate capacity which closely pursues one study must **infallibly** arrive at great

attainment [ətéinmənt] n.
학식, 재능, 조예
esteem [istíːm] n.
존중, 존경
conducive [kəndjúːsiv] adj.
도움이 되는, 이바지하는, 공헌하는
protract [proutrǽkt] v.
오래 끌게 하다, 연장하다

endue [indjúː, en-] v.
부여하다, 주다
whence [hwens] adv.
어디에서, 어디로부터
brink [briŋk] n.
가장자리, 언저리
revolve [riválv / -vólv] v.
궁리하다, 곰곰이 생각하다
physiology [fìziálədʒi / -ól-] n.
생리학

proficiency in that study; and I, who continually sought the **attainment** of one object of pursuit and was solely wrapped up in this, improved so rapidly that at the end of two years I made some discoveries in the improvement of some chemical instruments, which procured me great **esteem** and admiration at the university. When I had arrived at this point and had become as well acquainted with the theory and practice of natural philosophy as depended on the lessons of any of the professors at Ingolstadt, my residence there being no longer **conducive** to my improvements, I thought of returning to my friends and my native town, when an incident happened that **protracted** my stay.

One of the phenomena which had peculiarly attracted my attention was the structure of the human frame, and, indeed, any animal **endued** with life. **Whence**, I often asked myself, did the principle of life proceed? It was a bold question, and one which has ever been considered as a mystery; yet with how many things are we upon the **brink** of becoming acquainted, if cowardice or carelessness did not restrain our inquiries. I **revolved** these circumstances in my mind and determined thenceforth to apply myself more particularly to those branches of natural philosophy which relate to **physiology**. Unless I had been animated by an

supernatural [sù:pərnǽtʃərəl] adj. 초자연의, 불가사의한
irksome [ə́:rksəm] adj. 괴롭히는, 성가신
intolerable [intɑ́lərəbəl / -tɔ́l-] adj. 견딜 수 없는, 참을 수 없는
recourse [rí:kɔ:rs, rikɔ́:rs] n. 의지, 의뢰
precaution [prikɔ́:ʃən] n. 조심, 경계
insupportable [ìnsəpɔ́:rtəbəl] adj. 참을 수 없는, 견딜 수 없는. 지지할 수 없는
minutia [minjú:ʃiə, mai-] n. (pl. -tiae [-ʃiì:]) 사소한 점, 사소한 일
causation [kɔ:zéiʃən] n. 원인, 인과 관계
exemplify [igzémpləfài] v. 예증하다, 구현하다

almost **supernatural** enthusiasm, my application to this study would have been **irksome** and almost **intolerable**. To examine the causes of life, we must first have **recourse** to death. I became acquainted with the science of anatomy, but this was not sufficient; I must also observe the natural decay and corruption of the human body. In my education my father had taken the greatest **precautions** that my mind should be impressed with no supernatural horrors. I do not ever remember to have trembled at a tale of superstition or to have feared the apparition of a spirit. Darkness had no effect upon my fancy, and a churchyard was to me merely the receptacle of bodies deprived of life, which, from being the seat of beauty and strength, had become food for the worm. Now I was led to examine the cause and progress of this decay and forced to spend days and nights in vaults and charnel-houses. My attention was fixed upon every object the most **insupportable** to the delicacy of the human feelings. I saw how the fine form of man was degraded and wasted; I beheld the corruption of death succeed to the blooming cheek of life; I saw how the worm inherited the wonders of the eye and brain. I paused, examining and analysing all the **minutiae** of **causation**, as **exemplified** in the change from life to death, and death to life, until from the midst of this darkness a sudden light broke in upon me—a light so brilliant and wondrous, yet so simple, that while I became dizzy with the immensity of the prospect which it illustrated, I was surprised that among so many men of genius who had directed their inquiries towards the same science, that I alone should be reserved to discover so astonishing a secret.

Remember, I am not recording the **vision** of a madman. The sun does not more certainly shine in the heavens than that which I now affirm is true. Some miracle might have produced it, yet the stages of the discovery were distinct and probable. After days and nights of incredible labour and fatigue, I succeeded in discovering the cause of generation and life; **nay**, more, I became myself capable of **bestowing animation** upon lifeless matter.

The astonishment which I had at first experienced on this discovery soon gave place to delight and **rapture**. After so much time spent in painful labour, to arrive at once at the summit of my desires was the most **gratifying consummation** of my **toils**. But this discovery was so great and overwhelming that all the steps by which I had been progressively led to it were **obliterated**, and I beheld only the result. What had been the study and desire of

---

vision [víʒən] n.
환상, 환영
nay [nei] adv. n.
no
bestow [bistóu] v.
주다, 부여하다
animation [ænəméiʃən] n.
생기, 활기, 쾌활, 기운

rapture [ræptʃəːr] n.
큰 기쁨, 환희
gratifying [grǽtəfàiiŋ] adj.
만족을 주는, 흡족한, 유쾌한
consummation [kànsəméiʃən / kɔ̀n-] n.
완성, 달성, 성취, 마무리
toil [tɔil] n.
힘드는 일, 수고, 노고
obliterate [əblítərèit] v.
없애다

> I succeeded in discovering the cause of generation and life; nay, more, I became myself capable of bestowing animation upon lifeless matter.

perceive [pərsíːv] v.
알아차리다, 이해하다
reserved [rizə́ːrvd] adj.
마음을 털어놓지 않는, 조심스러운, 주저하는
lead on:
~하게 하다, ~로 이끌다
unguarded [ʌngɑ́ːrdid] adj.
부주의한, 무방비의
infallible [infǽləbəl] adj.
확실한, 결코 틀리지 않는
precept [príːsept] n.
교훈

the wisest men since the creation of the world was now within my grasp. Not that, like a magic scene, it all opened upon me at once: the information I had obtained was of a nature rather to direct my endeavours so soon as I should point them towards the object of my search than to exhibit that object already accomplished. I was like the Arabian who had been buried with the dead and found a passage to life, aided only by one glimmering and seemingly ineffectual light.

I see by your eagerness and the wonder and hope which your eyes express, my friend, that you expect to be informed of the secret with which I am acquainted; that cannot be; listen patiently until the end of my story, and you will easily **perceive** why I am **reserved** upon that subject. I will not **lead** you **on**, **unguarded** and ardent as I then was, to your destruction and **infallible** misery. Learn from me, if not by my **precepts**, at least by my example, how dangerous is the acquirement of knowledge and how much happier that man is who believes his native town to be the world, than he who aspires to become greater than his nature will allow.

When I found so astonishing a power placed within my hands, I hesitated a long time concerning the manner in which I should employ

intricacy [íntrikəsi] n.
얽히고 설킴, 복잡
inconceivable [ìnkənsí:vəbəl] adj. 상상도 할 수 없는, 믿을 수 없는
reverse [rivə́:rs] n.
불운, 실패, 패배
incessantly [insésəntli] adv
끊임없이, 계속해서
baffle [bǽfəl] v.
당황하게 하다, 좌절시키다
impracticability [impræ̀ktikəbíləti] n.
비실제성, 실행 불능
hindrance [híndrəns] n.
방해, 장애
stature [stǽtʃə:r] n.
키, 신장

it. Although I possessed the capacity of bestowing animation, yet to prepare a frame for the reception of it, with all its **intricacies** of fibres, muscles, and veins, still remained a work of **inconceivable** difficulty and labour. I doubted at first whether I should attempt the creation of a being like myself, or one of simpler organization; but my imagination was too much exalted by my first success to permit me to doubt of my ability to give life to an animal as complex and wonderful as man. The materials at present within my command hardly appeared adequate to so arduous an undertaking, but I doubted not that I should ultimately succeed. I prepared myself for a multitude of **reverses**; my operations might be **incessantly baffled**, and at last my work be imperfect, yet when I considered the improvement which every day takes place in science and mechanics, I was encouraged to hope my present attempts would at least lay the foundations of future success. Nor could I consider the magnitude and complexity of my plan as any argument of its **impracticability**. It was with these feelings that I began the creation of a human being. As the minuteness of the parts formed a great **hindrance** to my speed, I resolved, contrary to my first intention, to make the being of a gigantic **stature**, that is to say, about eight feet in height, and proportionably large. After having formed this determination and having spent some months in successfully collecting and arranging my materials, I began.

No one can conceive the variety of feelings which bore me onwards, like a hurricane, in the first enthusiasm of success. Life and death appeared to me ideal bounds, which I should first break through, and pour a **torrent** of light into our dark world. A new species would bless me as its creator and source; many happy and excellent natures would owe their being to me. No father could claim the **gratitude** of his child so completely as I should deserve theirs. Pursuing these reflections, I thought that if I could bestow animation upon lifeless matter, I might in process of time (although I now found it impossible) renew life where death had apparently devoted the body to corruption.

These thoughts supported my spirits, while I pursued my undertaking with **unremitting ardour**. My cheek had grown pale with study, and my person had become emaciated with **confinement**. Sometimes, on the very brink of certainty, I failed; yet still I clung to the hope which the next day or the next hour might realise. One secret which I alone possessed was the hope to which I had dedicated myself;

---

torrent [tɔ́:r-ənt, tár- / tɔ́r-] n.
급류, 분류
gratitude [grǽtətjù:d] n.
감사, 사의

Life and death appeared to me ideal bounds, which I should first break through, and pour a torrent of light into our dark world.

unremitting [ʌ̀nrimítiŋ] adj.
간단 없는, 끊임 없는
ardour [á:rdər] n.
열정, 열의
confinement [kənfáinmənt] n.
감금, 억류, 틀어박힘

unhallowed [ʌnhǽloud] adj.
사악한, 죄가 많은
frantic [frǽntik] adj.
미친, 광란의
impulse [ímpʌls] n.
충동, 일시적인 감정
trance [træns, trɑ:ns] n.
열중, 망연 자실
profane [prəféin, prou-] adj.
독신(瀆神)의, 모독적인, 불경스런

and the moon gazed on my midnight labours, while, with unrelaxed and breathless eagerness, I pursued nature to her hiding-places. Who shall conceive the horrors of my secret toil as I dabbled among the **unhallowed** damps of the grave or tortured the living animal to animate the lifeless clay? My limbs now tremble, and my eyes swim with the remembrance; but then a resistless and almost **frantic impulse** urged me forward; I seemed to have lost all soul or sensation but for this one pursuit. It was indeed but a passing **trance**, that only made me feel with renewed acuteness so soon as, the unnatural stimulus ceasing to operate, I had returned to my old habits. I collected bones from charnel-houses and disturbed, with **profane** fingers, the tremendous secrets of the human frame. In a solitary chamber, or rather cell, at the top of the house, and separated from all the other apartments by a gallery and staircase, I kept my workshop of filthy creation; my eyeballs were starting from their sockets in attending to the details of my employment. The dissecting room and the slaughter-house furnished many of my materials; and often did my human nature turn with loathing from my occupation, whilst, still urged on by an eagerness which perpetually increased, I brought my work near to a conclusion.

luxuriant [lʌgʒúəriənt, lʌkʃúər-] adj.
풍요한, 화려한
disquiet [diskwáiət] v.
불안하게 하다, 걱정시키다

loathsome [lóuðsəm] adj.
싫은, 지긋지긋한, 불쾌한
procrastinate [proukrǽstənèit] v. 지연하다, 꾸물거리다, 질질 끌다

ascribe [əskráib] v.
~의 탓으로 돌리다, ~에 기인하는 것으로 하다

The summer months passed while I was thus engaged, heart and soul, in one pursuit. It was a most beautiful season; never did the fields bestow a more plentiful harvest or the vines yield a more **luxuriant** vintage, but my eyes were insensible to the charms of nature. And the same feelings which made me neglect the scenes around me caused me also to forget those friends who were so many miles absent, and whom I had not seen for so long a time. I knew my silence **disquieted** them, and I well remembered the words of my father: "I know that while you are pleased with yourself you will think of us with affection, and we shall hear regularly from you. You must pardon me if I regard any interruption in your correspondence as a proof that your other duties are equally neglected."

I knew well therefore what would be my father's feelings, but I could not tear my thoughts from my employment, **loathsome** in itself, but which had taken an irresistible hold of my imagination. I wished, as it were, to **procrastinate** all that related to my feelings of affection until the great object, which swallowed up every habit of my nature, should be completed.

I then thought that my father would be unjust if he **ascribed** my neglect to vice or faultiness on my part, but I am now convinced that he was justified in conceiving that I should not be altogether free from blame. A human being in perfection ought always to preserve a calm and peaceful mind and never to allow passion or a **transitory** desire to **disturb** his **tranquillity**. I do not think that the pursuit of knowledge is an exception to this rule. If the study to which you apply yourself has a tendency to weaken your affections and to destroy your taste for those simple pleasures in which no **alloy** can possibly mix, then that study is certainly **unlawful**, that is to say, not **befitting** the human mind. If this rule were always observed; if no man allowed any pursuit whatsoever to interfere with the tranquillity of his domestic affections, Greece had not been enslaved, Caesar would have spared his country, America would have been discovered more gradually, and the empires of Mexico and Peru had not been destroyed.

But I forget that I am **moralizing** in the most interesting part of my tale, and your looks remind me to proceed.

My father made no **reproach** in his letters and only took notice of my silence by inquiring into my occupations more particularly than before. Winter, spring, and summer passed away during my labours; but I did not watch

engrossed [engróusd] adj.
몰두한
wither [wíðəːr] v.
시들다, 쇠퇴하다, 희박해지다
unwholesome [ʌnhóulsəm] adj. 불건전한, 해로운, 부패한
trade [treid] n.
직업, 일
shun [ʃʌn] v.
피하다, 비키다, 멀리하다
wreck [rek] n.
폐인, 병자
incipient [insípiənt] adj.
시초의, 발단의, 초기의

the blossom or the expanding leaves — sights which before always yielded me supreme delight — so deeply was I **engrossed** in my occupation. The leaves of that year had **withered** before my work drew near to a close, and now every day showed me more plainly how well I had succeeded. But my enthusiasm was checked by my anxiety, and I appeared rather like one doomed by slavery to toil in the mines, or any other **unwholesome trade** than an artist occupied by his favourite employment. Every night I was oppressed by a slow fever, and I became nervous to a most painful degree; the fall of a leaf startled me, and I **shunned** my fellow creatures as if I had been guilty of a crime. Sometimes I grew alarmed at the **wreck** I perceived that I had become; the energy of my purpose alone sustained me: my labours would soon end, and I believed that exercise and amusement would then drive away **incipient** disease; and I promised myself both of these when my creation should be complete.

Chapter 5

agony [ǽgəni] n.
고민, 고통
infuse [infjúːz] v.
주입하다, 불어넣다
patter [pǽtər] v.
또닥또닥 소리가 나다, (비가)
후두두 내리다
dismally [dízməli] adv.
음울하게, 황량하게, 쓸쓸하게
convulsive [kənválsiv] adj.
경련성인, 발작적인

delineate [dilínièit] v.
윤곽을 그리다, 묘사하다

It was on a dreary night of November that I beheld the accomplishment of my toils. With an anxiety that almost amounted to **agony**, I collected the instruments of life around me, that I might **infuse** a spark of being into the lifeless thing that lay at my feet. It was already one in the morning; the rain **pattered dismally** against the panes, and my candle was nearly burnt out, when, by the glimmer of the half-extinguished light, I saw the dull yellow eye of the creature open; it breathed hard, and a **convulsive** motion agitated its limbs.

How can I describe my emotions at this catastrophe, or how **delineate** the wretch whom with such infinite pains and care I had endeavoured to form? His limbs were in proportion, and I had selected his features as beautiful. Beautiful! Great God! His yellow skin scarcely covered the work of muscles and arteries beneath; his hair was of a lustrous black, and flowing; his teeth of a pearly whiteness; but these luxuriances only formed a more horrid contrast with his watery eyes, that seemed almost of the same colour as the dun-white sockets in which they were set, his shrivelled complexion and straight black lips.

The different accidents of life are not so changeable as the feelings of human nature. I had worked hard for nearly two years, for the sole purpose of infusing life into an **inanimate** body. For this I had deprived myself of rest and health. I had desired it with an ardour that far exceeded moderation; but now that I had finished, the beauty of the dream vanished, and breathless horror and disgust filled my heart. Unable to endure the aspect of the being I had created, I rushed out of the room and continued a long time traversing my bed-chamber, unable to **compose** my mind to sleep. **At length lassitude** succeeded to the tumult I had before endured, and I threw myself on the bed in my clothes, endeavouring to seek a few moments of forgetfulness. But it was **in vain**; I slept, indeed, but I was disturbed by the wildest

---

but now that I had finished, the beauty of the dream vanished, and breathless horror and disgust filled my heart.

inanimate [inǽnəmit] adj.
생명 없는, 무생물의
compose [kəmpóuz] v.
가라앉히다, 정돈하다, 진정시키다
at length:
드디어, 마침내
lassitude [lǽsitjùːd] n.
나른함, 권태, 피로
in vain:
효과 없이, 보람 없이, 헛되이

mutter [mʌ́tə:r] v.
낮고 불명확한 소리로 말하다,
중얼중얼 말하다
inarticulate [ìnɑ:rtíkjəlit] adj.
분명치 않은
detain [ditéin] v.
붙들다, 구류하다
demoniacal [dì:mənáiəkəl] adj.
악마의, 악마와 같은, 귀신들린

His jaws opened, and he muttered some inarticulate sounds, while a grin wrinkled his cheeks. He might have spoken, but I did not hear; one hand was stretched out, seemingly to detain me, but I escaped and rushed downstairs.

dreams. I thought I saw Elizabeth, in the bloom of health, walking in the streets of Ingolstadt. Delighted and surprised, I embraced her, but as I imprinted the first kiss on her lips, they became livid with the hue of death; her features appeared to change, and I thought that I held the corpse of my dead mother in my arms; a shroud enveloped her form, and I saw the grave-worms crawling in the folds of the flannel. I started from my sleep with horror; a cold dew covered my forehead, my teeth chattered, and every limb became convulsed; when, by the dim and yellow light of the moon, as it forced its way through the window shutters, I beheld the wretch—the miserable monster whom I had created. He held up the curtain of the bed; and his eyes, if eyes they may be called, were fixed on me. His jaws opened, and he **muttered** some **inarticulate** sounds, while a grin wrinkled his cheeks. He might have spoken, but I did not hear; one hand was stretched out, seemingly to **detain** me, but I escaped and rushed downstairs. I took refuge in the courtyard belonging to the house which I inhabited, where I remained during the rest of the night, walking up and down in the greatest agitation, listening attentively, catching and fearing each sound as if it were to announce the approach of the **demoniacal** corpse to which I had so

mummy [mʌ́mi] n.
미라
endue [indjúː, en-] v.
부여하다, 주다
hideous [hídiəs] adj.
무서운, 몹시 추한, 극악 무도한

palpitation [pæ̀lpətéiʃən] n.
고동, 두근거림, 떨림
languor [lǽŋgəːr] n.
피로, 무기력함
overthrow [óuvərəròu] n.
타도, 패배, 멸망

asylum [əsáiləm] n.
도피처, 은신처, 피난처

dreams that had been my food and pleasant rest for so long a space were now become a hell to me; and the change was so rapid, the overthrow so complete!

miserably given life.

Oh! No mortal could support the horror of that countenance. A **mummy** again **endued** with animation could not be so **hideous** as that wretch. I had gazed on him while unfinished; he was ugly then, but when those muscles and joints were rendered capable of motion, it became a thing such as even Dante could not have conceived.

I passed the night wretchedly. Sometimes my pulse beat so quickly and hardly that I felt the **palpitation** of every artery; at others, I nearly sank to the ground through **languor** and extreme weakness. Mingled with this horror, I felt the bitterness of disappointment; dreams that had been my food and pleasant rest for so long a space were now become a hell to me; and the change was so rapid, the **overthrow** so complete!

Morning, dismal and wet, at length dawned and discovered to my sleepless and aching eyes the church of Ingolstadt, its white steeple and clock, which indicated the sixth hour. The porter opened the gates of the court, which had that night been my **asylum**, and I issued into the streets, pacing them with quick steps, as if I sought to avoid the wretch whom I feared every turning of the street would present to my view. I did not dare return to the apartment

impel [impél] v.
재촉하다, 몰아대다, 강제하다

which I inhabited, but felt **impelled** to hurry on, although drenched by the rain which poured from a black and comfortless sky.

I continued walking in this manner for some time, endeavouring by bodily exercise to ease the load that weighed upon my mind. I traversed the streets without any clear conception of where I was or what I was doing. My heart palpitated in the sickness of fear, and I hurried on with irregular steps, not daring to look about me:

doth [dʌθ, dəθ] v.
(고어) do의 3인칭단수·직설법·현재
fiend [fi:nd] n.
마귀, 악령, 악한
tread [tred] v.
걷다

> Like one who, on a lonely road,
> **Doth** walk in fear and dread,
> And, having once turned round, walks on,
> And turns no more his head;
> Because he knows a frightful **fiend**
> Doth close behind him **tread**.*

diligence [díladʒɑ̀:ns, -dʒəns] n. (프랑스 등에서 사용된) 승합 마차

Because he knows a frightful fiend
Doth close behind him tread.

Continuing thus, I came at length opposite to the inn at which the various **diligences** and carriages usually stopped. Here I paused, I knew not why; but I remained some minutes with my eyes fixed on a coach that was coming towards me from the other end of the street. As it drew nearer I observed that it was the Swiss diligence; it stopped just where I was standing, and on the door being opened, I

---

* Coleridge's "Ancient Mariner."

perceived Henry Clerval, who, on seeing me, instantly sprung out. "My dear Frankenstein," exclaimed he, "how glad I am to see you! How fortunate that you should be here at the very moment of my alighting!"

Nothing could equal my delight on seeing Clerval; his presence brought back to my thoughts my father, Elizabeth, and all those scenes of home so dear to my recollection. I grasped his hand, and in a moment forgot my horror and misfortune; I felt suddenly, and for the first time during many months, calm and **serene** joy. I welcomed my friend, therefore, in the most **cordial** manner, and we walked towards my college. Clerval continued talking for some time about our mutual friends and his own good fortune in being permitted to come to Ingolstadt. "You may easily believe," said he, "how great was the difficulty to persuade my father that all necessary knowledge was not comprised in the noble art of book-keeping; and, indeed, I believe I left him **incredulous** to the last, for his constant answer to my unwearied entreaties was the same as that of the Dutch schoolmaster in *The Vicar of Wakefield*: 'I have ten thousand **florins** a year without Greek, I eat heartily without Greek.' But his affection for me at length overcame his dislike of learning, and he has permitted me to

---

serene [sirí:n] adj.
조용한, 고요한, 평온한
cordial [kɔ́:rdʒəl / -diəl] adj.
진심에서 우러난
incredulous [inkrédʒələs] adj.
믿으려 하지 않는, 의심하는
florin [flɔ́(:)rin, flár-] n.
플로린(1252년 Florence에서 발행한 금화)

undertake a voyage of discovery to the land of knowledge."

"It gives me the greatest delight to see you; but tell me how you left my father, brothers, and Elizabeth."

"Very well, and very happy, only a little uneasy that they hear from you so seldom. **By the by**, I mean to lecture you a little upon their account myself. But, my dear Frankenstein," continued he, stopping short and gazing full in my face, "I did not before **remark** how very ill you appear; so thin and pale; you look as if you had been watching for several nights."

"You have guessed right; I have lately been so deeply engaged in one occupation that I have not allowed myself sufficient rest, as you see; but I hope, I sincerely hope, that all these employments are now **at an end** and that I am **at length** free."

I trembled excessively; I could not endure to think of, and far less to **allude** to, the occurrences of the **preceding** night. I walked with a quick pace, and we soon arrived at my college. I then reflected, and the thought made me shiver, that the creature whom I had left in my apartment might still be there, alive and walking about. I **dreaded** to behold this monster, but I feared still more that Henry should see him. Entreating him, therefore, to remain

---

by the by:
그런데, 덧붙여서
remark [rimá:rk] v.
주목하다, 알아차리다

at an end:
끝나다, 다하다
at length:
드디어, 마침내

allude [əlú:d] v.
넌지시 말하다, 언급하다
preceding [prisí:diŋ] adj.
이전의, 바로 전의
dread [dred] n.
무서워하다, 싫어하다

a few minutes at the bottom of the stairs, I darted up towards my own room. My hand was already on the lock of the door before I **recollected** myself. I then paused, and a cold shivering came over me. I threw the door forcibly open, as children are accustomed to do when they expect a **spectre** to stand in waiting for them on the other side; but nothing appeared. I stepped fearfully in: the apartment was empty, and my bedroom was also freed from its hideous guest. I could hardly believe that so great a good fortune could have **befallen** me, but when I became assured that my enemy had indeed fled, I clapped my hands for joy and ran down to Clerval.

We ascended into my room, and the servant presently brought breakfast; but I was unable to **contain** myself. It was not joy only that possessed me; I felt my flesh **tingle** with excess of sensitiveness, and my pulse beat rapidly. I was unable to remain for a single instant in the same place; I jumped over the chairs, clapped my hands, and laughed aloud. Clerval at first **attributed** my unusual spirits to joy on his arrival, but when he observed me more **attentively**, he saw a wildness in my eyes for which he could not **account**, and my loud, unrestrained, heartless laughter frightened and astonished him.

---

recollect [rìːkəlékt] v.
다시 모으다, 마음을 가라앉히다, (힘, 용기를) 불러일으키다
specter [spéktəːr] n.
유령, 망령, 요괴
befall [bifɔ́ːl] v.
발생하다, 일어나다

contain [kəntéin] v.
(감정 따위를) 안으로 억누르다, 참다, 자제하다
tingle [tíŋ-əl] v.
쑤시다, 욱신거리다, 따끔거리다
attribute [ətríbjuːt] v.
~에 기인한다고 생각하다, ~의 결과라고 생각하다
attentively [əténtivli] adv.
주의 깊게, 세심하게
account [əkáunt] v.
설명하다, 이유를 밝히다

"My dear Victor," cried he, "what, for God's sake, is the matter? Do not laugh in that manner. How ill you are! What is the cause of all this?"

"Do not ask me," cried I, putting my hands before my eyes, for I thought I saw the dreaded spectre glide into the room; "*he* can tell. Oh, save me! Save me!" I imagined that the monster seized me; I struggled furiously and fell down in a **fit**.

Poor Clerval! What must have been his feelings? A meeting, which he anticipated with such joy, so strangely turned to bitterness. But I was not the witness of his grief, for I was lifeless and did not recover my senses for a long, long time.

This was the commencement of a nervous fever which **confined** me for several months. During all that time Henry was my only nurse. I afterwards learned that, knowing my father's advanced age and unfitness for so long a journey, and how **wretched** my sickness would make Elizabeth, he spared them this grief by concealing the extent of my **disorder**. He knew that I could not have a more kind and attentive nurse than himself; and, firm in the hope he felt of my recovery, he did not doubt that, instead of doing harm, he performed the kindest action that he could towards them.

---

fit [fit] n.
발작, 경련

confine [kənfáin] v.
제한하다, 가둬 넣다, 틀어박히게 하다
wretched [rétʃid] adj.
불행한, 비참한, 불쌍한
disorder [disɔ́ːrdər] n.
병, 장애, 이상

But I was in reality very ill, and surely nothing but the **unbounded** and **unremitting** attentions of my friend could have restored me to life. The form of the monster on whom I had bestowed existence was for ever before my eyes, and I **raved** incessantly concerning him. Doubtless my words surprised Henry; he at first believed them to be the wanderings of my disturbed imagination, but the **pertinacity** with which I continually **recurred** to the same subject persuaded him that my disorder indeed owed its origin to some uncommon and terrible event.

By very slow degrees, and with frequent **relapses** that alarmed and grieved my friend, I recovered. I remember the first time I became capable of observing outward objects with any kind of pleasure, I **perceived** that the fallen leaves had disappeared and that the young buds were shooting forth from the trees that shaded my window. It was a divine spring, and the season contributed greatly to my **convalescence**. I felt also sentiments of joy and affection **revive** in my bosom; my gloom disappeared, and in a short time I became as cheerful as before I was attacked by the fatal passion.

"Dearest Clerval," exclaimed I, "how kind, how very good you are to me. This whole winter, instead of being spent in study, as you promised yourself, has been consumed in my sick room. How shall I ever repay you? I feel the greatest **remorse** for the disappointment of which I have been the **occasion**, but you will forgive me."

"You will repay me entirely if you do not **discompose** yourself, but get well as fast as you can; and since you appear in such good spirits, I may speak to you on one subject, may I not?"

I trembled. One subject! What could it be? Could he allude to an object on whom I dared not even think?

"Compose yourself," said Clerval, who observed my change of colour, "I will not mention it if it agitates you; but your father and cousin would be very happy if they received a letter from you in your own handwriting. They hardly know how ill you have been and are uneasy at your long silence."

"Is that all, my dear Henry? How could you suppose that my first thought would not fly towards those dear, dear friends whom I love and who are so deserving of my love?"

"If this is your present temper, my friend, you will perhaps be glad to see a letter that has been lying here some days for you; it is from your cousin, I believe."

---

remorse [rimɔ́ːrs] n.
후회, 양심의 가책
occasion [əkéiʒən] n.
이유, 근거, 원인

discompose [dìskəmpóuz] v.
불안하게 하다, 뒤숭숭하게 하다, 괴롭히다

The form of the monster on whom I had bestowed existence was for ever before my eyes, and I raved incessantly concerning him.

Chapter 6

Clerval then put the following letter into my hands. It was from my own Elizabeth:

"My dearest Cousin,

"You have been ill, very ill, and even the constant letters of dear kind Henry are not sufficient to **reassure** me **on your account**. You are forbidden to write—to hold a pen; yet one word from you, dear Victor, is necessary to calm our **apprehensions**. For a long time I have thought that each post would bring this line, and my persuasions have **restrained** my uncle from undertaking a journey to Ingolstadt. I have prevented his encountering the inconveniences and perhaps dangers of so long a

reassure [rìːəʃúəːr] v.
안심시키다, 장담하다, 기운을 돋우다
on someone's account/ on account of someone:
~을 위하여
apprehension [æprihénʃən] n.
불안, 걱정
restrain [ristréin] v.
제지하다, 억누르다, 억제하다

devolve [diválv / -vólv] v.
맡겨지다, 귀속하다
mercenary [mə́:rsənèri] adj.
돈을 목적으로 하는, 고용된, 물질적인
minister [mínistər] v.
섬기다, 봉사하다, 보살펴 주다
intelligence [intéləd ʒəns] n.
정보, 소식, 보도

application [æ̀plikéiʃən] n.
열심, 근면
odious [óudiəs] adj.
싫은, 미운, 가증스러운
fetter [fétər] v.
차꼬, 족쇄, 속박
idler [áidlər] n.
게으름뱅이
yield [ji:ld] v.
양보하다, 굴복하다, 인정하다

journey, yet how often have I regretted not being able to perform it myself! I figure to myself that the task of attending on your sickbed has **devolved** on some **mercenary** old nurse, who could never guess your wishes nor **minister** to them with the care and affection of your poor cousin. Yet that is over now: Clerval writes that indeed you are getting better. I eagerly hope that you will confirm this **intelligence** soon in your own handwriting.

"Get well — and return to us. You will find a happy, cheerful home and friends who love you dearly. Your father's health is vigorous, and he asks but to see you, but to be assured that you are well; and not a care will ever cloud his benevolent countenance. How pleased you would be to remark the improvement of our Ernest! He is now sixteen and full of activity and spirit. He is desirous to be a true Swiss and to enter into foreign service, but we cannot part with him, at least until his elder brother returns to us. My uncle is not pleased with the idea of a military career in a distant country, but Ernest never had your powers of **application**. He looks upon study as an **odious fetter**; his time is spent in the open air, climbing the hills or rowing on the lake. I fear that he will become an **idler** unless we **yield** the point and permit him to enter on the profession which he has selected.

"Little **alteration**, except the growth of our dear children, has taken place since you left us. The blue lake and snow-clad mountains — they never change; and I think our placid home and our contented hearts are regulated by the same **immutable** laws. My **trifling occupations** take up my time and amuse me, and I am rewarded for any **exertions** by seeing none but happy, kind faces around me. Since you left us, but one change has taken place in our little household. Do you remember on what occasion Justine Moritz entered our family? Probably you do not; I will relate her history, therefore in a few words. Madame Moritz, her mother, was a widow with four children, of whom Justine was the third. This girl had always been the favourite of her father, but through a strange **perversity**, her mother could not endure her, and after the death of M. Moritz, treated her very ill. My aunt observed this, and when Justine was twelve years of age, **prevailed** on her mother to allow her to live at our house. The **republican institutions** of our country have produced simpler and happier manners than those which prevail in the great **monarchies** that surround it. Hence there is less distinction between the several classes of its inhabitants; and the lower **orders**, being

---

alteration [ɔ̀:ltəréiʃən] n.
변화, 변경, 수정
immutable [imjú:təbəl] adj.
변치 않는
trifling [tráifliŋ] adj.
하찮은, 시시한
occupation [àkjəpéiʃən / ɔ̀k-] n.
일, 업무, 활동
exertion [igzə́:rʃən] n.
노력, 진력, 고된 일
perversity [pərvə́:rsəti] n.
심술궂음, 외고집
prevail [privéil] v.
설복하다, 설득하다
republican [ripʌ́blikən] adj.
공화국의, 공화주의의
institution [ìnstətjú:ʃən] n.
제도, 관습, 법령
monarchy [mánərki / mɔ́n-] n.
군주제, 군주 정치, 군주국
order [ɔ́:rdər] n.
지위, 신분, 계급

refined [rifáind] adj.
고상한, 세련된, 우아한
dignity [dígnəti] n.
위엄, 존엄성, 품위

recollect [rèkəlékt] v.
생각해 내다, 회상하다
dissipate [dísəpèit] v.
흩뜨리다, 일소하다
attachment [ətǽtʃmənt] n.
애정, 사모, 애착
profession [prəféʃən] n.
공언, 언명, 고백
protectress [prətéktris] n.
protector의 여성형; 보호자, 후원자
disposition [dìspəzíʃən] n.
기질, 성미, 성격
inconsiderate [ìnkənsídərit] adj. 헤아림이 없는, 분별이 없는, 경솔한
phraseology [frèiziálədʒi / -ól-] n. 표현, 문구, 어법

neither so poor nor so despised, their manners are more **refined** and moral. A servant in Geneva does not mean the same thing as a servant in France and England. Justine, thus received in our family, learned the duties of a servant, a condition which, in our fortunate country, does not include the idea of ignorance and a sacrifice of the **dignity** of a human being.

"Justine, you may remember, was a great favourite of yours; and I **recollect** you once remarked that if you were in an ill humour, one glance from Justine could **dissipate** it, for the same reason that Ariosto gives concerning the beauty of Angelica — she looked so frank-hearted and happy. My aunt conceived a great **attachment** for her, by which she was induced to give her an education superior to that which she had at first intended. This benefit was fully repaid; Justine was the most grateful little creature in the world: I do not mean that she made any **professions** I never heard one pass her lips, but you could see by her eyes that she almost adored her **protectress**. Although her **disposition** was gay and in many respects **inconsiderate**, yet she paid the greatest attention to every gesture of my aunt. She thought her the model of all excellence and endeavoured to imitate her **phraseology** and manners, so that even now she often reminds me of her.

"When my dearest aunt died every one was too much occupied in their own grief to notice poor Justine, who had attended her during her illness with the most anxious affection. Poor Justine was very ill; but other trials were reserved for her.

"One by one, her brothers and sister died; and her mother, with the exception of her neglected daughter, was left childless. The conscience of the woman was troubled; she began to think that the deaths of her favourites was a judgement from heaven to **chastise** her **partiality**. She was a Roman Catholic; and I believe her **confessor confirmed** the idea which she had conceived. Accordingly, a few months after your departure for Ingolstadt, Justine was called home by her **repentant** mother. Poor girl! She wept when she **quitted** our house; she was much altered since the death of my aunt; grief had given softness and a **winning** mildness to her manners, which had before been remarkable for vivacity. Nor was her residence at her mother's house of a nature to restore her gaiety. The poor woman was very **vacillating** in her repentance. She sometimes begged Justine to forgive her unkindness, but much oftener accused her of having caused

irritability [ìrətəbíləti] n.
성마름, 민감함
mien [mi:n] n.
풍채, 태도, 모습

the deaths of her brothers and sister. Perpetual fretting at length threw Madame Moritz into a decline, which at first increased her **irritability**, but she is now at peace for ever. She died on the first approach of cold weather, at the beginning of this last winter. Justine has just returned to us; and I assure you I love her tenderly. She is very clever and gentle, and extremely pretty; as I mentioned before, her **mien** and her expression continually remind me of my dear aunt.

"I must say also a few words to you, my dear cousin, of little darling William. I wish you could see him; he is very tall of his age, with sweet laughing blue eyes, dark eyelashes, and curling hair. When he smiles, two little dimples appear on each cheek, which are rosy with health. He has already had one or two little *wives*, but Louisa Biron is his favourite, a pretty little girl of five years of age.

"Now, dear Victor, I dare say you wish to be indulged in a little gossip concerning the good people of Geneva. The pretty Miss Mansfield has already received the congratulatory visits on her approaching marriage with a young Englishman, John Melbourne, Esq. Her ugly sister, Manon, married M. Duvillard, the rich banker, last autumn. Your favourite schoolfellow, Louis Manoir, has suffered several misfortunes since the departure of Clerval from Geneva. But he has already recovered his spirits, and is reported to be on the point of marrying a lively pretty Frenchwoman, Madame Tavernier. She is a widow, and much older than Manoir; but she is very much admired, and a favourite with everybody.

"I have written myself into better spirits, dear cousin; but my anxiety returns upon me as I conclude. Write, dearest Victor, — one line — one word will be a blessing to us. Ten thousand thanks to Henry for his kindness, his affection, and his many letters; we are sincerely grateful. Adieu! my cousin; take care of yourself; and, I entreat you, write!

Elizabeth Lavenza.

Geneva, March 18th, 17—.

"Dear, dear Elizabeth!" I exclaimed, when I had read her letter: "I will write instantly and **relieve** them from the anxiety they must feel." I wrote, and this **exertion** greatly fatigued me; but my **convalescence** had commenced, and proceeded regularly. In another fortnight I was able to leave my chamber.

One of my first duties on my recovery was to introduce Clerval to the several professors of the university. In doing this, I **underwent**

---

relieve [rilíːv] v.
(고통, 부탁, 걱정 따위를) 경감하다, 덜다, 해방하다
exertion [igzə́ːrʃən] n.
노력, 진력, 고된 일
convalescence [kànvəlésns / kɔ̀n-] n.
회복, 요양

undergo [ʌ̀ndərgóu] v.
경험하다, 겪다

antipathy [æntípəθi] n.
반감, 혐오
natural philosophy:
자연 철학(natural science)
renew [rinjú:] v.
부활시키다, 다시 살아나게 하다
apparatus [æpəréitəs, -rǽtəs] n. 장치, 기계, 기구
inflict [inflíkt] v.
(고통, 타격) 등을 가하다, 입히다
draw out:
꾀어서 말하게 하다, 털어놓게 하다
writhe [raið] v.
몸부림치다, 괴로워하다, 고민하다

a kind of rough usage, ill befitting the wounds that my mind had sustained. Ever since the fatal night, the end of my labours, and the beginning of my misfortunes, I had conceived a violent **antipathy** even to the name of **natural philosophy**. When I was otherwise quite restored to health, the sight of a chemical instrument would **renew** all the agony of my nervous symptoms. Henry saw this, and had removed all my **apparatus** from my view. He had also changed my apartment; for he perceived that I had acquired a dislike for the room which had previously been my laboratory. But these cares of Clerval were made of no avail when I visited the professors. M. Waldman **inflicted** torture when he praised, with kindness and warmth, the astonishing progress I had made in the sciences. He soon perceived that I disliked the subject; but not guessing the real cause, he attributed my feelings to modesty, and changed the subject from my improvement, to the science itself, with a desire, as I evidently saw, of **drawing** me **out**. What could I do? He meant to please, and he tormented me. I felt as if he had placed carefully, one by one, in my view those instruments which were to be afterwards used in putting me to a slow and cruel death. I **writhed** under his words, yet dared not exhibit the pain I felt. Clerval, whose

discern [disə́ːrn, -zə́ːrn] v.
알아보다, 알아내다, 식별하다
allege [əlédʒ] v.
(변명으로) 내세우다, 구실로 삼다
confide [kənfáid] v.
비밀을 털어놓다, 개인 일을 이야기하다

docile [dásəl / dóusail] adj.
유순한, 다루기 쉬운
encomium [enkóumiəm] n.
찬사, 칭찬, 찬미
approbation [æproubéiʃən] n.
찬성, 시인, 칭찬
outstrip [àutstríp] v.
앞지르다, 낫다, 능가하다
youngster [jʌ́ŋstəːr] n.
젊은이
out of countenace:
당황하는, 놀라는
diffident [dífidənt] adj.
자신 없는, 사양하는, 수줍은

eyes and feelings were always quick in **discerning** the sensations of others, declined the subject, **alleging**, in excuse, his total ignorance; and the conversation took a more general turn. I thanked my friend from my heart, but I did not speak. I saw plainly that he was surprised, but he never attempted to draw my secret from me; and although I loved him with a mixture of affection and reverence that knew no bounds, yet I could never persuade myself to **confide** in him that event which was so often present to my recollection, but which I feared the detail to another would only impress more deeply.

M. Krempe was not equally **docile**; and in my condition at that time, of almost insupportable sensitiveness, his harsh blunt **encomiums** gave me even more pain than the benevolent **approbation** of M. Waldman. "D—n the fellow!" cried he; "why, M. Clerval, I assure you he has **outstript** us all. Ay, stare if you please; but it is nevertheless true. A **youngster** who, but a few years ago, believed in Cornelius Agrippa as firmly as in the gospel, has now set himself at the head of the university; and if he is not soon pulled down, we shall all be **out of countenance**. Ay, ay," continued he, observing my face expressive of suffering, "M. Frankenstein is modest; an excellent quality in a young man. Young men should be **diffident** of themselves,

wear out:
닳아 없어지다, 다하다

eulogy [júːlədʒi] n.
찬사, 칭송, 칭찬

inglorious [inglɔ́ːriəs] adj.
불명예스러운, 면목없는, 창피스러운

enter on:
시작하다, 착수하다

irksome [ə́ːrksəm] adj.
괴롭히는, 귀찮은, 성가신

dialect [dáiəlèkt] n.
방언, 지방 사투리, 통용어

you know, M. Clerval: I was myself when young; but that **wears out** in a very short time."

M. Krempe had now commenced a **eulogy** on himself, which happily turned the conversation from a subject that was so annoying to me.

Clerval had never sympathised in my tastes for natural science; and his literary pursuits differed wholly from those which had occupied me. He came to the university with the design of making himself complete master of the oriental languages, and thus he should open a field for the plan of life he had marked out for himself. Resolved to pursue no **inglorious** career, he turned his eyes toward the East, as affording scope for his spirit of enterprise. The Persian, Arabic, and Sanskrit languages engaged his attention, and I was easily induced to **enter on** the same studies. Idleness had ever been **irksome** to me, and now that I wished to fly from reflection, and hated my former studies, I felt great relief in being the fellow-pupil with my friend, and found not only instruction but consolation in the works of the orientalists. I did not, like him, attempt a critical knowledge of their **dialects**, for I did not contemplate making any other use of them than temporary amusement. I read merely to understand their meaning, and they well repaid my labours.

melancholy [mélənkàli / -kɔ̀li]
n. 우울, 구슬픔, 애수

impassable [impǽsəbəl, -pàːs-]
adj. 지날 수 없는
retard [ritáːrd] v.
늦추다, 더디게 하다
dilatoriness [dilətɔːrinis /
-tərinis] n.
지연, 지체

Their **melancholy** is soothing, and their joy elevating, to a degree I never experienced in studying the authors of any other country. When you read their writings, life appears to consist in a warm sun and a garden of roses, in the smiles and frowns of a fair enemy, and the fire that consumes your own heart. How different from the manly and heroical poetry of Greece and Rome!

Summer passed away in these occupations, and my return to Geneva was fixed for the latter end of autumn; but being delayed by several accidents, winter and snow arrived, the roads were deemed **impassable**, and my journey was **retarded** until the ensuing spring. I felt this delay very bitterly; for I longed to see my native town and my beloved friends. My return had only been delayed so long, from an unwillingness to leave Clerval in a strange place, before he had become acquainted with any of its inhabitants. The winter, however, was spent cheerfully; and although the spring was uncommonly late, when it came its beauty compensated for its **dilatoriness**.

The month of May had already commenced, and I expected the letter daily which was to fix the date of my departure, when Henry proposed a pedestrian tour in the environs of Ingolstadt, that I might bid a personal farewell

accede [æksíːd] v.
동의하다, 응하다
ramble[rǽmb-əl] n.
소요, 산책

perambulation [pəræmb-jəléiʃən] n.
배회, 거닐기
salubrious [səlúːbriəs] adj.
건강에 좋은, 상쾌한, 유익한
seclude [siklúːd] v.
분리하다, 격리하다
cramp [kræmp] v.
꺾쇠로 죄다, 속박하다, 제한하다
serene [siríːn] adj.
조용한, 평온한, 화창한
verdant [vɔ́ːrdənt] adj.
푸릇푸릇한, 푸른 잎이 무성한, 신록의

to the country I had so long inhabited. I **acceded** with pleasure to this proposition: I was fond of exercise, and Clerval had always been my favourite companion in the **ramble** of this nature that I had taken among the scenes of my native country.

We passed a fortnight in these **perambulations**: my health and spirits had long been restored, and they gained additional strength from the **salubrious** air I breathed, the natural incidents of our progress, and the conversation of my friend. Study had before **secluded** me from the intercourse of my fellow-creatures, and rendered me unsocial; but Clerval called forth the better feelings of my heart; he again taught me to love the aspect of nature, and the cheerful faces of children. Excellent friend! How sincerely you did love me, and endeavour to elevate my mind until it was on a level with your own! A selfish pursuit had **cramped** and narrowed me, until your gentleness and affection warmed and opened my senses; I became the same happy creature who, a few years ago, loved and beloved by all, had no sorrow or care. When happy, inanimate nature had the power of bestowing on me the most delightful sensations. A **serene** sky and **verdant** fields filled me with ecstasy. The present season was indeed divine; the flowers of spring bloomed

undisturbed [ʌndistə́:rbd] adj.
방해되지 않은, 평온한
invincible [invínsəbəl] adj.
정복할 수 없는, 무적의, 극복할 수 없는

ingenuity [ìndʒənjú:əti] n.
현명함, 재간, 교묘함

unbridled [ʌnbráidld] adj.
재갈을 물리지 않은, 구속되지 않은, 억제되지 않은
hilarity [hilǽrəti, hai-] n.
환희, 유쾌한 기분

in the hedges, while those of summer were already in bud. I was **undisturbed** by thoughts which during the preceding year had pressed upon me, notwithstanding my endeavours to throw them off, with an **invincible** burden.

Henry rejoiced in my gaiety, and sincerely sympathised in my feelings: he exerted himself to amuse me, while he expressed the sensations that filled his soul. The resources of his mind on this occasion were truly astonishing: his conversation was full of imagination; and very often, in imitation of the Persian and Arabic writers, he invented tales of wonderful fancy and passion. At other times he repeated my favourite poems, or drew me out into arguments, which he supported with great **ingenuity**.

We returned to our college on a Sunday afternoon: the peasants were dancing, and every one we met appeared gay and happy. My own spirits were high, and I bounded along with feelings of **unbridled** joy and **hilarity**.

Chapter 7

On my return, I found the following letter from my father:

"My dear Victor,

"You have probably waited impatiently for a letter to fix the date of your return to us, and I was at first tempted to write only a few lines, merely mentioning the day on which I should expect you. But that would be a cruel kindness, and I dare not do it. What would be your surprise, my son, when you expected a happy and glad welcome, to behold, **on the contrary**, tears and wretchedness? And how, Victor, can I **relate** our misfortune? Absence cannot have rendered you **callous** to our joys and griefs;

---

on the contrary:
반대로
relate [riléit] v.
이야기하다, 말하다
callous [kǽləs] adj.
무감각한, 냉담한

and how shall I **inflict** pain on my long absent son? I wish to prepare you for the **woeful** news, but I know it is impossible; even now your eye **skims** over the page to seek the words which are to convey to you the horrible **tidings**.

"William is dead! That sweet child, whose smiles delighted and warmed my heart, who was so gentle, yet so gay! Victor, he is murdered!

"I will not attempt to **console** you; but will simply relate the circumstances of the transaction.

"Last Thursday (May 7th), I, my niece, and your two brothers, went to walk in Plainpalais. The evening was warm and serene, and we **prolonged** our walk farther than usual. It was already dusk before we thought of returning; and then we discovered that William and Ernest, who had gone on before, were not to be found. We accordingly rested on a seat until they should return. Presently Ernest came, and enquired if we had seen his brother; he said, that he had been playing with him, that William had run away to hide himself, and that he vainly sought for him, and afterwards waited for a long time, but that he did not return.

"This account rather alarmed us, and we continued to search for him until night fell, when Elizabeth conjectured that he might have returned to the house. He was not there. We

---

inflict [inflíkt] v.
(고통, 타격) 등을 가하다, 입히다
woeful [wóufəl] adj.
슬픈, 비참한, 애처로운
skim [skim] v.
대강 훑어 읽다, 대충 보다
tiding [taidiŋ] n.
소식, 정보, 뉴스

console [kənsóul] v.
위로하다, 위안하다

prolong [proulɔ́:ŋ, -láŋ] v.
늘이다, 연장하다, 오래 끌다

anguish [ǽŋgwiʃ] n.
(심신의) 고통, 괴로움, 번민

returned again, with torches; for I could not rest, when I thought that my sweet boy had lost himself, and was exposed to all the damps and dews of night; Elizabeth also suffered extreme **anguish**. About five in the morning I discovered my lovely boy, whom the night before I had seen blooming and active in health, stretched on the grass livid and motionless; the print of the murder's finger was on his neck.

"He was conveyed home, and the anguish that was visible in my countenance betrayed the secret to Elizabeth. She was very earnest to see the corpse. At first I attempted to prevent her but she persisted, and entering the room where it lay, hastily examined the neck of the victim, and clasping her hands exclaimed, 'O God! I have murdered my darling child!'

unremitted [Ànrimítid] adj.
부단한, 끊임없는

"She fainted, and was restored with extreme difficulty. When she again lived, it was only to weep and sigh. She told me, that that same evening William had teased her to let him wear a very valuable miniature that she possessed of your mother. This picture is gone, and was doubtless the temptation which urged the murderer to the deed. We have no trace of him at present, although our exertions to discover him are **unremitted**; but they will not restore my beloved William!

"Come, dearest Victor; you alone can console Elizabeth. She weeps continually, and accuses herself unjustly as the cause of his death; her words pierce my heart. We are all unhappy; but will not that be an additional motive for you, my son, to return and be our comforter? Your dear mother! Alas, Victor! I now say, Thank God she did not live to witness the cruel, miserable death of her youngest darling!

"Come, Victor; not brooding thoughts of vengeance against the assassin, but with feelings of peace and gentleness, that will heal, instead of **festering**, the wounds of our minds. Enter the house of mourning, my friend, but with kindness and affection for those who love you, and not with hatred for your enemies.

Your affectionate and afflicted father,
Alphonse Frankenstein.

Geneva, May 12th, 17—."

Clerval, who had watched my countenance as I read this letter, was surprised to observe the despair that succeeded the joy I at first expressed on receiving news from my friends. I threw the letter on the table, and covered my face with my hands.

"My dear Frankenstein," exclaimed Henry, when he perceived me weep with bitterness,

fester [féstər] v.
(상처가) 곪다, 곪게 하다, 괴롭히다

"are you always to be unhappy? My dear friend, what has happened?"

I motioned him to take up the letter, while I walked up and down the room in the extremest agitation. Tears also gushed from the eyes of Clerval, as he read the account of my misfortune.

"I can offer you no consolation, my friend," said he; "your disaster is **irreparable**. What do you intend to do?"

"To go instantly to Geneva: come with me, Henry, to order the horses."

During our walk, Clerval endeavoured to say a few words of consolation; he could only express his heartfelt sympathy. "Poor William!" said he, "dear lovely child, he now sleeps with his angel mother! Who that had seen him bright and joyous in his young beauty, but must weep over his untimely loss! To die so miserably; to feel the murderer's grasp! How much more a murderer, that could destroy such 7radiant innocence! Poor little fellow! One only consolation have we; his friends mourn and weep, but he is at rest. The pang is over, his sufferings are at an end for ever. A **sod** covers his gentle form, and he knows no pain. He can no longer be a subject for pity; we must reserve that for his miserable survivors."

Clerval spoke thus as we hurried through

---

irreparable [irépərəbəl] adj.
돌이킬 수 없는

sod [sɑd / sɔd] n.
뗏장, 떼, 잔디

the streets; the words impressed themselves on my mind and I remembered them afterwards in solitude. But now, as soon as the horses arrived, I hurried into a **cabriolet**, and bade farewell to my friend.

My journey was very melancholy. At first I wished to hurry on, for I longed to console and sympathise with my loved and sorrowing friends; but when I drew near my native town, I **slackened** my progress. I could hardly sustain the multitude of feelings that crowded into my mind. I passed through scenes familiar to my youth, but which I had not seen for nearly six years. How altered every thing might be during that time! One sudden and desolating change had taken place; but a thousand little circumstances might have by degrees worked other alterations, which, although they were done more tranquilly, might not be the less decisive. Fear overcame me; I dared no advance, dreading a thousand nameless evils that made me tremble, although I was unable to define them.

I remained two days at Lausanne, in this painful state of mind. I contemplated the lake: the waters were placid; all around was calm; and the snowy mountains, "the palaces of nature," were not changed. By degrees the calm and heavenly scene restored me, and I continued my journey towards Geneva.

prognosticate [prɑgnɑ́stikèit / prɔgnɔ́sti-] v.
예언하다, 예측하다, 전조가 되다
mock [mɑk / mɔ(:)k] v.
조롱하다, 놀리다

The road ran by the side of the lake, which became narrower as I approached my native town. I discovered more distinctly the black sides of Jura, and the bright summit of Mont Blanc. I wept like a child. “Dear mountains! My own beautiful lake! How do you welcome your wanderer? Your summits are clear; the sky and lake are blue and placid. Is this to **prognosticate** peace, or to **mock** at my unhappiness?”

render [réndəːr] v.
~이 되게 하다
tedious [tíːdiəs, -dʒəs] adj.
지루한, 싫증나는, 장황한
dwell on:
깊이 생각하다, 상세히 말하다

I fear, my friend, that I shall **render** myself **tedious** by **dwelling on** these preliminary circumstances; but they were days of comparative happiness, and I think of them with pleasure. My country, my beloved country! Who but a native can tell the delight I took in again beholding thy streams, thy mountains, and, more than all, thy lovely lake!

prophesy [prɑ́fəsài / prɔ́] v.
예언하다, 예측하다

Yet, as I drew nearer home, grief and fear again overcame me. Night also closed around; and when I could hardly see the dark mountains, I felt still more gloomily. The picture appeared a vast and dim scene of evil, and I foresaw obscurely that I was destined to become the most wretched of human beings. Alas! I **prophesied** truly, and failed only in one single circumstance, that in all the misery I imagined and dreaded, I did not conceive the hundredth part of the anguish I was destined to endure.

ascend [əsénd] v.
올라가다, 오르다

It was completely dark when I arrived in the environs of Geneva; the gates of the town were already shut; and I was obliged to pass the night at Secheron, a village at the distance of half a league from the city. The sky was serene; and, as I was unable to rest, I resolved to visit the spot where my poor William had been murdered. As I could not pass through the town, I was obliged to cross the lake in a boat to arrive at Plainpalais. During this short voyage I saw the lightning playing on the summit of Mont Blanc in the most beautiful figures. The storm appeared to approach rapidly, and, on landing, I **ascended** a low hill, that I might observe its progress. It advanced; the heavens were clouded, and I soon felt the rain coming slowly in large drops, but its violence quickly increased.

pitchy [pítʃi] adj.
새까만, 캄캄한

I quitted my seat, and walked on, although the darkness and storm increased every minute, and the thunder burst with a terrific crash over my head. It was echoed from Salêve, the Juras, and the Alps of Savoy; vivid flashes of lightning dazzled my eyes, illuminating the lake, making it appear like a vast sheet of fire; then for an instant every thing seemed of a **pitchy** darkness, until the eye recovered itself from the preceding flash. The storm, as is often the case in Switzerland, appeared at once in

promontory [práməntɔ̀:ri / prɔ́məntəri] n.
곶, 갑(岬)

tempest [témpist] n.
사나운 비바람, 폭풍우
terrific [tərífik] adj.
무시무시한, 소름끼치는
dirge [də:rdʒ] n.
만가, 애도가, 장송가
steal [sti:l] v.
몰래 움직이다, 숨어 들어가다
shudder [ʃʌ́də:r] v.
떨다, 몸서리치다
conception [kənsépʃən] n.
개념, 생각, 상상

...its gigantic stature, and the deformity of its aspect more hideous than belongs to humanity, instantly informed me that it was the wretch, the filthy daemon, to whom I had given life.

various parts of the heavens. The most violent storm hung exactly north of the town, over the part of the lake which lies between the **promontory** of Belrive and the village of Copêt. Another storm enlightened Jura with faint flashes; and another darkened and sometimes disclosed the Môle, a peaked mountain to the east of the lake.

While I watched the **tempest**, so beautiful yet **terrific**, I wandered on with a hasty step. This noble war in the sky elevated my spirits; I clasped my hands, and exclaimed aloud, "William, dear angel! This is thy funeral, this thy **dirge**!" As I said these words, I perceived in the gloom a figure which **stole** from behind a clump of trees near me; I stood fixed, gazing intently: I could not be mistaken. A flash of lightning illuminated the object, and discovered its shape plainly to me; its gigantic stature, and the deformity of its aspect more hideous than belongs to humanity, instantly informed me that it was the wretch, the filthy daemon, to whom I had given life. What did he there? Could he be (I **shuddered** at the **conception**) the murderer of my brother? No sooner did that idea cross my imagination, than I became convinced of its truth; my teeth chattered, and I was forced to lean against a tree for support. The figure passed me quickly, and I lost it in

presence [prézəns] n.
존재, 실재
irresistible [ìrizístəbəl] adj.
저항할 수 없는, 억누를 수 없는, 압도적인

Alas! I had turned loose into the world a depraved wretch, ...

envelop [envéləp] vt.
싸다, 봉하다, 포위하다
impenetrable [impénətrəbəl] adj. 꿰뚫을 수 없는, 들어갈 수 없는
revolve [riválv / -vólv] v.
궁리하다, 곰곰이 생각하다
train[trein] n.
연속, 과정, 맥락
elapse [iléps] v.
지나다, 경과하다
turn loose:
해방하다, 자유롭게 하다
depraved [dipréivd] adj.
타락한, 사악한, 저열한
wretch [retʃ] n.
천박한 사람, 비열한(漢)
carnage [ká:rnidʒ] n.
대학살

the gloom. Nothing in human shape could have destroyed the fair child. *He* was the murderer! I could not doubt it. The mere **presence** of the idea was an **irresistible** proof of the fact. I thought of pursuing the devil; but it would have been in vain, for another flash discovered him to me hanging among the rocks of the nearly perpendicular ascent of Mont Salêve, a hill that bounds Plainpalais on the south. He soon reached the summit, and disappeared.

I remained motionless. The thunder ceased; but the rain still continued, and the scene was **enveloped** in an **impenetrable** darkness. I **revolved** in my mind the events which I had until now sought to forget: the whole **train** of my progress toward the creation; the appearance of the works of my own hands at my bedside; its departure. Two years had now nearly **elapsed** since the night on which he first received life; and was this his first crime? Alas! I had **turned loose** into the world a **depraved wretch**, whose delight was in **carnage** and misery; had he not murdered my brother?

No one can conceive the anguish I suffered during the remainder of the night, which I spent, cold and wet, in the open air. But I did not feel the inconvenience of the weather; my imagination was busy in scenes of evil and despair. I considered the being whom I had

effect [ifékt] v.
초래하다, 가져오다
in the light of:
~에 비추어, ~을 생각하면, ~의 모습으로

endue [indjú:, en-] v.
부여하다, 주다
precipice [présəpis] n.
벼랑, 절벽
inaccessible [ìnəksésəbəl] adj. 접근하기 어려운
delirium [dilíriəm] n.
환영, 섬망, 열광
utterly [ʌ́tərli] adv.
아주, 완전히
improbable [imprábəbəl / -prɔ́b-] adj.
있을 법하지 않은
relation [riléiʃ-ən] n.
설화, 진술; 이야기
raving [réiviŋ] n.
헛소리, 광란

cast among mankind, and endowed with the will and power to **effect** purposes of horror, such as the deed which he had now done, nearly **in the light of** my own vampire, my own spirit let loose from the grave, and forced to destroy all that was dear to me.

Day dawned; and I directed my steps towards the town. The gates were open, and I hastened to my father's house. My first thought was to discover what I knew of the murderer, and cause instant pursuit to be made. But I paused when I reflected on the story that I had to tell. A being whom I myself had formed, and **endued** with life, had met me at midnight among the **precipices** of an **inaccessible** mountain. I remembered also the nervous fever with which I had been seized just at the time that I dated my creation, and which would give an air of **delirium** to a tale otherwise so **utterly improbable**. I well knew that if any other had communicated such a **relation** to me, I should have looked upon it as the **ravings** of insanity. Besides, the strange nature of the animal would elude all pursuit, even if I were so far credited as to persuade my relatives to commence it. And then of what use would be pursuit? Who could arrest a creature capable of scaling the overhanging sides of Mont Salêve? These reflections determined me, and I resolved to remain silent.

It was about five in the morning when I entered my father's house. I told the servants not to disturb the family, and went into the library to attend their usual hour of rising.

Six years had elapsed, passed in a dream but for one **indelible** trace, and I stood in the same place where I had last embraced my father before my departure for Ingolstadt. Beloved and **venerable** parent! He still remained to me. I gazed on the picture of my mother, which stood over the mantel-piece. It was an historical subject, painted at my father's desire, and represented Caroline Beaufort in an agony of despair, kneeling by the coffin of her dead father. Her **garb** was **rustic**, and her cheek pale; but there was an air of dignity and beauty, that hardly permitted the sentiment of pity. Below this picture was a miniature of William; and my tears flowed when I looked upon it. While I was thus engaged, Ernest entered: he had heard me arrive, and hastened to welcome me: "Welcome, my dearest Victor," said he. "Ah! I wish you had come three months ago, and then you would have found us all joyous and delighted. You come to us now to share a misery which nothing can **alleviate**; yet your presence will, I hope, revive our father, who seems sinking under his misfortune; and your persuasions

---

indelible [indéləbəl] adj.
지울 수 없는
venerable [vénərəbəl] adj.
존경할 만한
garb [gɑːrb] n.
복장, 옷차림
rustic [rʌ́stik] adj.
시골의, 단순한, 소박한
alleviate [əlíːvièit] v.
경감하다, 완화하다, 누그러뜨리다

will induce poor Elizabeth to cease her vain and tormenting self-accusations. Poor William! He was our darling and our pride!"

Tears, **unrestrained**, fell from my brother's eyes; a sense of mortal agony crept over my frame. Before, I had only imagined the wretchedness of my desolated home; the reality came on me as a new, and a not less terrible, disaster. I tried to calm Ernest; I **enquired** more minutely concerning my father, and here I named my cousin.

"She most of all," said Ernest, "requires consolation; she accused herself of having caused the death of my brother, and that made her very wretched. But since the murderer has been discovered —"

"The murderer discovered! Good God! How can that be? Who could attempt to pursue him? It is impossible; one might as well try to overtake the winds, or confine a mountain-stream with a straw. I saw him too; he was free last night!"

"I do not know what you mean," replied my brother, in accents of wonder, "but to us the discovery we have made completes our misery. No one would believe it at first; and even now Elizabeth will not be convinced, **notwithstanding** all the evidence. Indeed, who would credit that Justine Moritz, who was so **amiable**, and

---

unrestrained [Ànristréind] adj.
억제되지 않은, 무제한의, 제멋대로의
inquire/enquire [inkwáiər] v.
묻다, 조사하다

notwithstanding [nɑ̀twiðstǽndiŋ, -wiɵ- / nɔ̀tch-] prep. ~에도 불구하고(in spite of)
amiable [éimiəbəl] adj.
상냥한, 호의적인

fond of all the family, could suddenly become so capable of so frightful, so **appalling** a crime?"

"Justine Moritz! Poor, poor girl, is she the accused? But it is wrongfully; every one knows that; no one believes it, surely, Ernest?"

"No one did at first; but several circumstances came out, that have almost forced conviction upon us; and her own behaviour has been so confused, as to add to the evidence of facts a weight that, I fear, leaves no hope for doubt. But she will be tried today, and you will then hear all."

He then related that, the morning on which the murder of poor William had been discovered, Justine had been taken ill, and confined to her bed for several days. During this interval, one of the servants, happening to examine the **apparel** she had worn on the night of the murder, had discovered in her pocket the picture of my mother, which had been judged to be the **temptation** of the murderer. The servant instantly showed it to one of the others, who, without saying a word to any of the family, went to a **magistrate**; and, upon their **deposition**, Justine was **apprehended**. On being charged with the fact, the poor girl confirmed the suspicion in a great measure by her extreme confusion of manner.

This was a strange tale, but it did not shake

---

appalling [əpɔ́:liŋ] adj.
무서운, 끔찍한, 놀랄만한, 지독한

"Justine Moritz! Poor, poor girl, is she the accused? But it is wrongfully ...

apparel [əpǽrəl] n.
의복, 의상
temptation [temptéiʃ-ən] n.
유혹
magistrate [mǽdʒəstrèit, -trit] n. 법관, 판사, 행정관
deposition [dèpəzíʃən, dì:p-] n. (법정 등에서의) 증언
apprehend [æ̀prihénd] v.
체포하다, 구금하다

my faith; and I replied earnestly, "You are all mistaken; I know the murderer. Justine, poor, good Justine, is innocent."

At that instant my father entered. I saw unhappiness deeply impressed on his countenance, but he endeavoured to welcome me cheerfully; and, after we had exchanged our mournful greeting, would have introduced some other topic than that of our disaster, had not Ernest exclaimed, "Good God, papa! Victor says that he knows who was the murderer of poor William."

"We do also, unfortunately," replied my father, "for indeed I **had rather** have been for ever ignorant than have discovered so much **depravity** and **ingratitude** in one I valued so highly."

"My dear father, you are mistaken; Justine is innocent."

"If she is, God forbid that she should suffer as guilty. She is to be tried today, and I hope, I sincerely hope, that she will be **acquitted**."

This speech calmed me. I was firmly convinced in my own mind that Justine, and indeed every human being, was guiltless of this murder. I had no fear, therefore, that any **circumstantial evidence** could be brought forward strong enough to **convict** her. My tale was not one to announce publicly; its

presumption [prizʌ́mpʃən] n.
주제넘음, 뻔뻔스러움
rash [ræʃ] adj.
무모한, 무분별한
ignorance [íɡnərəns] n.
무식, 무지, 모름

candor/candour [kǽndər] n.
공정, 정직, 솔직
vivacity [vivǽsəti, vai-] n.
쾌활, 활발, 발랄
condemn [kəndém] v.
유죄 판결을 내리다

astounding horror would be looked upon as madness by the vulgar. Did any one indeed exist, except I, the creator, who would believe, unless his senses convinced him, in the existence of the living monument of **presumption** and **rash ignorance** which I had let loose upon the world?

We were soon joined by Elizabeth. Time had altered her since I last beheld her; it had endowed her with loveliness surpassing the beauty of her childish years. There was the same **candour**, the same **vivacity**, but it was allied to an expression more full of sensibility and intellect. She welcomed me with the greatest affection. "Your arrival, my dear cousin," said she, "fills me with hope. You perhaps will find some means to justify my poor guiltless Justine. Alas! Who is safe, if she be convicted of crime? I rely on her innocence as certainly as I do upon my own. Our misfortune is doubly hard to us; we have not only lost that lovely darling boy, but this poor girl, whom I sincerely love, is to be torn away by even a worse fate. If she is **condemned**, I never shall know joy more. But she will not, I am sure she will not; and then I shall be happy again, even after the sad death of my little William."

"She is innocent, my Elizabeth," said I, "and that shall be proved; fear nothing, but let your

acquittal [əkwítəl] n.
무죄, 방면, 석방

despairing [dispéəriŋ] adj.
절망적인, 자포자기의

partiality [pɑ̀:rʃiǽləti] n.
불완전함, 불공평, 편파적임

spirits be cheered by the assurance of her **acquittal**."

"How kind and generous you are! Every one else believes in her guilt, and that made me wretched, for I knew that it was impossible; and to see every one else prejudiced in so deadly a manner rendered me hopeless and **despairing**." She wept.

"Dearest niece," said my father, "dry your tears. If she is, as you believe, innocent, rely on the justice of our laws, and the activity with which I shall prevent the slightest shadow of **partiality**."

Chapter 8

commence [kəméns] v.
시작하다
mockery [mákəri, mɔ́(:)k-] n.
엉터리, 흉내만 낸 것
lawless [lɔ́:lis] adj.
무법의, 제어할 수 없는, 제멋대로의
aggravation [ægrəvéiʃən] n.
악화, 심화
infamy [ínfəmi] n.
악명, 오명

We passed a few sad hours until eleven o'clock, when the trial was to **commence**. My father and the rest of the family being obliged to attend as witnesses, I accompanied them to the court. During the whole of this wretched **mockery** of justice I suffered living torture. It was to be decided whether the result of my curiosity and **lawless** devices would cause the death of two of my fellow beings: one a smiling babe full of innocence and joy, the other far more dreadfully murdered, with every **aggravation** of **infamy** that could make the murder memorable in horror. Justine also was a girl of merit and possessed qualities which promised to render her life happy; now

obliterate [əblítərèit] v.
없애다
ignominious [ìgnəmíniəs] adj.
수치스러운, 불명예스러운
ascribe [əskráib] v.
~의 탓으로 돌리다, ~에 기인하는 것으로 하다
exculpate [ékskʌlpèit, iksˊ-] v.
무죄로 하다, 무죄를 증명하다

execrate [éksikrèit] v.
통렬히 비난하다, 혐오하다, 저주하다
enormity [inɔ́:rməti] n.
무법, 극악, 중대한 범죄
constrained [kənstréind] adj.
부자연스러운, 어색한, 경직한
adduce [ədjú:s] v.
(이유, 증거 따위를) 제시하다, 예증으로서 들다
attest [ətést] v.
증명하다, 입증하다, 증언하다
utter [ʌ́tər] adj.
완전한, 절대적인

all was to be **obliterated** in an **ignominious** grave, and I the cause! A thousand times rather would I have confessed myself guilty of the crime **ascribed** to Justine, but I was absent when it was committed, and such a declaration would have been considered as the ravings of a madman and would not have **exculpated** her who suffered through me.

The appearance of Justine was calm. She was dressed in mourning, and her countenance, always engaging, was rendered, by the solemnity of her feelings, exquisitely beautiful. Yet she appeared confident in innocence and did not tremble, although gazed on and **execrated** by thousands, for all the kindness which her beauty might otherwise have excited was obliterated in the minds of the spectators by the imagination of the **enormity** she was supposed to have committed. She was tranquil, yet her tranquillity was evidently **constrained**; and as her confusion had before been **adduced** as a proof of her guilt, she worked up her mind to an appearance of courage. When she entered the court she threw her eyes round it and quickly discovered where we were seated. A tear seemed to dim her eye when she saw us, but she quickly recovered herself, and a look of sorrowful affection seemed to **attest** her **utter** guiltlessness.

advocate [ǽdvəkit, -kèit] n.
변호사, 법률가
charge [tʃɑːrdʒ] n.
고발, 고소, 혐의
stagger [stǽgər] v.
흔들리게 하다, 동요하게 하다, 놀라게 하다
unintelligible [ʌ̀nintélədʒəbəl] adj. 알기 힘든, 난해한
indignation [ìndignéiʃən] n.
분개, 분노

The trial began, and after the **advocate** against her had stated the **charge**, several witnesses were called. Several strange facts combined against her, which might have **staggered** anyone who had not such proof of her innocence as I had. She had been out the whole of the night on which the murder had been committed and towards morning had been perceived by a market-woman not far from the spot where the body of the murdered child had been afterwards found. The woman asked her what she did there, but she looked very strangely and only returned a confused and **unintelligible** answer. She returned to the house about eight o'clock, and when one inquired where she had passed the night, she replied that she had been looking for the child and demanded earnestly if anything had been heard concerning him. When shown the body, she fell into violent hysterics and kept her bed for several days. The picture was then produced which the servant had found in her pocket; and when Elizabeth, in a faltering voice, proved that it was the same which, an hour before the child had been missed, she had placed round his neck, a murmur of horror and **indignation** filled the court.

Justine was called on for her defence. As the trial had proceeded, her countenance had

plead [pli:d] v.
변호하다, 변론하다

protestation [prὰtistéiʃən, pròutes- / pròt-] n.
주장, 항의

acquit [əkwít] v.
무죄 선고하다, 석방하다

adduce [ədjú:s] v.
(이유, 증거 따위를) 제시하다, 예증으로서 들다

incline [inkláin] v.
(마음을) 내키게 하다, ~할 마음이 일게 하다

barn [bɑ:rn] n.
헛간, 광

altered. Surprise, horror, and misery were strongly expressed. Sometimes she struggled with her tears, but when she was desired to **plead**, she collected her powers and spoke in an audible although variable voice.

"God knows," she said, "how entirely I am innocent. But I do not pretend that my **protestations** should **acquit** me; I rest my innocence on a plain and simple explanation of the facts which have been **adduced** against me, and I hope the character I have always borne will **incline** my judges to a favourable interpretation where any circumstance appears doubtful or suspicious."

She then related that, by the permission of Elizabeth, she had passed the evening of the night on which the murder had been committed at the house of an aunt at Chêne, a village situated at about a league from Geneva. On her return, at about nine o'clock, she met a man who asked her if she had seen anything of the child who was lost. She was alarmed by this account and passed several hours in looking for him, when the gates of Geneva were shut, and she was forced to remain several hours of the night in a **barn** belonging to a cottage, being unwilling to call up the inhabitants, to whom she was well known. Most of the night she spent here watching; towards morning she believed

asylum [əsáiləm] n.
도피처, 은신처, 피난처
bewilder [biwíldər] v.
당황하다
account [əkáunt] n.
이유, 근거, 동기

that she slept for a few minutes; some steps disturbed her, and she awoke. It was dawn, and she quitted her **asylum**, that she might again endeavour to find my brother. If she had gone near the spot where his body lay, it was without her knowledge. That she had been **bewildered** when questioned by the market-woman was not surprising, since she had passed a sleepless night and the fate of poor William was yet uncertain. Concerning the picture she could give no **account**.

"I know," continued the unhappy victim, "how heavily and fatally this one circumstance weighs against me, but I have no power of explaining it; and when I have expressed my utter ignorance, I am only left to conjecture concerning the probabilities by which it might have been placed in my pocket. But here also I am checked. I believe that I have no enemy on earth, and none surely would have been so wicked as to destroy me **wantonly**. Did the murderer place it there? I know of no opportunity **afforded** him for so doing; or, if I had, why should he have stolen the jewel, to part with it again so soon?

wantonly [wɔ́(:)nt-ənli, wán-] adv.
제멋대로, 변덕스럽게, 방자하게
afford [əfɔ́:rd] v.
주다, 제공하다

"I commit my cause to the justice of my judges, yet I see no **room** for hope. I beg permission to have a few witnesses examined concerning my character, and if their **testimony** shall not

room [ru:m, rum] n.
여지, 경우, 가능성
testimony [téstəmòuni / -məni] n.
증언, 증거, 증명

overweigh [òuvərwéi] v.
~보다 무겁다, ~보다 가치가 있다, 압도하다
pledge [pledʒ] v.
서약하다, 맹세하다
salvation [sælvéiʃ-ən] n.
구제, 구원
timorous [tím-ərəs] adj.
마음이 약한, 소심한, 겁 많은
resource [ríːsɔːrs, -zɔːrs, rizɔ́ːrs, -zɔ́ːrs] n.
수단, 방편, 방책
irreproachable [iripróutʃəbəl] adj. 비난할 수 없는, 흠잡을 데 없는
fail [feil] v.
기대를 어기다, 도움이 되지 않다, 저버리다
indecent [indíːsnt] adj.
버릇없는, 품위없는, 꼴 사나운
pretended [priténdid] adj.
외양만의, 거짓의, 겉치레의
be acquainted with:
~을 알고 있다, 정통하다

overweigh my supposed guilt, I must be condemned, although I would **pledge** my **salvation** on my innocence."

Several witnesses were called who had known her for many years, and they spoke well of her; but fear and hatred of the crime of which they supposed her guilty rendered them **timorous** and unwilling to come forward. Elizabeth saw even this last **resource**, her excellent dispositions and **irreproachable** conduct, about to **fail** the accused, when, although violently agitated, she desired permission to address the court.

"I am," said she, "the cousin of the unhappy child who was murdered, or rather his sister, for I was educated by and have lived with his parents ever since and even long before his birth. It may therefore be judged **indecent** in me to come forward on this occasion, but when I see a fellow creature about to perish through the cowardice of her **pretended** friends, I wish to be allowed to speak, that I may say what I know of her character. I **am** well **acquainted with** the accused. I have lived in the same house with her, at one time for five and at another for nearly two years. During all that period she appeared to me the most amiable and benevolent of human creatures. She nursed Madame Frankenstein, my aunt, in her last

affectionate [əfékʃənit] adj.
다정한, 인정 많은
bauble [bɔ́:bəl] n.
싸구려, 시시한 것, 장난감
esteem [istí:m] v.
존경하다, 존중하다

illness, with the greatest affection and care and afterwards attended her own mother during a tedious illness, in a manner that excited the admiration of all who knew her, after which she again lived in my uncle's house, where she was beloved by all the family. She was warmly attached to the child who is now dead and acted towards him like a most **affectionate** mother. For my own part, I do not hesitate to say that, notwithstanding all the evidence produced against her, I believe and rely on her perfect innocence. She had no temptation for such an action; as to the **bauble** on which the chief proof rests, if she had earnestly desired it, I should have willingly given it to her, so much do I **esteem** and value her."

murmur [mə́:rmə:r] n.
속삭임, 중얼거림
approbation [æ̀proubéiʃən] n.
찬성, 시인, 칭찬
ingratitude [ingrǽtətjùːd] n.
배은망덕, 은혜를 모름
betray [bitréi] v.
팔아넘기다

A **murmur** of **approbation** followed Elizabeth's simple and powerful appeal, but it was excited by her generous interference, and not in favour of poor Justine, on whom the public indignation was turned with renewed violence, charging her with the blackest **ingratitude**. She herself wept as Elizabeth spoke, but she did not answer. My own agitation and anguish was extreme during the whole trial. I believed in her innocence; I knew it. Could the daemon who had (I did not for a minute doubt) murdered my brother also in his hellish sport have **betrayed** the innocent to death and

ignominy [íɡnəmìni] n.
치욕, 불명예
fang [fæŋ] n.
엄니, 송곳니
remorse [rimɔ́:rs] n.
후회, 양심의 가책
forgo [fɔ:rɡóu] v.
삼가다, 그만두다

ballot [bǽlət] n.
투표
condemn [kəndém] v.
유죄 판결을 내리다, 형(특히 사형)을 선고하다

glaring [ɡléəriŋ] adj.
틀림없는, 명백한, 빤한
decisive [disáisiv] adj.
결정적인, 의심할 여지가 없는

ignominy? I could not sustain the horror of my situation, and when I perceived that the popular voice and the countenances of the judges had already condemned my unhappy victim, I rushed out of the court in agony. The tortures of the accused did not equal mine; she was sustained by innocence, but the **fangs** of **remorse** tore my bosom and would not **forgo** their hold.

I passed a night of unmingled wretchedness. In the morning I went to the court; my lips and throat were parched. I dared not ask the fatal question, but I was known, and the officer guessed the cause of my visit. The **ballots** had been thrown; they were all black, and Justine was **condemned**.

I cannot pretend to describe what I then felt. I had before experienced sensations of horror, and I have endeavoured to bestow upon them adequate expressions, but words cannot convey an idea of the heart-sickening despair that I then endured. The person to whom I addressed myself added that Justine had already confessed her guilt.

"That evidence," he observed, "was hardly required in so **glaring** a case, but I am glad of it, and, indeed, none of our judges like to condemn a criminal upon circumstantial evidence, be it ever so **decisive**."

This was strange and unexpected **intelligence**; what could it mean? Had my eyes deceived me? And was I really as mad as the whole world would believe me to be if I disclosed the object of my suspicions? I hastened to return home, and Elizabeth eagerly demanded the result.

"My cousin," replied I, "it is decided as you may have expected; all judges **had rather** that **ten innocent should suffer** than that one guilty should escape. But she has confessed."

This was a **dire** blow to poor Elizabeth, who had relied with firmness upon Justine's innocence. "Alas!" said she. "How shall I ever again believe in human goodness? Justine, whom I loved and esteemed as my sister, how could she put on those smiles of innocence only to betray? Her mild eyes seemed incapable of any **severity** or **guile**, and yet she has committed a murder."

Soon after we heard that the poor victim had expressed a desire to see my cousin. My father wished her not to go but said that he left it to her own judgment and feelings to decide. "Yes," said Elizabeth, "I will go, although she is guilty; and you, Victor, shall accompany me; I cannot go alone." The idea of this visit was torture to me, yet I could not refuse.

We entered the gloomy prison chamber and

---

intelligence [ínteledʒens] n.
정보, 보도

had rather:
오히려 ~하려 하다, 차라리 ~하려 하다
ten innocent sould suffer~:
"It is better that ten guilty persons escape than that one innocent suffer."(열 명의 죄인이 빠져나가더라도 한 명의 무고한 사람이 억울한 처벌을 받지 말아야 한다)라는 말의 반어적 재인용
dire [daiər] adj.
무서운, 심각한
severity [sivérəti] n.
심각함, 가혹함
guile [gail] n.
교활, 간계, 기만

... all judges had rather that ten innocent should suffer than that one guilty should escape. But she has confessed."

manacle [mǽnəkl] v.
수갑을 채우다, 족쇄를 채우다

beheld Justine sitting on some straw at the farther end; her hands were **manacled**, and her head rested on her knees. She rose on seeing us enter, and when we were left alone with her, she threw herself at the feet of Elizabeth, weeping bitterly. My cousin wept also.

"Oh, Justine!" said she. "Why did you rob me of my last consolation? I relied on your innocence, and although I was then very wretched, I was not so miserable as I am now."

"And do you also believe that I am so very, very wicked? Do you also join with my enemies to crush me, to condemn me as a murderer?" Her voice was suffocated with sobs.

"Rise, my poor girl," said Elizabeth; "why do you kneel, if you are innocent? I am not one of your enemies, I believed you guiltless, notwithstanding every evidence, until I heard that you had yourself declared your guilt. That report, you say, is false; and be assured, dear Justine, that nothing can shake my confidence in you for a moment, but your own confession."

absolution [æ̀bsəlúːʃən] n.
죄의 사함, 사죄(赦罪)
confessor [kənfésər] n.
고해 신부
besiege [bisíːdʒ] v.
공세를 퍼붓다, 괴롭히다

"I did confess, but I confessed a lie. I confessed, that I might obtain **absolution**; but now that falsehood lies heavier at my heart than all my other sins. The God of heaven forgive me! Ever since I was condemned, my **confessor** has **besieged** me; he threatened and menaced, until I almost began to think that I was the

excommunication [èkskəm-jùːnəkéiʃən] n.
파문, 제명, 축출
obdurate [ábdjurit / ób-] adj.
완고한, 고집센
perdition [pərdíʃən] n.
멸망, 파멸, 지옥
subscribe [səbskráib] v.
서명하다, 동의하다, 찬성하다

perpetrate [pə́ːrpətrèit] v.
범하다, 저지르다
console [kənsóul] v.
위로하다, 위안하다

distrust [distrʌ́st] v.
믿지 않다, 의심하다, 의아스럽게 여기다

"... He threatened excommunication and hell fire in my last moments if I continued obdurate. ..."

pang [pæŋ] n.
상심, 비통, 번민

monster that he said I was. He threatened **excommunication** and hell fire in my last moments if I continued **obdurate**. Dear lady, I had none to support me; all looked on me as a wretch doomed to ignominy and **perdition**. What could I do? In an evil hour I **subscribed** to a lie; and now only am I truly miserable."

She paused, weeping, and then continued, "I thought with horror, my sweet lady, that you should believe your Justine, whom your blessed aunt had so highly honoured, and whom you loved, was a creature capable of a crime which none but the devil himself could have **perpetrated**. Dear William! Dearest blessed child! I soon shall see you again in heaven, where we shall all be happy; and that **consoles** me, going as I am to suffer ignominy and death."

"Oh, Justine! Forgive me for having for one moment **distrusted** you. Why did you confess? But do not mourn, dear girl. Do not fear. I will proclaim, I will prove your innocence. I will melt the stony hearts of your enemies by my tears and prayers. You shall not die! You, my playfellow, my companion, my sister, perish on the scaffold! No! No! I never could survive so horrible a misfortune."

Justine shook her head mournfully. "I do not fear to die," she said; "that **pang** is past. God raises my weakness and gives me courage

resigned [rizáind] adj.
순종하는, 체념한, 묵묵히 따르는
submit [səbmít] v.
복종하다, 굴복하다, 감수하다

horrid [hɔ́:rid, hár-] adj.
진저리나는, 지독한
anguish [ǽŋgwiʃ] n.
(심신의) 고통, 괴로움, 번민
gnash [næʃ] v.
(이를) 갈다
utter [ʌ́tər] v.
(목소리나 말 따위를) 내다, 입 밖에 내다

to endure the worst. I leave a sad and bitter world; and if you remember me and think of me as of one unjustly condemned, I am **resigned** to the fate awaiting me. Learn from me, dear lady, to **submit** in patience to the will of heaven!"

During this conversation I had retired to a corner of the prison room, where I could conceal the **horrid anguish** that possessed me. Despair! Who dared talk of that? The poor victim, who on the morrow was to pass the awful boundary between life and death, felt not, as I did, such deep and bitter agony. I **gnashed** my teeth and ground them together, **uttering** a groan that came from my inmost soul. Justine started. When she saw who it was, she approached me and said, "Dear sir, you are very kind to visit me; you, I hope, do not believe that I am guilty?"

I could not answer. "No, Justine," said Elizabeth; "he is more convinced of your innocence than I was, for even when he heard that you had confessed, he did not credit it."

"I truly thank him. In these last moments I feel the sincerest gratitude towards those who think of me with kindness. How sweet is the affection of others to such a wretch as I am! It removes more than half my misfortune, and I feel as if I could die in peace now that my innocence is acknowledged by you, dear lady, and your cousin."

Thus the poor sufferer tried to comfort others and herself. She indeed gained the **resignation** she desired. But I, the true murderer, felt the never-dying worm alive in my bosom, which allowed of no hope or consolation. Elizabeth also wept and was unhappy, but hers also was the misery of innocence, which, like a cloud that passes over the fair moon, for a while hides but cannot **tarnish** its brightness. Anguish and despair had penetrated into the core of my heart; I bore a hell within me which nothing could extinguish. We stayed several hours with Justine, and it was with great difficulty that Elizabeth could tear herself away. "I wish," cried she, "that I were to die with you; I cannot live in this world of misery."

Justine assumed an air of cheerfulness, while she with difficulty **repressed** her bitter tears. She embraced Elizabeth and said in a voice of half-suppressed emotion, "Farewell, sweet lady, dearest Elizabeth, my beloved and only friend; may heaven, in its **bounty**, bless and preserve you; may this be the last misfortune that you will ever suffer! Live, and be happy, and make others so."

And on the morrow Justine died. Elizabeth's heart-rending **eloquence** failed to move the

---

resignation [rèzignéiʃ-ən] n.
포기, 단념, 체념
tarnish [tá:rniʃ] v.
흐리게 하다, 녹슬게 하다, 변색시키다

repress [riprés] v.
억누르다, 저지하다
bounty [báunti] n.
활수함, 관대함, 박애

eloquence [éləkwəns] n.
웅변, 능변

avowal [əváuəl] n.
공언, 언명
revoke [rivóuk] v.
철회하다, 폐지하다, 취소하다

woe [wou] n.
비애, 비통, 고뇌
desolation [dèsəléiʃən] n.
공허함, 황량함, 적막함
wail [weil] n.
울부짖음, 통곡, 구슬픈 소리
lamentation [læməntéiʃ-ən, -men-] n.
슬퍼함, 한탄, 비탄
inexorable [inéksərəbəl] adj.
가차없는, 냉혹한, 움직이지 않는

judges from their settled conviction in the criminality of the saintly sufferer. My passionate and indignant appeals were lost upon them. And when I received their cold answers and heard the harsh, unfeeling reasoning of these men, my purposed **avowal** died away on my lips. Thus I might proclaim myself a madman, but not **revoke** the sentence passed upon my wretched victim. She perished on the scaffold as a murderess!

From the tortures of my own heart, I turned to contemplate the deep and voiceless grief of my Elizabeth. This also was my doing! And my father's **woe**, and the **desolation** of that late so smiling home — all was the work of my thrice-accursed hands! Ye weep, unhappy ones, but these are not your last tears! Again shall you raise the funeral **wail**, and the sound of your **lamentations** shall again and again be heard! Frankenstein, your son, your kinsman, your early, much-loved friend; he who would spend each vital drop of blood for your sakes, — who has no thought nor sense of joy except as it is mirrored also in your dear countenances, — who would fill the air with blessings and spend his life in serving you — he bids you weep, to shed countless tears; happy beyond his hopes, if thus **inexorable** fate be satisfied, and if the destruction pause before the peace of the grave have succeeded to your sad torments!

Thus spoke my prophetic soul, as, torn by remorse, horror, and despair, I beheld those I loved spend vain sorrow upon the graves of William and Justine, the first **hapless** victims to my **unhallowed** arts.

---

hapless [hǽplis] adj.
불운한, 불행한

unhallowed [ʌnhǽloud] adj.
사악한, 죄가 많은

Chapter 9

inaction [inǽkʃən] n.
무위, 정지, 휴식
mischief [místʃif] n.
손해, 위해, 악영향

Nothing is more painful to the human mind than, after the feelings have been worked up by a quick succession of events, the dead calmness of **inaction** and certainty which follows and deprives the soul both of hope and fear. Justine died, she rested, and I was alive. The blood flowed freely in my veins, but a weight of despair and remorse pressed on my heart which nothing could remove. Sleep fled from my eyes; I wandered like an evil spirit, for I had committed deeds of **mischief** beyond description horrible, and more, much more (I persuaded myself) was yet behind. Yet my heart overflowed with kindness and the love of virtue. I had begun life with benevolent intentions

serenity [sirénəti] n.
고요함, 평온, 침착
conscience [kánʃəns / kɔ́n-] n.
양심, 도덕심
thence [ðens] adv.
거기서부터, 그 때부터

prey [prei] v.
괴롭히다, 해치다
shun [ʃʌn] v.
피하다, 비키다, 멀리하다
complacency [kəmpléisənsi] n.
만족감, 자기 도취
solitude [sálitjùːd / sɔ́li-] n.
고독, 홀로 삶
alteration [ɔ̀ːltəréiʃən] n.
변경, 변화, 변질
fortitude [fɔ́ːrtətjùːd] n.
용기, 불굴의 정신, 인내
augment [ɔːgmént] v.
늘리다, 증대하다
immoderate [imádərit / imɔ́d-] adj.
무절제한, 과도한, 엄청난

and thirsted for the moment when I should put them in practice and make myself useful to my fellow beings. Now all was blasted; instead of that **serenity** of **conscience** which allowed me to look back upon the past with self-satisfaction, and from **thence** to gather promise of new hopes, I was seized by remorse and the sense of guilt, which hurried me away to a hell of intense tortures such as no language can describe.

This state of mind **preyed** upon my health, which had perhaps never entirely recovered from the first shock it had sustained. I **shunned** the face of man; all sound of joy or **complacency** was torture to me; **solitude** was my only consolation — deep, dark, deathlike solitude.

My father observed with pain the **alteration** perceptible in my disposition and habits and endeavoured by arguments deduced from the feelings of his serene conscience and guiltless life to inspire me with **fortitude** and awaken in me the courage to dispel the dark cloud which brooded over me. "Do you think, Victor," said he, "that I do not suffer also? No one could love a child more than I loved your brother" — tears came into his eyes as he spoke — "but is it not a duty to the survivors that we should refrain from **augmenting** their unhappiness by an appearance of **immoderate** grief? It is also a duty owed to yourself, for excessive sorrow prevents improvement or enjoyment, or even the discharge of daily usefulness, without which no man is fit for society."

This advice, although good, was totally **inapplicable** to my case; I should have been the first to hide my grief and console my friends if remorse had not mingled its bitterness, and terror its alarm, with my other sensations. Now I could only answer my father with a look of despair and endeavour to hide myself from his view.

About this time we retired to our house at Belrive. This change was particularly agreeable to me. The shutting of the gates regularly at ten o'clock and the impossibility of remaining on the lake after that hour had rendered our residence within the walls of Geneva very **irksome** to me. I was now free. Often, after the rest of the family had retired for the night, I took the boat and passed many hours upon the water. Sometimes, with my **sails** set, I was carried by the wind; and sometimes, after rowing into the middle of the lake, I left the boat to pursue its own course and **gave way** to my own miserable reflections. I was often tempted, when all was at peace around me, and I the only **unquiet** thing that wandered restless in a scene so beautiful and heavenly — if I except

---

inapplicable [inǽplikəbəl] adj.
적용할 수 없는, 들어맞지 않는, 부적당한

irksome [ə́:rksəm] adj.
괴롭히는, 성가신
sail [seil] n.
(배의) 돛
give way:
무너지다, (감정 등에) 빠져들다
unquiet [ʌnkwáiət] adj.
동요하는, 설레는, 불안한

some bat, or the frogs, whose harsh and interrupted croaking was heard only when I approached the shore — often, I say, I was tempted to plunge into the silent lake, that the waters might close over me and my **calamities** for ever. But I was restrained, when I thought of the heroic and suffering Elizabeth, whom I tenderly loved, and whose existence was bound up in mine. I thought also of my father and surviving brother; should I by my **base desertion** leave them exposed and unprotected to the **malice** of the **fiend** whom I had let loose among them?

At these moments I wept bitterly and wished that peace would revisit my mind only that I might afford them consolation and happiness. But that could not be. Remorse **extinguished** every hope. I had been the **author** of **unalterable** evils, and I lived in daily fear **lest** the monster whom I had created should **perpetrate** some new wickedness. I had an obscure feeling that all was not over and that he would still commit some **signal** crime, which by its enormity should almost **efface** the recollection of the past. There was always scope for fear so long as anything I loved remained behind. My **abhorrence** of this fiend cannot be conceived. When I thought of him I gnashed my teeth, my eyes became inflamed, and I ardently wished

---

calamity [kəlǽməti] n.
재난, 불행, 비운
base [beis] adj.
천한, 비열한, 하등의
desertion [dizə́ːrʃən] n.
버림, 유기, 도망
malice [mǽlis] n.
악의, 적의
fiend [fiːnd] n.
마귀, 악령, 악한

extinguish [ikstíŋgwiʃ] v.
끄다, 소멸시키다, 잃게 하다
author [ɔ́ːθər] n.
창조자, 장본인
unalterable [ʌnɔ́ːltərəbəl] adj.
변경할 수 없는, 불변의
lest [lest] conj.
~하지 않을까(라는)
perpetrate [pə́ːrpətrèit] v.
범하다, 저지르다
signal [sígn-əl] adj.
두드러진, 현저한, 주목할 만한
efface [iféis] v.
지우다, 없애다
abhorrence [æbhɔ́ːrəns, -hár-]
n. 혐오, 질색, 증오

precipitate [prisípətèit] v.
곤두박이치게 하다, 떨어뜨리다
wreak [riːk] v.
(벌, 복수 등을) 가하다, (분노 등을) 터뜨리다
avenge [əvéndʒ] v.
복수하다, 보복하다

sacrilege [sǽkrəlidʒ] n.
신성 모독, 벌받을 행위
quench [kwentʃ] v
(불 따위를) 끄다, 억누르다

I wished to see him again, that I might wreak the utmost extent of abhorrence on his head and avenge the deaths of William and Justine.

to extinguish that life which I had so thoughtlessly bestowed. When I reflected on his crimes and malice, my hatred and revenge burst all bounds of moderation. I would have made a pilgrimage to the highest peak of the Andes, could I, when there, have **precipitated** him to their base. I wished to see him again, that I might **wreak** the utmost extent of abhorrence on his head and **avenge** the deaths of William and Justine.

Our house was the house of mourning. My father's health was deeply shaken by the horror of the recent events. Elizabeth was sad and desponding; she no longer took delight in her ordinary occupations; all pleasure seemed to her **sacrilege** toward the dead; eternal woe and tears she then thought was the just tribute she should pay to innocence so blasted and destroyed. She was no longer that happy creature who in earlier youth wandered with me on the banks of the lake and talked with ecstasy of our future prospects. The first of those sorrows which are sent to wean us from the earth had visited her, and its dimming influence **quenched** her dearest smiles.

"When I reflect, my dear cousin," said she, "on the miserable death of Justine Moritz, I no longer see the world and its works as they before appeared to me. Before, I looked upon

misery [mízəri] n.
불행, 고뇌, 비참함
come home:
절실히 느껴지다, 분명해지다
precipice [présəpis] n.
벼랑, 절벽
abyss [əbís] n.
심해, 심연, 한없이 깊은 구렁텅이

the accounts of vice and injustice that I read in books or heard from others as tales of ancient days or imaginary evils; at least they were remote and more familiar to reason than to the imagination; but now **misery** has **come home**, and men appear to me as monsters thirsting for each other's blood. Yet I am certainly unjust. Everybody believed that poor girl to be guilty; and if she could have committed the crime for which she suffered, assuredly she would have been the most depraved of human creatures. For the sake of a few jewels, to have murdered the son of her benefactor and friend, a child whom she had nursed from its birth, and appeared to love as if it had been her own! I could not consent to the death of any human being, but certainly I should have thought such a creature unfit to remain in the society of men. But she was innocent. I know, I feel she was innocent; you are of the same opinion, and that confirms me. Alas! Victor, when falsehood can look so like the truth, who can assure themselves of certain happiness? I feel as if I were walking on the edge of a **precipice**, towards which thousands are crowding and endeavouring to plunge me into the **abyss**. William and Justine were assassinated, and the murderer escapes; he walks about the world free, and perhaps respected. But even if I were condemned to suffer on the scaffold for the same crimes, I would not change places with such a wretch."

I listened to this **discourse** with the extremest agony. I, not in deed, but in effect, was the true murderer. Elizabeth read my anguish in my countenance, and kindly taking my hand, said, "My dearest friend, you must calm yourself. These events have affected me, God knows how deeply; but I am not so **wretched** as you are. There is an expression of despair, and sometimes of revenge, in your countenance that makes me tremble. Dear Victor, **banish** these dark passions. Remember the friends around you, who centre all their hopes in you. Have we lost the power of rendering you happy? Ah! While we love, while we are true to each other, here in this land of peace and beauty, your native country, we may **reap** every tranquil blessing — what can disturb our peace?"

And could not such words from her whom I fondly prized before every other gift of fortune **suffice** to chase away the fiend that **lurked** in my heart? Even as she spoke I drew near to her, as if in terror, lest at that very moment the destroyer had been near to rob me of her.

Thus not the tenderness of friendship, nor the beauty of earth, nor of heaven, could **redeem** my soul from woe; the very **accents** of

---

discourse [dískɔːrs] n.
회화, 이야기, 담화
wretched [rétʃid] adj.
불행한, 비참한, 불쌍한
banish [bǽniʃ] v.
멀리하다, 쫓아버리다, 떨쳐버리다
reap [riːp] v.
거두다, 획득하다

suffice [səfáis, -fáiz] v.
족하다, 충분하다
lurk [ləːrk] v.
숨어있다, 잠재하다t

redeem [ridíːm] v.
구해내다, 구하다
accent [ǽksent / -sənt] n.
말, 언어

love were **ineffectual**. I was encompassed by a cloud which no beneficial influence could penetrate. The wounded deer dragging its fainting limbs to some untrodden **brake**, there to gaze upon the arrow which had pierced it, and to die, was but a type of me.

Sometimes I could **cope** with the sullen despair that overwhelmed me, but sometimes the whirlwind passions of my soul drove me to seek, by bodily exercise and by change of place, some relief from my **intolerable** sensations. It was during an **access** of this kind that I suddenly left my home, and bending my steps towards the near Alpine valleys, sought in the magnificence, the eternity of such scenes, to forget myself and my **ephemeral**, because human, sorrows. My wanderings were directed towards the valley of Chamounix. I had visited it frequently during my boyhood. Six years had passed since then: *I was a wreck*, but **nought** had changed in those savage and enduring scenes.

I performed the first part of my journey on horseback. I afterwards hired a mule, as the more sure-footed and least **liable** to receive injury on these rugged roads. The weather was fine; it was about the middle of the month of August, nearly two months after the death of Justine, that miserable **epoch** from which I dated all my woe. The weight upon my spirit

---

ineffectual [ìnifékt∫uəl] adj.
효과 없는, 헛된, 무력한
brake [breik] n.
숲, 덤불

cope [koup] v.
대처하다, 극복하다
intolerable [intάlərəbəl / -tɔ́l-] adj. 견딜 수 없는, 참을 수 없는
access [ǽkses] n.
(병, 노여움 등의) 발작, 격발
ephemeral [ifémərəl] adj.
덧없는, 단명한
nought [nɔːt, nɑːt] n.
제로, 무(無)

liable [láiəb-əl] adj.
~하기 쉬운
epoch [épək / íːpɔk] n.
획기적인 사건, 중요한 순간

ravine [rəví:n] n.
계곡, 협곡
omnipotence [ɑmnípətəns / ɔm-] n.
전능; 전능의 신
guise [gaiz] n.
외관, 모습, 겉보기
piny [páini] adj.
소나무의, 소나무가 무성한
impetuous [impétʃuəs] adj.
격렬한, 맹렬한
sublime [səbláim] adj.
장대한, 웅대한, 장엄한
habitation [hæ̀bətéiʃən] n.
거주지, 사는 곳

picturesque [pìktʃərésk] adj.
그림같은, 아름다운

was sensibly lightened as I plunged yet deeper in the **ravine** of Arve. The immense mountains and precipices that overhung me on every side, the sound of the river raging among the rocks, and the dashing of the waterfalls around spoke of a power mighty as **Omnipotence** — and I ceased to fear or to bend before any being less almighty than that which had created and ruled the elements, here displayed in their most terrific **guise**. Still, as I ascended higher, the valley assumed a more magnificent and astonishing character. Ruined castles hanging on the precipices of **piny** mountains, the **impetuous** Arve, and cottages every here and there peeping forth from among the trees formed a scene of singular beauty. But it was augmented and rendered **sublime** by the mighty Alps, whose white and shining pyramids and domes towered above all, as belonging to another earth, the **habitations** of another race of beings.

I passed the bridge of Pélissier, where the ravine, which the river forms, opened before me, and I began to ascend the mountain that overhangs it. Soon after, I entered the valley of Chamounix. This valley is more wonderful and sublime, but not so beautiful and **picturesque** as that of Servox, through which I had just passed. The high and snowy mountains were its immediate boundaries, but I saw no

glacier [gléiʃər, gléisjər] n.
빙하
avalanche [ǽvəlæntʃ / -là:nʃ] n.
눈사태
aiguille [eigwí:l] n.
뾰족한 산봉우리

fetter [fétər] v.
차꼬(족쇄)를 채우다, 속박하다, 구속하다
spur [spə:r] v. 박차를 가하다, 박차를 가하여 질주하다

pallid [pǽlid] adj.
창백한, 흐린, 희미한

more ruined castles and fertile fields. Immense **glaciers** approached the road; I heard the rumbling thunder of the falling **avalanche** and marked the smoke of its passage. Mont Blanc, the supreme and magnificent Mont Blanc, raised itself from the surrounding *aiguilles*, and its tremendous dôme overlooked the valley.

A tingling long-lost sense of pleasure often came across me during this journey. Some turn in the road, some new object suddenly perceived and recognised, reminded me of days gone by, and were associated with the light-hearted gaiety of boyhood. The very winds whispered in soothing accents, and maternal Nature bade me weep no more. Then again the kindly influence ceased to act—I found myself **fettered** again to grief and indulging in all the misery of reflection. Then I **spurred** on my animal, striving so to forget the world, my fears, and more than all, myself—or, in a more desperate fashion, I alighted and threw myself on the grass, weighed down by horror and despair.

At length I arrived at the village of Chamounix. Exhaustion succeeded to the extreme fatigue both of body and of mind which I had endured. For a short space of time I remained at the window watching the **pallid** lightnings that played above Mont Blanc and listening to the

lullaby [lʌ́ləbài] n.
자장가

oblivion [əblíviən] n.
망각, 잊혀짐

rushing of the Arve, which pursued its noisy way beneath. The same lulling sounds acted as a **lullaby** to my too keen sensations; when I placed my head upon my pillow, sleep crept over me; I felt it as it came and blessed the giver of **oblivion**.

Chapter 10

roam [roum] v.
돌아다니다, 방랑하다
presence chamber:
알현실
reverberate [rivə́:rb-ərèit] v.
반향하다, 울려 퍼지다
immutable [imjú:təbəl] adj.
변치 않는

I spent the following day **roaming** through the valley. I stood beside the sources of the Arveiron, which take their rise in a glacier, that with slow pace is advancing down from the summit of the hills to barricade the valley. The abrupt sides of vast mountains were before me; the icy wall of the glacier overhung me; a few shattered pines were scattered around; and the solemn silence of this glorious **presence-chamber** of imperial Nature was broken only by the brawling waves or the fall of some vast fragment, the thunder sound of the avalanche or the cracking, **reverberated** along the mountains, of the accumulated ice, which, through the silent working of **immutable** laws,

ever and anon:
때때로, 이따금
divert [divə́:rt, dai-] v.
전환시키다, 돌리다
assemblance [əsɛmbləns] n.
모임, 집합
congregate [káŋgrigèit / kɔ́ŋ-]
v. 모이다, 집합하다

melancholy [mélənkàli / -kòli]
n. 우울, 구슬픔, 애수
torrent [tɔ́:r-ənt, tár- / tɔ́r-] n.
급류, 분류

was **ever and anon** rent and torn, as if it had been but a plaything in their hands. These sublime and magnificent scenes afforded me the greatest consolation that I was capable of receiving. They elevated me from all littleness of feeling, and although they did not remove my grief, they subdued and tranquillised it. In some degree, also, they **diverted** my mind from the thoughts over which it had brooded for the last month. I retired to rest at night; my slumbers, as it were, waited on and ministered to by the **assemblance** of grand shapes which I had contemplated during the day. They **congregated** round me; the unstained snowy mountain-top, the glittering pinnacle, the pine woods, and ragged bare ravine, the eagle, soaring amidst the clouds — they all gathered round me and bade me be at peace.

Where had they fled when the next morning I awoke? All of soul-inspiring fled with sleep, and dark **melancholy** clouded every thought. The rain was pouring in **torrents**, and thick mists hid the summits of the mountains, so that I even saw not the faces of those mighty friends. Still I would penetrate their misty veil and seek them in their cloudy retreats. What were rain and storm to me? My mule was brought to the door, and I resolved to ascend to the summit of Montanvert. I remembered

solemnize [sάləmnàiz / sɔ́l-] v.
엄숙하게 하다, 장엄하게 하다
passing [pǽsiŋ, pάːs-] adj.
일시적인, 한때의
be acquainted with:
~을 알고 있다, 정통하다
grandeur [grǽndʒər, -dʒuər] n.
위대함, 위엄, 웅장함

the effect that the view of the tremendous and ever-moving glacier had produced upon my mind when I first saw it. It had then filled me with a sublime ecstasy that gave wings to the soul and allowed it to soar from the obscure world to light and joy. The sight of the awful and majestic in nature had indeed always the effect of **solemnising** my mind and causing me to forget the **passing** cares of life. I determined to go without a guide, for I **was** well **acquainted with** the path, and the presence of another would destroy the solitary **grandeur** of the scene.

precipitous [prisípətəs] adj.
절벽의, 깎아지른 듯한
surmount [sərmáunt] v.
이겨내다, 극복하다
perpendicularity
[pəːrpəndikjəlǽrəti] n.
수직, 직립
concussion [kənkʌ́ʃən] n.
진동, 격동, 충격

The ascent is **precipitous**, but the path is cut into continual and short windings, which enable you to **surmount** the **perpendicularity** of the mountain. It is a scene terrifically desolate. In a thousand spots the traces of the winter avalanche may be perceived, where trees lie broken and strewed on the ground, some entirely destroyed, others bent, leaning upon the jutting rocks of the mountain or transversely upon other trees. The path, as you ascend higher, is intersected by ravines of snow, down which stones continually roll from above; one of them is particularly dangerous, as the slightest sound, such as even speaking in a loud voice, produces a **concussion** of air sufficient to draw destruction upon the head

luxuriant [lʌgʒúəriənt, lʌkʃúər-] adj.
번성한, 울창한
severity [sivérəti] n.
엄격, 엄중
impulse [ímpʌls] n.
충동, 일시적인 감정

of the speaker. The pines are not tall or **luxuriant**, but they are sombre and add an air of **severity** to the scene. I looked on the valley beneath; vast mists were rising from the rivers which ran through it and curling in thick wreaths around the opposite mountains, whose summits were hid in the uniform clouds, while rain poured from the dark sky and added to the melancholy impression I received from the objects around me. Alas! Why does man boast of sensibilities superior to those apparent in the brute; it only renders them more necessary beings. If our **impulses** were confined to hunger, thirst, and desire, we might be nearly free; but now we are moved by every wind that blows and a chance word or scene that that word may convey to us.

pollute [pəlú:t] v.
더럽히다, 불결하게 하다, 오염시키다
nought [nɔ:t, nɑ:t] n.
제로, 무(無)
mutability [mjù:təbíləti] n.
변하기 쉬움; 변덕

 We rest; a dream has power to poison sleep.
 We rise; one wand'ring thought **pollutes** the day.
 We feel, conceive, or reason; laugh or weep,
 Embrace fond woe, or cast our cares away;
 It is the same: for, be it joy or sorrow,
 The path of its departure still is free.
 Man's yesterday may ne'er be like his morrow;
 Nought may endure but **mutability**!

ascent [əsént] n.
상승, 비탈, 오르막
dissipate [dísəpèit] v.
흩뜨리다, (군중 따위를) 쫓아 흩어버리다
intersperse [ìntərspə́:rs] v.
흩뿌리다, 산재시키다
rift [rift] n.
갈라진 틈, 균열
stupendous [stju:péndəs] adj.
엄청난, 굉장한

It was nearly noon when I arrived at the top of the **ascent**. For some time I sat upon the rock that overlooks the sea of ice. A mist covered both that and the surrounding mountains. Presently a breeze **dissipated** the cloud, and I descended upon the glacier. The surface is very uneven, rising like the waves of a troubled sea, descending low, and **interspersed** by **rifts** that sink deep. The field of ice is almost a league in width, but I spent nearly two hours in crossing it. The opposite mountain is a bare perpendicular rock. From the side where I now stood Montanvert was exactly opposite, at the distance of a league; and above it rose Mont Blanc, in awful majesty. I remained in a recess of the rock, gazing on this wonderful and **stupendous** scene. The sea, or rather the vast river of ice, wound among its dependent mountains, whose aerial summits hung over its recesses. Their icy and glittering peaks shone in the sunlight over the clouds. My heart, which was before sorrowful, now swelled with something like joy; I exclaimed, "Wandering spirits, if indeed ye wander, and do not rest in your narrow beds, allow me this faint happiness, or take me, as your companion, away from the joys of life."

As I said this I suddenly beheld the figure of a man, at some distance, advancing towards

crevice [krévis] n.
갈라진 틈
stature [stǽtʃəːr] n.
키, 신장
close with:
맞붙어 싸우다, 접근전을 펴다
mortal combat:
목숨을 건 싸움
bespeak [bispíːk] v.
나타내다
disdain [disdéin] n.
경멸, 모멸
malignity [məlígnəti] n.
악의, 원한

I trembled with rage and horror, resolving to wait his approach and then close with him in mortal combat.

begone [bigɔ́(ː)n, -gán] v.
떠나다, 물러가다
extinction [ikstíŋkʃən] n.
사멸, 절멸, 폐절

me with superhuman speed. He bounded over the **crevices** in the ice, among which I had walked with caution; his **stature**, also, as he approached, seemed to exceed that of man. I was troubled; a mist came over my eyes, and I felt a faintness seize me, but I was quickly restored by the cold gale of the mountains. I perceived, as the shape came nearer (sight tremendous and abhorred!) that it was the wretch whom I had created. I trembled with rage and horror, resolving to wait his approach and then **close with** him in **mortal combat**. He approached; his countenance **bespoke** bitter anguish, combined with **disdain** and **malignity**, while its unearthly ugliness rendered it almost too horrible for human eyes. But I scarcely observed this; rage and hatred had at first deprived me of utterance, and I recovered only to overwhelm him with words expressive of furious detestation and contempt.

"Devil," I exclaimed, "do you dare approach me? And do not you fear the fierce vengeance of my arm wreaked on your miserable head? **Begone**, vile insect! Or rather, stay, that I may trample you to dust! And, oh! That I could, with the **extinction** of your miserable existence, restore those victims whom you have so diabolically murdered!"

"I expected this reception," said the daemon.

detest [ditést] v.
몹시 싫어하다, 혐오하다
spurn [spəːrn] v.
퇴짜놓다, 걷어차다
dissoluble [disÁljəbəl / -sɔ́l-]
adj. 분해할 수 있는, 해소할 수 있는
annihilation [ənàiəléiʃən] n.
멸망, 소멸
purpose [pə́ːrpəs] v.
의도하다, 꾀하다
sport [spɔːrt] v.
놀다, 장난치다, 농락하다
comply [kəmplái] v.
따르다, 응하다
glut [glʌt] v.
물리게 하다, 가득 채우다
maw [mɔː] n.
목구멍; 심연, 깊은 구렁
negligently [néglidʒəntli] adv.
소홀하게, 태만하게, 부주의하게

give vent to:
(노여움 따위를) 터뜨리다, ~을 나타내다

"All men hate the wretched; how, then, must I be hated, who am miserable beyond all living things! Yet you, my creator, **detest** and **spurn** me, thy creature, to whom thou art bound by ties only **dissoluble** by the **annihilation** of one of us. You **purpose** to kill me. How dare you **sport** thus with life? Do your duty towards me, and I will do mine towards you and the rest of mankind. If you will **comply** with my conditions, I will leave them and you at peace; but if you refuse, I will **glut** the **maw** of death, until it be satiated with the blood of your remaining friends."

"Abhorred monster! Fiend that thou art! The tortures of hell are too mild a vengeance for thy crimes. Wretched devil! You reproach me with your creation, come on, then, that I may extinguish the spark which I so **negligently** bestowed."

My rage was without bounds; I sprang on him, impelled by all the feelings which can arm one being against the existence of another.

He easily eluded me and said,

"Be calm! I entreat you to hear me before you **give vent to** your hatred on my devoted head. Have I not suffered enough, that you seek to increase my misery? Life, although it may only be an accumulation of anguish, is dear to me, and I will defend it. Remember, thou hast made me more powerful than thyself; my height is superior to thine, my joints more **supple**. But I will not be tempted to set myself in opposition to thee. I am thy creature, and I will be even mild and docile to my natural lord and king if thou wilt also perform thy part, the which thou owest me. Oh, Frankenstein, be not **equitable** to every other and trample upon me alone, to whom thy justice, and even thy **clemency** and affection, is most due. Remember that I am thy creature; I ought to be thy Adam, but I am rather the fallen angel, whom thou drivest from joy for no **misdeed**. Everywhere I see bliss, from which I alone am **irrevocably** excluded. I was benevolent and good; misery made me a fiend. Make me happy, and I shall again be virtuous."

"Begone! I will not hear you. There can be no **community** between you and me; we are enemies. Begone, or let us try our strength in a fight, in which one must fall."

"How can I move thee? Will no entreaties cause thee to turn a favourable eye upon thy creature, who **implores** thy goodness and **compassion**? Believe me, Frankenstein, I was benevolent; my soul glowed with love and humanity; but am I not alone, miserably alone? You, my creator, **abhor** me; what hope can I gather from your fellow creatures, who owe me nothing? They **spurn** and hate me. The desert mountains and dreary glaciers are my refuge. I have wandered here many days; the caves of ice, which I only do not fear, are a dwelling to me, and the only one which man does not grudge. These bleak skies I **hail**, for they are kinder to me than your fellow beings. If the multitude of mankind knew of my existence, they would do as you do, and arm themselves for my destruction. Shall I not then hate them who abhor me? I will keep no terms with my enemies. I am miserable, and they shall share my wretchedness. Yet it is in your power to **recompense** me, and deliver them from an evil which it only remains for you to make so great, that not only you and your family, but thousands of others, shall be swallowed up in the whirlwinds of its rage. Let your compassion be moved, and do not disdain me. Listen to my tale; when you have heard that, abandon or **commiserate** me, as you shall judge that I deserve. But hear me. The guilty are allowed, by human laws, bloody as they are, to speak in their own defence before they are condemned. Listen to me, Frankenstein. You accuse me of murder, and yet you would, with a **satisfied** conscience, destroy your own creature. Oh, praise the eternal justice of man! Yet I ask you not to spare me; listen to me, and then, if

---

spurn [spə:rn] v.
퇴짜놓다, 걷어차다
hail [heil] v.
환영하다, 갈채하다
recompense [rékəmpèns] v.
보상하다, 보답하다
commiserate [kəmízərèit] v.
가엾게 여기다, 불쌍하게 생각하다
satisfied [sǽtisfàid] adj.
만족한, 깨끗이 치른, 납득되는

Remember that I am thy creature; I ought to be thy Adam, but I am rather the fallen angel, whom thou drivest from joy for no misdeed.

rejoin [riːdʒɔ́in] v.
대답하다

"... Listen to me, Frankenstein. You accuse me of murder, and yet you would, with a satisfied conscience, destroy your own creature. Oh, praise the eternal justice of man!

quit [kwit] v.
떠나다, 물러나다
scourge [skəːrdʒ] n.
하늘의 응징, 천벌, 징벌

you can, and if you will, destroy the work of your hands."

"Why do you call to my remembrance," I **rejoined**, "circumstances of which I shudder to reflect, that I have been the miserable origin and author? Cursed be the day, abhorred devil, in which you first saw light! Cursed (although I curse myself) be the hands that formed you! You have made me wretched beyond expression. You have left me no power to consider whether I am just to you or not. Begone! Relieve me from the sight of your detested form."

"Thus I relieve thee, my creator," he said, and placed his hated hands before my eyes, which I flung from me with violence; "thus I take from thee a sight which you abhor. Still thou canst listen to me and grant me thy compassion. By the virtues that I once possessed, I demand this from you. Hear my tale; it is long and strange, and the temperature of this place is not fitting to your fine sensations; come to the hut upon the mountain. The sun is yet high in the heavens; before it descends to hide itself behind your snowy precipices and illuminate another world, you will have heard my story and can decide. On you it rests, whether I **quit** for ever the neighbourhood of man and lead a harmless life, or become the **scourge** of your fellow creatures and the author of your own speedy ruin."

As he said this he led the way across the ice; I followed. My heart was full, and I did not answer him, but as I proceeded, I **weighed** the various arguments that he had used and determined at least to listen to his tale. I was partly **urged** by curiosity, and compassion confirmed my **resolution**. I had hitherto supposed him to be the murderer of my brother, and I eagerly sought a **confirmation** or denial of this opinion. For the first time, also, I felt what the duties of a creator towards his creature were, and that I ought to render him happy before I complained of his wickedness. These motives urged me to **comply** with his demand. We crossed the ice, therefore, and ascended the opposite rock. The air was cold, and the rain again began to descend; we entered the hut, the fiend with an air of exultation, I with a heavy heart and depressed spirits. But I consented to listen, and seating myself by the fire which my **odious** companion had lighted, he thus began his tale.

---

weigh [wei] v.
숙고하다, 고찰하다, 비교 평가하다
urge [əːrdʒ] v.
재촉하다, 다그치다, 촉구하다
resolution [rèzəlúːʃ-ən] n.
결심, 단호함, 의지
confirmation [kànfərméiʃən / kòn-] n.
확인, 확정
comply [kəmplái] v.
따르다, 응하다
odious [óudiəs] adj.
싫은, 미운, 가증스러운

Chapter 11

indistinct [ìndistíŋkt] adj.
불분명한, 희미한

"It is with considerable difficulty that I remember the original era of my being; all the events of that period appear confused and **indistinct**. A strange multiplicity of sensations seized me, and I saw, felt, heard, and smelt at the same time; and it was, indeed, a long time before I learned to distinguish between the operations of my various senses. By degrees, I remember, a stronger light pressed upon my nerves, so that I was obliged to shut my eyes. Darkness then came over me and troubled me, but hardly had I felt this when, by opening my eyes, as I now suppose, the light poured in upon me again. I walked and, I believe, descended, but I presently found a great

alteration [ɔ̀:ltəréiʃən] n.
변경, 변화, 변질
opaque [oupéik] adj.
불투명한, 분명치 않은
impervious [impə́:rviəs] adj.
통하지 않는, 영향을 받지 않는, 느끼지 못하는
at liberty:
자유로운, 해방된
dormant [dɔ́:rmənt] adj.
잠자는, 동면의
slake [sleik] v.
갈증을 풀다

desolate [désəlit] adj.
고독한, 쓸쓸한, 비참한

steal [sti:l] v.
모르는 사이에 지나가다(오다), 어느새 엄습하다

alteration in my sensations. Before, dark and **opaque** bodies had surrounded me, **impervious** to my touch or sight; but I now found that I could wander on **at liberty**, with no obstacles which I could not either surmount or avoid. The light became more and more oppressive to me, and the heat wearying me as I walked, I sought a place where I could receive shade. This was the forest near Ingolstadt; and here I lay by the side of a brook resting from my fatigue, until I felt tormented by hunger and thirst. This roused me from my nearly **dormant** state, and I ate some berries which I found hanging on the trees or lying on the ground. I **slaked** my thirst at the brook, and then lying down, was overcome by sleep.

"It was dark when I awoke; I felt cold also, and half frightened, as it were, instinctively, finding myself so **desolate**. Before I had quitted your apartment, on a sensation of cold, I had covered myself with some clothes, but these were insufficient to secure me from the dews of night. I was a poor, helpless, miserable wretch; I knew, and could distinguish, nothing; but feeling pain invade me on all sides, I sat down and wept.

"Soon a gentle light **stole** over the heavens and gave me a sensation of pleasure. I started up and beheld a radiant form rise from among

distinct [distíŋkt] adj. 뚜렷한, 명백한, 명확한
innumerable [injú:mərəbəl] adj. 무수한, 셀 수 없이 많은

foliage [fóuliidʒ] n. 녹음, 산림, 신록

the trees*. I gazed with a kind of wonder. It moved slowly, but it enlightened my path, and I again went out in search of berries. I was still cold when under one of the trees I found a huge cloak, with which I covered myself, and sat down upon the ground. No **distinct** ideas occupied my mind; all was confused. I felt light, and hunger, and thirst, and darkness; **innumerable** sounds rang in my ears, and on all sides various scents saluted me; the only object that I could distinguish was the bright moon, and I fixed my eyes on that with pleasure.

"Several changes of day and night passed, and the orb of night had greatly lessened, when I began to distinguish my sensations from each other. I gradually saw plainly the clear stream that supplied me with drink and the trees that shaded me with their **foliage**. I was delighted when I first discovered that a pleasant sound, which often saluted my ears, proceeded from the throats of the little winged animals who had often intercepted the light from my eyes. I began also to observe, with greater accuracy, the forms that surrounded me and to perceive the boundaries of the radiant roof of light which canopied me. Sometimes I tried to imitate the pleasant songs of the birds but was unable. Sometimes I wished to express my sensations

---

* The moon [author's footnote].

uncouth [ʌnkúːθ] adj.
어색한, 괴상한
inarticulate [ìnɑːrtíkjəlit] adj.
분명치 않은

ember [émbər] n.
타다 남은 것, 깜부기불

in my own mode, but the **uncouth** and **inarticulate** sounds which broke from me frightened me into silence again.

"The moon had disappeared from the night, and again, with a lessened form, showed itself, while I still remained in the forest. My sensations had by this time become distinct, and my mind received every day additional ideas. My eyes became accustomed to the light and to perceive objects in their right forms; I distinguished the insect from the herb, and by degrees, one herb from another. I found that the sparrow uttered none but harsh notes, whilst those of the blackbird and thrush were sweet and enticing.

"One day, when I was oppressed by cold, I found a fire which had been left by some wandering beggars, and was overcome with delight at the warmth I experienced from it. In my joy I thrust my hand into the live **embers**, but quickly drew it out again with a cry of pain. How strange, I thought, that the same cause should produce such opposite effects! I examined the materials of the fire, and to my joy found it to be composed of wood. I quickly collected some branches, but they were wet and would not burn. I was pained at this and sat still watching the operation of the fire. The wet wood which I had placed near the heat dried and itself became inflamed. I reflected on this, and by touching the various branches, I discovered the cause and busied myself in collecting a great quantity of wood, that I might dry it and have a plentiful supply of fire. When night came on and brought sleep with it, I was in the greatest fear lest my fire should be extinguished. I covered it carefully with dry wood and leaves and placed wet branches upon it; and then, spreading my cloak, I lay on the ground and sank into sleep.

"It was morning when I awoke, and my first care was to visit the fire. I uncovered it, and a gentle breeze quickly fanned it into a flame. I observed this also and **contrived** a fan of branches, which roused the embers when they were nearly extinguished. When night came again I found, with pleasure, that the fire gave light as well as heat and that the discovery of this element was useful to me in my food, for I found some of the **offals** that the travellers had left had been roasted, and tasted much more **savoury** than the berries I gathered from the trees. I tried, therefore, to dress my food in the same manner, placing it on the live embers. I found that the berries were spoiled by this operation, and the nuts and roots much improved.

"Food, however, became scarce, and I often

---

contrive [kəntráiv] v.
고안하다, 설계하다
offal [ɔ́(:)fəl, ɑ́fəl] n.
고기부스러기, (짐승의) 내장
savory [séiv-əri] adj.
풍미 있는, 맛좋은

assuage [əswéidʒ] v.
누그러뜨리다, 완화시키다
relinquish [rilíŋkwiʃ] v.
포기하다, 그만두다, 버리다
ramble[rǽmb-əl] n.
소요, 산책
disconsolate [diskánsəlit / -kón-] adj.
어두운, 우울한

spent the whole day searching in vain for a few acorns to **assuage** the pangs of hunger. When I found this, I resolved to quit the place that I had hitherto inhabited, to seek for one where the few wants I experienced would be more easily satisfied. In this emigration I exceedingly lamented the loss of the fire which I had obtained through accident and knew not how to reproduce it. I gave several hours to the serious consideration of this difficulty, but I was obliged to **relinquish** all attempt to supply it, and wrapping myself up in my cloak, I struck across the wood towards the setting sun. I passed three days in these **rambles** and at length discovered the open country. A great fall of snow had taken place the night before, and the fields were of one uniform white; the appearance was **disconsolate**, and I found my feet chilled by the cold damp substance that covered the ground.

"It was about seven in the morning, and I longed to obtain food and shelter; at length I perceived a small hut, on a rising ground, which had doubtless been built for the convenience of some shepherd. This was a new sight to me, and I examined the structure with great curiosity. Finding the door open, I entered. An old man sat in it, near a fire, over which he was preparing his breakfast. He turned on hearing

exquisite [ikskwízit, ékskwi-] adj. 매우 아름다운, 훌륭한
retreat [ritrí:t] n. 은신처, 피난처
pandemonium [pæ̀ndəmóuniəm] n. 복마전, 지옥
remnant [rémnənt] n. 나머지, 잔여

allure [əlúər] v. 꾀다, 부추기다, 유혹하다
recommence [rì:kəméns] v. 재개하다, 다시 시작하다
engage [engéidʒ] v. 끌다, 사로잡다, 매혹하다

a noise, and perceiving me, shrieked loudly, and quitting the hut, ran across the fields with a speed of which his debilitated form hardly appeared capable. His appearance, different from any I had ever before seen, and his flight somewhat surprised me. But I was enchanted by the appearance of the hut; here the snow and rain could not penetrate; the ground was dry; and it presented to me then as **exquisite** and divine a **retreat** as **Pandaemonium** appeared to the daemons of hell after their sufferings in the lake of fire. I greedily devoured the **remnants** of the shepherd's breakfast, which consisted of bread, cheese, milk, and wine; the latter, however, I did not like. Then, overcome by fatigue, I lay down among some straw and fell asleep.

"It was noon when I awoke, and **allured** by the warmth of the sun, which shone brightly on the white ground, I determined to **recommence** my travels; and, depositing the remains of the peasant's breakfast in a wallet I found, I proceeded across the fields for several hours, until at sunset I arrived at a village. How miraculous did this appear! The huts, the neater cottages, and stately houses **engaged** my admiration by turns. The vegetables in the gardens, the milk and cheese that I saw placed at the windows of some of the cottages, allured my

hovel [hʌ́vəl, hάv-] n.
광, 헛간, 오두막집

appetite. One of the best of these I entered, but I had hardly placed my foot within the door before the children shrieked, and one of the women fainted. The whole village was roused; some fled, some attacked me, until, grievously bruised by stones and many other kinds of missile weapons, I escaped to the open country and fearfully took refuge in a low **hovel**, quite bare, and making a wretched appearance after the palaces I had beheld in the village. This hovel however, joined a cottage of a neat and pleasant appearance, but after my late dearly bought experience, I dared not enter it. My place of refuge was constructed of wood, but so low that I could with difficulty sit upright in it. No wood, however, was placed on the earth, which formed the floor, but it was dry; and although the wind entered it by innumerable chinks, I found it an agreeable asylum from the snow and rain.

inclemency [inklémənsi] n.
(날씨의) 험악; 무자비, 가혹
barbarity [bɑːrbǽrəti] n.
야만, 만행

"Here, then, I retreated and lay down happy to have found a shelter, however miserable, from the **inclemency** of the season, and still more from the **barbarity** of man.

kennel [kénəl] n.
초라한 집, 누옥

"As soon as morning dawned I crept from my **kennel**, that I might view the adjacent cottage and discover if I could remain in the habitation I had found. It was situated against the back of the cottage and surrounded on the sides which were exposed by a pig sty and a clear pool of water. One part was open, and by that I had crept in; but now I covered every crevice by which I might be perceived with stones and wood, yet in such a manner that I might move them on occasion to pass out; all the light I enjoyed came through the sty, and that was sufficient for me.

"Having thus arranged my dwelling and carpeted it with clean straw, I retired, for I saw the figure of a man at a distance, and I remembered too well my treatment the night before to trust myself in his power. I had first, however, provided for my **sustenance** for that day by a loaf of coarse bread, which I **purloined**, and a cup with which I could drink more conveniently than from my hand of the pure water which flowed by my retreat. The floor was a little raised, so that it was kept perfectly dry, and by its vicinity to the chimney of the cottage it was tolerably warm.

"Being thus provided, I resolved to reside in this hovel until something should occur which might alter my determination. It was indeed a paradise compared to the bleak forest, my former residence, the rain-dropping branches, and **dank** earth. I ate my breakfast with pleasure and was about to remove a plank to procure myself a little water when I heard a step, and

sustenance [sʌ́stənəns] n.
생계수단, 음식물
purloin [pərlɔ́in, pə́:r-] v.
훔치다

dank [dæŋk] adj.
습한, 축축한

pail [peil] n.
원통형 용기; 버킷
incommode [ìnkəmóud] v.
불편을 느끼게 하다, 폐를 끼치다, 방해하다
despondence [dispʌ́ndəns / -spɔ́nd-] n.
낙담, 의기소침

looking through a small chink, I beheld a young creature, with a **pail** on her head, passing before my hovel. The girl was young and of gentle demeanour, unlike what I have since found cottagers and farmhouse servants to be. Yet she was meanly dressed, a coarse blue petticoat and a linen jacket being her only garb; her fair hair was plaited but not adorned: she looked patient yet sad. I lost sight of her, and in about a quarter of an hour she returned bearing the pail, which was now partly filled with milk. As she walked along, seemingly **incommoded** by the burden, a young man met her, whose countenance expressed a deeper **despondence**. Uttering a few sounds with an air of melancholy, he took the pail from her head and bore it to the cottage himself. She followed, and they disappeared. Presently I saw the young man again, with some tools in his hand, cross the field behind the cottage; and the girl was also busied, sometimes in the house and sometimes in the yard.

"On examining my dwelling, I found that one of the windows of the cottage had formerly occupied a part of it, but the panes had been filled up with wood. In one of these was a small and almost imperceptible chink through which the eye could just penetrate. Through this crevice a small room was visible, whitewashed and

aught [ɔːt] pron.
어떤 일, 무언가
reverence [rév-ərəns] n.
경의, 숭배

clean but very bare of furniture. In one corner, near a small fire, sat an old man, leaning his head on his hands in a disconsolate attitude. The young girl was occupied in arranging the cottage; but presently she took something out of a drawer, which employed her hands, and she sat down beside the old man, who, taking up an instrument, began to play and to produce sounds sweeter than the voice of the thrush or the nightingale. It was a lovely sight, even to me, poor wretch who had never beheld **aught** beautiful before. The silver hair and benevolent countenance of the aged cottager won my **reverence**, while the gentle manners of the girl enticed my love. He played a sweet mournful air which I perceived drew tears from the eyes of his amiable companion, of which the old man took no notice, until she sobbed audibly; he then pronounced a few sounds, and the fair creature, leaving her work, knelt at his feet. He raised her and smiled with such kindness and affection that I felt sensations of a peculiar and overpowering nature; they were a mixture of pain and pleasure, such as I had never before experienced, either from hunger or cold, warmth or food; and I withdrew from the window, unable to bear these emotions.

"Soon after this the young man returned, bearing on his shoulders a load of wood. The girl met him at the door, helped to relieve him of his burden, and taking some of the fuel into the cottage, placed it on the fire; then she and the youth went apart into a **nook** of the cottage, and he showed her a large loaf and a piece of cheese. She seemed pleased and went into the garden for some roots and plants, which she placed in water, and then upon the fire. She afterwards continued her work, whilst the young man went into the garden and appeared busily employed in digging and pulling up roots. After he had been employed thus about an hour, the young woman joined him and they entered the cottage together.

"The old man had, in the meantime, been **pensive**, but on the appearance of his companions he assumed a more cheerful air, and they sat down to eat. The meal was quickly dispatched. The young woman was again occupied in arranging the cottage, the old man walked before the cottage in the sun for a few minutes, leaning on the arm of the youth. Nothing could exceed in beauty the contrast between these two excellent creatures. One was old, with silver hairs and a countenance beaming with benevolence and love; the younger was slight and graceful in his figure, and his features were moulded with the finest symmetry, yet his eyes and attitude expressed the utmost

---

nook [nuk] n.
구석

pensive [pénsiv] adj.
생각에 잠긴, 수심에 잠긴

taper [téipə:r] n.
가는 양초
utter [ʌ́tər] v.
(목소리나 말 따위를) 내다, 입 밖에 내다

sadness and despondency. The old man returned to the cottage, and the youth, with tools different from those he had used in the morning, directed his steps across the fields.

"Night quickly shut in, but to my extreme wonder, I found that the cottagers had a means of prolonging light by the use of **tapers**, and was delighted to find that the setting of the sun did not put an end to the pleasure I experienced in watching my human neighbours. In the evening the young girl and her companion were employed in various occupations which I did not understand; and the old man again took up the instrument which produced the divine sounds that had enchanted me in the morning. So soon as he had finished, the youth began, not to play, but to **utter** sounds that were monotonous, and neither resembling the harmony of the old man's instrument nor the songs of the birds; I since found that he read aloud, but at that time I knew nothing of the science of words or letters.

"The family, after having been thus occupied for a short time, extinguished their lights and retired, as I conjectured, to rest."

Chapter 12

"I lay on my straw, but I could not sleep. I thought of the occurrences of the day. What chiefly struck me was the gentle manners of these people, and I longed to join them, but dared not. I remembered too well the treatment I had suffered the night before from the barbarous villagers, and resolved, whatever course of conduct I might hereafter think it right to pursue, that for the present I would remain quietly in my hovel, watching and endeavouring to discover the motives which influenced their actions.

"The cottagers arose the next morning before the sun. The young woman arranged the cottage and prepared the food, and the youth

precede [prisíːd] v.
선행하다, 앞서다, 먼저 일어나다
venerable [vénərəbəl] adj.
존경할 만한

viand [váiənd] n.
식품, 음식
imply [implái] v.
암시하다, 의미하다

departed after the first meal.

"This day was passed in the same routine as that which **preceded** it. The young man was constantly employed out of doors, and the girl in various laborious occupations within. The old man, whom I soon perceived to be blind, employed his leisure hours on his instrument or in contemplation. Nothing could exceed the love and respect which the younger cottagers exhibited towards their **venerable** companion. They performed towards him every little office of affection and duty with gentleness, and he rewarded them by his benevolent smiles.

"They were not entirely happy. The young man and his companion often went apart and appeared to weep. I saw no cause for their unhappiness, but I was deeply affected by it. If such lovely creatures were miserable, it was less strange that I, an imperfect and solitary being, should be wretched. Yet why were these gentle beings unhappy? They possessed a delightful house (for such it was in my eyes) and every luxury; they had a fire to warm them when chill and delicious **viands** when hungry; they were dressed in excellent clothes; and, still more, they enjoyed one another's company and speech, interchanging each day looks of affection and kindness. What did their tears **imply**? Did they really express pain? I was at

perpetual [pərpétʃuəl] adj.
부단한, 끊임없는
enigmatic [ènigmǽtik, ìn-] adj.
수수께끼의, 불가사의한

elapse [ilǽps] v.
지나다, 경과하다

inflict [inflíkt] v.
(고통, 타격) 등을 가하다, 입히다
abstain [æbstéin] v.
그만두다, 끊다, 삼가다

first unable to solve these questions, but **perpetual** attention and time explained to me many appearances which were at first **enigmatic**.

"A considerable period **elapsed** before I discovered one of the causes of the uneasiness of this amiable family: it was poverty, and they suffered that evil in a very distressing degree. Their nourishment consisted entirely of the vegetables of their garden and the milk of one cow, which gave very little during the winter, when its masters could scarcely procure food to support it. They often, I believe, suffered the pangs of hunger very poignantly, especially the two younger cottagers, for several times they placed food before the old man when they reserved none for themselves.

"This trait of kindness moved me sensibly. I had been accustomed, during the night, to steal a part of their store for my own consumption, but when I found that in doing this I **inflicted** pain on the cottagers, I **abstained** and satisfied myself with berries, nuts, and roots which I gathered from a neighbouring wood.

"I discovered also another means through which I was enabled to assist their labours. I found that the youth spent a great part of each day in collecting wood for the family fire, and during the night I often took his tools, the use

firing [fáiəriŋ] n.
장작, 연료, 땔감

of which I quickly discovered, and brought home **firing** sufficient for the consumption of several days.

"I remember, the first time that I did this, the young woman, when she opened the door in the morning, appeared greatly astonished on seeing a great pile of wood on the outside. She uttered some words in a loud voice, and the youth joined her, who also expressed surprise. I observed, with pleasure, that he did not go to the forest that day, but spent it in repairing the cottage and cultivating the garden.

moment [móumənt] n.
중요성, 중대사
articulate [ɑ:rtíkjəlit] adj.
명확한, 분명한
baffle [bǽfəl] v.
당황하게 하다, 좌절시키다
unravel [ʌnrǽvəl] v.
풀다, 해결하다
application [æplikéiʃən] n.
열심, 근면

"By degrees I made a discovery of still greater **moment**. I found that these people possessed a method of communicating their experience and feelings to one another by **articulate** sounds. I perceived that the words they spoke sometimes produced pleasure or pain, smiles or sadness, in the minds and countenances of the hearers. This was indeed a godlike science, and I ardently desired to become acquainted with it. But I was **baffled** in every attempt I made for this purpose. Their pronunciation was quick, and the words they uttered, not having any apparent connection with visible objects, I was unable to discover any clue by which I could **unravel** the mystery of their reference. By great **application**, however, and after having remained during the space of

discourse [dískɔːrs] n.
회화, 이야기, 담화
appropriate [əpróuprièit] v.
(어떤 목적에) 충당하다, 사용하다

endear [endíər] v.
애정을 느끼게 하다
accomplishment [əkámplíʃmənt / əkɔ́m-] n.
지식, 소양, 교양

several revolutions of the moon in my hovel, I discovered the names that were given to some of the most familiar objects of **discourse**; I learned and applied the words, "fire", "milk", "bread", and "wood". I learned also the names of the cottagers themselves. The youth and his companion had each of them several names, but the old man had only one, which was "father". The girl was called "sister" or "Agatha", and the youth "Felix", "brother", or "son". I cannot describe the delight I felt when I learned the ideas **appropriated** to each of these sounds and was able to pronounce them. I distinguished several other words without being able as yet to understand or apply them, such as "good", "dearest", "unhappy".

"I spent the winter in this manner. The gentle manners and beauty of the cottagers greatly **endeared** them to me; when they were unhappy, I felt depressed; when they rejoiced, I sympathised in their joys. I saw few human beings besides them, and if any other happened to enter the cottage, their harsh manners and rude gait only enhanced to me the superior **accomplishments** of my friends. The old man, I could perceive, often endeavoured to encourage his children, as sometimes I found that he called them, to cast off their melancholy. He would talk in a cheerful accent, with an

exhortation [èɡzɔːrtéiʃən, èksɔːr-] n.
간곡한 권유, 권고

expression of goodness that bestowed pleasure even upon me. Agatha listened with respect, her eyes sometimes filled with tears, which she endeavoured to wipe away unperceived; but I generally found that her countenance and tone were more cheerful after having listened to the **exhortations** of her father. It was not thus with Felix. He was always the saddest of the group, and even to my unpractised senses, he appeared to have suffered more deeply than his friends. But if his countenance was more sorrowful, his voice was more cheerful than that of his sister, especially when he addressed the old man.

innumerable [injúːmərəbəl] adj. 무수한, 셀 수 없이 많은
disposition [dìspəzíʃən] n. 기질, 성미, 성격
outhouse [áuthàus] n. 딴채, 헛간
replenish [ripléniʃ] v. 다시 채우다, 계속 공급하다

"I could mention **innumerable** instances which, although slight, marked the **dispositions** of these amiable cottagers. In the midst of poverty and want, Felix carried with pleasure to his sister the first little white flower that peeped out from beneath the snowy ground. Early in the morning, before she had risen, he cleared away the snow that obstructed her path to the milk-house, drew water from the well, and brought the wood from the **outhouse**, where, to his perpetual astonishment, he found his store always **replenished** by an invisible hand. In the day, I believe, he worked sometimes for a neighbouring farmer, because he often went forth and did not return until dinner, yet brought no wood with him. At other times he worked in the garden, but as there was little to do in the frosty season, he read to the old man and Agatha.

"This reading had puzzled me extremely at first, but by degrees I discovered that he uttered many of the same sounds when he read as when he talked. I **conjectured**, therefore, that he found on the paper signs for speech which he understood, and I ardently longed to comprehend these also; but how was that possible when I did not even understand the sounds for which they stood as signs? I improved, however, sensibly in this science, but not sufficiently to follow up any kind of conversation, although I applied my whole mind to the endeavour, for I easily perceived that, although I eagerly longed to discover myself to the cottagers, I ought not to make the attempt until I had first become master of their language, which knowledge might enable me to make them **overlook** the **deformity** of my figure, for with this also the contrast perpetually presented to my eyes had made me acquainted.

"I had admired the perfect forms of my cottagers — their grace, beauty, and delicate complexions; but how was I terrified when I viewed myself in a transparent pool! At first I started back, unable to believe that it was

---

conjecture [kəndʒéktʃər] v.
추측하다
overlook [òuvərlúk] v.
관대히 봐주다, 눈감아주다
deformity [difɔ́:rməti] n.
기형, 불구, 보기 흉한 것

despondence [dispándəns / -spónd-] n.
낙담, 의기소침
mortification [mɔ̀:rtəfikéiʃ-ən] n.
굴욕, 수치

famine [fǽmin] n.
기근, 굶주림, 기아

mode [moud] n.
양식, 형식, 방법

indeed I who was reflected in the mirror; and when I became fully convinced that I was in reality the monster that I am, I was filled with the bitterest sensations of **despondence** and **mortification**. Alas! I did not yet entirely know the fatal effects of this miserable deformity.

"As the sun became warmer and the light of day longer, the snow vanished, and I beheld the bare trees and the black earth. From this time Felix was more employed, and the heart-moving indications of impending **famine** disappeared. Their food, as I afterwards found, was coarse, but it was wholesome; and they procured a sufficiency of it. Several new kinds of plants sprang up in the garden, which they dressed; and these signs of comfort increased daily as the season advanced.

"The old man, leaning on his son, walked each day at noon, when it did not rain, as I found it was called when the heavens poured forth its waters. This frequently took place, but a high wind quickly dried the earth, and the season became far more pleasant than it had been.

"My **mode** of life in my hovel was uniform. During the morning I attended the motions of the cottagers, and when they were dispersed in various occupations, I slept; the remainder of the day was spent in observing my friends. When they had retired to rest, if there was any moon or the night was star-light, I went into the woods and collected my own food and fuel for the cottage. When I returned, as often as it was necessary, I cleared their path from the snow and performed those offices that I had seen done by Felix. I afterwards found that these labours, performed by an invisible hand, greatly astonished them; and once or twice I heard them, on these occasions, utter the words "good spirit", "wonderful"; but I did not then understand the signification of these terms.

"My thoughts now became more active, and I longed to discover the motives and feelings of these lovely creatures; I was **inquisitive** to know why Felix appeared so miserable and Agatha so sad. I thought (foolish wretch!) that it might be in my power to restore happiness to these deserving people. When I slept or was absent, the forms of the venerable blind father, the gentle Agatha, and the excellent Felix flitted before me. I looked upon them as superior beings who would be the **arbiters** of my future destiny. I formed in my imagination a thousand pictures of presenting myself to them, and their reception of me. I imagined that they would be disgusted, until, by my gentle **demeanour** and conciliating words, I should first win their favour and afterwards their love.

"These thoughts **exhilarated** me and led me

---

inquisitive [inkwízətiv] adj.
캐묻는, 탐구적인
arbiter [á:rbitər] n.
중재인, 조정자
demeanor [dimí:nər] n.
태도, 품행

exhilarate [igzílərèit] v.
기분을 돋우다, 유쾌하게 하다

execration [eksikréiʃən] n. 매도, 통렬한 비난

to apply with fresh ardour to the acquiring the art of language. My organs were indeed harsh, but supple; and although my voice was very unlike the soft music of their tones, yet I pronounced such words as I understood with tolerable ease. It was as the ass and the lap-dog; yet surely the gentle ass whose intentions were affectionate, although his manners were rude, deserved better treatment than blows and **execration**.

"The pleasant showers and genial warmth of spring greatly altered the aspect of the earth. Men who before this change seemed to have been hid in caves dispersed themselves and were employed in various arts of cultivation. The birds sang in more cheerful notes, and the leaves began to bud forth on the trees. Happy, happy earth! Fit habitation for gods, which, so short a time before, was bleak, damp, and unwholesome. My spirits were elevated by the enchanting appearance of nature; the past was blotted from my memory, the present was tranquil, and the future gilded by bright rays of hope and anticipations of joy."

Chapter 13

"I now hasten to the more moving part of my story. I shall relate events that impressed me with feelings which, from what I had been, have made me what I am.

"Spring advanced rapidly; the weather became fine and the skies cloudless. It surprised me that what before was desert and gloomy should now bloom with the most beautiful flowers and **verdure**. My senses were gratified and refreshed by a thousand scents of delight and a thousand sights of beauty.

"It was on one of these days, when my cottagers periodically rested from labour — the old man played on his guitar, and the children listened to him — that I observed the

verdure [və́:rdʒər] n. (초목의) 푸르름, 신록

countenance of Felix was melancholy beyond expression; he sighed frequently, and once his father paused in his music, and I conjectured by his manner that he inquired the cause of his son's sorrow. Felix replied in a cheerful accent, and the old man was recommencing his music when someone tapped at the door.

"It was a lady on horseback, accompanied by a country-man as a guide. The lady was dressed in a dark suit and covered with a thick black veil. Agatha asked a question, to which the stranger only replied by pronouncing, in a sweet accent, the name of Felix. Her voice was musical but unlike that of either of my friends. On hearing this word, Felix came up hastily to the lady, who, when she saw him, threw up her veil, and I beheld a countenance of angelic beauty and expression. Her hair of a shining raven black, and curiously braided; her eyes were dark, but gentle, although animated; her features of a regular proportion, and her complexion wondrously fair, each cheek tinged with a lovely pink.

"Felix seemed **ravished** with delight when he saw her, every trait of sorrow vanished from his face, and it instantly expressed a degree of ecstatic joy, of which I could hardly have believed it capable; his eyes sparkled, as his cheek flushed with pleasure; and at that moment I

ravish [rǽviʃ] v.
황홀하게 하다, 몹시 기쁘게 하다

dismount [dismáunt] v.
(말, 자전거 따위에서) 내리다
conduct [kəndʌ́kt] v.
인도하다, 안내하다
take place:
발생하다, 일어나다

thought him as beautiful as the stranger. She appeared affected by different feelings; wiping a few tears from her lovely eyes, she held out her hand to Felix, who kissed it rapturously and called her, as well as I could distinguish, his sweet Arabian. She did not appear to understand him, but smiled. He assisted her to **dismount**, and dismissing her guide, **conducted** her into the cottage. Some conversation **took place** between him and his father, and the young stranger knelt at the old man's feet and would have kissed his hand, but he raised her and embraced her affectionately.

articulate [ɑ:rtíkjəlit] adj.
명확한, 분명한
diffuse [difjú:z] v.
흩뜨리다, 발산하다
dissipate [dísəpèit] v.
사라지다, 흩어져 없어지다

"I soon perceived that although the stranger uttered **articulate** sounds and appeared to have a language of her own, she was neither understood by nor herself understood the cottagers. They made many signs which I did not comprehend, but I saw that her presence **diffused** gladness through the cottage, dispelling their sorrow as the sun **dissipates** the morning mists. Felix seemed peculiarly happy and with smiles of delight welcomed his Arabian. Agatha, the ever-gentle Agatha, kissed the hands of the lovely stranger, and pointing to her brother, made signs which appeared to me to mean that he had been sorrowful until she came. Some hours passed thus, while they, by their countenances, expressed joy, the cause of which I

recurrence [riká:rəns, -kʌ́r-] n.
재현, 재발, 반복

make use of:
~을 이용하다, 사용하다

did not comprehend. Presently I found, by the frequent **recurrence** of some sound which the stranger repeated after them, that she was endeavouring to learn their language; and the idea instantly occurred to me that I should **make use of** the same instructions to the same end. The stranger learned about twenty words at the first lesson; most of them, indeed, were those which I had before understood, but I profited by the others.

"As night came on, Agatha and the Arabian retired early. When they separated Felix kissed the hand of the stranger and said, 'Good night sweet Safie.' He sat up much longer, conversing with his father, and by the frequent repetition of her name I conjectured that their lovely guest was the subject of their conversation. I ardently desired to understand them, and bent every faculty towards that purpose, but found it utterly impossible.

cadence [kéidəns] n.
운율, 박자

"The next morning Felix went out to his work, and after the usual occupations of Agatha were finished, the Arabian sat at the feet of the old man, and taking his guitar, played some airs so entrancingly beautiful that they at once drew tears of sorrow and delight from my eyes. She sang, and her voice flowed in a rich **cadence**, swelling or dying away like a nightingale of the woods.

air [ɛər] n.
멜로디, 가락, 곡조

herbage [hə́:rbidʒ] n.
풀, 목초

intersperse [ìntərspə́:rs] v.
흩뿌리다, 산재시키다

"When she had finished, she gave the guitar to Agatha, who at first declined it. She played a simple **air**, and her voice accompanied it in sweet accents, but unlike the wondrous strain of the stranger. The old man appeared enraptured and said some words which Agatha endeavoured to explain to Safie, and by which he appeared to wish to express that she bestowed on him the greatest delight by her music.

"The days now passed as peaceably as before, with the sole alteration that joy had taken place of sadness in the countenances of my friends. Safie was always gay and happy; she and I improved rapidly in the knowledge of language, so that in two months I began to comprehend most of the words uttered by my protectors.

"In the meanwhile also the black ground was covered with **herbage**, and the green banks **interspersed** with innumerable flowers, sweet to the scent and the eyes, stars of pale radiance among the moonlight woods; the sun became warmer, the nights clear and balmy; and my nocturnal rambles were an extreme pleasure to me, although they were considerably shortened by the late setting and early rising of the sun, for I never ventured abroad during daylight, fearful of meeting with the same treatment I had formerly endured in the first village which I entered.

"My days were spent in close attention, that I might more speedily master the language; and I may boast that I improved more rapidly than the Arabian, who understood very little and conversed in broken accents, whilst I comprehended and could imitate almost every word that was spoken.

"While I improved in speech, I also learned the science of letters as it was taught to the stranger, and this opened before me a wide field for wonder and delight.

"The book from which Felix instructed Safie was Volney's *Ruins of Empires*. I should not have understood the **purport** of this book **had not Felix**, in reading it, given very **minute** explanations. He had chosen this work, he said, because the **declamatory** style was framed in imitation of the Eastern authors. Through this work I obtained a **cursory** knowledge of history and a view of the several empires at present existing in the world; it gave me an **insight** into the manners, governments, and religions of the different nations of the earth. I heard of the **slothful Asiatics**, of the **stupendous** genius and mental activity of the Grecians, of the wars and wonderful virtue of the early Romans — of their subsequent degenerating — of the decline of that mighty empire, of

---

purport [pərpɔ́ːrt, pɔ́ːrpɔːrt] n.
의미, 의도
had not Felix:
if Flex had not
minute [mainjúːt, mi-] adj.
상세한, 정밀한, 세심한
declamatory [diklǽmətɔ̀ːri / -təri] adj.
연설조의, 웅변가투의
cursory [kə́ːrsəri] adj.
몹시 서두른, 조잡한, 피상적인
insight [ínsàit] n.
통찰, 통찰력
slothful [slóuθfəl, slɔ́ː-] adj.
나태한, 게으른, 굼뜬
Asiatic [èiʒiǽtik / -ʃi-] n.
아시아인
stupendous [stjuːpéndəs] adj.
엄청난, 굉장한

chivalry, Christianity, and kings. I heard of the discovery of the American hemisphere and wept with Safie over the **hapless** fate of its original inhabitants.

"These wonderful narrations inspired me with strange feelings. Was man, indeed, at once so powerful, so virtuous and magnificent, yet so vicious and base? He appeared at one time a mere **scion** of the evil principle and at another as all that can be conceived of noble and godlike. To be a great and virtuous man appeared the highest honour that can befall a sensitive being; to be base and vicious, as many on record have been, appeared the lowest **degradation**, a condition more **abject** than that of the blind mole or harmless worm. For a long time I could not conceive how one man could go forth to murder his fellow, or even why there were laws and governments; but when I heard details of vice and bloodshed, my wonder ceased and I turned away with disgust and loathing.

"Every conversation of the cottagers now opened new wonders to me. While I listened to the instructions which Felix bestowed upon the Arabian, the strange system of human society was explained to me. I heard of the division of property, of immense wealth and **squalid** poverty, of rank, **descent**, and noble

---

hapless [hǽplis] adj.
불운한, 불행한

scion [sáiən] n.
자손
degradation [dègrədéiʃən] n.
하강, 타락, 퇴화
abject [ǽbdʒekt] adj.
영락한, 비참한, 비열한

squalid [skwɑ́lid / skwɔ́l-] adj.
더러운, 누추한, 비열한
descent [disént] n.
가계, 혈통, 출신

unsullied [ʌnsʌ́lid] adj.
오점이 없는, 결백한
endue [indjúː, en-] v.
부여하다, 주다
deformed [difɔ́ːrmd] adj.
볼품없는, 불구의, 기형의
loathsome [lóuðsəm] adj.
싫은, 지긋지긋한, 불쾌한
subsist [səbsíst] v.
살아가다
blot [blɑt / blɔt] n.
얼룩, 더러움, 오점

blood.

"The words induced me to turn towards myself. I learned that the possessions most esteemed by your fellow creatures were high and **unsullied** descent united with riches. A man might be respected with only one of these advantages, but without either he was considered, except in very rare instances, as a vagabond and a slave, doomed to waste his powers for the profits of the chosen few! And what was I? Of my creation and creator I was absolutely ignorant, but I knew that I possessed no money, no friends, no kind of property. I was, besides, **endued** with a figure hideously **deformed** and **loathsome**; I was not even of the same nature as man. I was more agile than they and could **subsist** upon coarser diet; I bore the extremes of heat and cold with less injury to my frame; my stature far exceeded theirs. When I looked around I saw and heard of none like me. Was I, then, a monster, a **blot** upon the earth, from which all men fled and whom all men disowned?

"I cannot describe to you the agony that these reflections inflicted upon me; I tried to dispel them, but sorrow only increased with knowledge. Oh, that I had for ever remained in my native wood, nor known nor felt beyond the sensations of hunger, thirst, and heat!

"Of what a strange nature is knowledge! It clings to the mind when it has once seized on it like a **lichen** on the rock. I wished sometimes to shake off all thought and feeling, but I learned that there was but one means to overcome the sensation of pain, and that was death—a state which I feared yet did not understand. I admired virtue and good feelings and loved the gentle manners and amiable qualities of my cottagers, but I was shut out from intercourse with them, except through means which I obtained by stealth, when I was unseen and unknown, and which rather increased than satisfied the desire I had of becoming one among my fellows. The gentle words of Agatha and the animated smiles of the charming Arabian were not for me. The mild **exhortations** of the old man and the lively conversation of the loved Felix were not for me. Miserable, unhappy wretch!

"Other lessons were impressed upon me even more deeply. I heard of the difference of sexes, and the birth and growth of children, how the father **doted** on the smiles of the infant, and the lively sallies of the older child, how all the life and cares of the mother were wrapped up in the precious charge, how the mind of youth expanded and gained knowledge, of brother, sister, and all the various relationships which

recur [rikə́:r] v.
되풀이되다

bind one human being to another in mutual bonds.

"But where were my friends and relations? No father had watched my infant days, no mother had blessed me with smiles and caresses; or if they had, all my past life was now a blot, a blind vacancy in which I distinguished nothing. From my earliest remembrance I had been as I then was in height and proportion. I had never yet seen a being resembling me or who claimed any intercourse with me. What was I? The question again **recurred**, to be answered only with groans.

"I will soon explain to what these feelings tended, but allow me now to return to the cottagers, whose story excited in me such various feelings of indignation, delight, and wonder, but which all terminated in additional love and reverence for my protectors (for so I loved, in an innocent, half-painful self-deceit, to call them)."

Chapter 14

unfold [ʌ̀nfóuld] v.
드러나다, 밝혀지다

"Some time elapsed before I learned the history of my friends. It was one which could not fail to impress itself deeply on my mind, **unfolding** as it did a number of circumstances, each interesting and wonderful to one so utterly inexperienced as I was.

affluence [ǽflu(:)əns, əflú:-] n.
풍부함, 풍요, 유복
distinction [distíŋkʃən] n.
탁월함, 우수함, 고귀함

"The name of the old man was De Lacey. He was descended from a good family in France, where he had lived for many years in **affluence**, respected by his superiors and beloved by his equals. His son was bred in the service of his country, and Agatha had ranked with ladies of the highest **distinction**. A few months before my arrival they had lived in a large and luxurious city called Paris, surrounded by friends

obnoxious [əbnákʃəs / -nók-] adj. 밉살스러운, 불쾌한
flagrant [fléigrənt] adj. 현저하게 눈에 띄는, 명백한
indignant [indígnənt] adj. 성난, 화난

fruitless [frúːtlis] adj. 소용 없는, 무익한, 헛된
dungeon [dʌ́ndʒən] n. 지하 감옥
Muhammadan [muhǽmədən] n. 이슬람교도

and possessed of every enjoyment which virtue, refinement of intellect, or taste, accompanied by a moderate fortune, could afford.

"The father of Safie had been the cause of their ruin. He was a Turkish merchant and had inhabited Paris for many years, when, for some reason which I could not learn, he became **obnoxious** to the government. He was seized and cast into prison the very day that Safie arrived from Constantinople to join him. He was tried and condemned to death. The injustice of his sentence was very **flagrant**; all Paris was **indignant**; and it was judged that his religion and wealth rather than the crime alleged against him had been the cause of his condemnation.

"Felix had accidentally been present at the trial; his horror and indignation were uncontrollable when he heard the decision of the court. He made, at that moment, a solemn vow to deliver him and then looked around for the means. After many **fruitless** attempts to gain admittance to the prison, he found a strongly grated window in an unguarded part of the building, which lighted the **dungeon** of the unfortunate **Muhammadan**, who, loaded with chains, waited in despair the execution of the barbarous sentence. Felix visited the grate at night and made known to the prisoner his intentions in his favour. The Turk, amazed and delighted, endeavoured to kindle the zeal of his deliverer by promises of reward and wealth. Felix rejected his offers with contempt, yet when he saw the lovely Safie, who was allowed to visit her father and who by her gestures expressed her lively gratitude, the youth could not help owning to his own mind that the captive possessed a treasure which would fully reward his toil and hazard.

"The Turk quickly perceived the impression that his daughter had made on the heart of Felix and endeavoured to secure him more entirely in his interests by the promise of her hand in marriage so soon as he should be conveyed to a place of safety. Felix was too delicate to accept this offer, yet he **looked forward to** the probability of the event as to the **consummation** of his happiness.

"During the ensuing days, while the preparations were going forward for the escape of the merchant, the zeal of Felix was warmed by several letters that he received from this lovely girl, who found means to express her thoughts in the language of her lover by the aid of an old man, a servant of her father who understood French. She thanked him in the most ardent terms for his intended services towards her parent, and at the same time she

---

look forward to:
기대하다, 예상하다, 기다리다
consummation [kɑ̀nsəméiʃən / kɔ̀n-] n.
완성, 달성, 성취, 마무리

procure [proukjúər, prə-] v.
입수하다, 손에 넣다, 획득하다
substance [sʌ́bstəns] n.
요지, 요점, 골자

tenet [ténət, tíː-] n.
주의, 신조, 교리
indelibly [indéləbəli] adv.
지울 수 없게, 지워지지 않게, 씻을 수 없이
immure [imjúər] v.
감금하다, 가두다
infantile [ínfəntàil, -til] adj.
어린애 같은
emulation [èmjəléiʃən] n.
경쟁, 겨룸

gently deplored her own fate.

"I have copies of these letters, for I found means, during my residence in the hovel, to **procure** the implements of writing; and the letters were often in the hands of Felix or Agatha. Before I depart I will give them to you; they will prove the truth of my tale; but at present, as the sun is already far declined, I shall only have time to repeat the **substance** of them to you.

"Safie related that her mother was a Christian Arab, seized and made a slave by the Turks; recommended by her beauty, she had won the heart of the father of Safie, who married her. The young girl spoke in high and enthusiastic terms of her mother, who, born in freedom, spurned the bondage to which she was now reduced. She instructed her daughter in the **tenets** of her religion and taught her to aspire to higher powers of intellect and an independence of spirit forbidden to the female followers of Muhammad. This lady died, but her lessons were **indelibly** impressed on the mind of Safie, who sickened at the prospect of again returning to Asia and being **immured** within the walls of a harem, allowed only to occupy herself with **infantile** amusements, ill-suited to the temper of her soul, now accustomed to grand ideas and a noble **emulation** for virtue. The prospect of marrying a Christian and remaining in a country where women were allowed to take a rank in society was enchanting to her.

"The day for the execution of the Turk was fixed, but on the night previous to it he **quitted** his prison and before morning was distant many leagues from Paris. Felix had procured passports in the name of his father, sister, and himself. He had previously communicated his plan to the former, who aided the deceit by quitting his house, under the **pretence** of a journey and concealed himself, with his daughter, in an obscure part of Paris.

"Felix conducted the **fugitives** through France to Lyons and across Mont Cenis to Leghorn, where the merchant had decided to wait a favourable opportunity of passing into some part of the Turkish **dominions**.

"Safie resolved to remain with her father until the moment of his departure, before which time the Turk renewed his promise that she should be united to his deliverer; and Felix remained with them in expectation of that event; and in the meantime he enjoyed the society of the Arabian, who exhibited towards him the simplest and tenderest affection. They conversed with one another through the means of an interpreter, and sometimes with the interpretation of looks; and Safie sang to him the

---

quit [kwit] v.
떠나다, 물러나다
pretence [priténs] n.
구실, 핑계

fugitive [fjú:dʒətiv] n.
도주자, 도피자
dominion [dəmínjən] n.
지배, 통치, 주권

air [εər] n.
멜로디, 가락, 곡조
resentment [rizéntmənt] n.
노함, 분개
lukewarm [lú:kwɔ̀:rm] adj.
미온적인
betray [bitréi] v.
누설하다, 폭로하다
revolve [riválv / -vɔ́lv] v.
궁리하다, 곰곰이 생각하다
facilitate [fəsílətèit] v.
손쉽게 하다, 돕다, 촉진하다

enrage [enréidʒ] v.
노하게 하다, 분격시키다
spare [spεə:r] v.
아끼다, 삼가다
noisome [nɔ́isəm] adj.
해로운, 유독한, 불쾌한

divine **airs** of her native country.

"The Turk allowed this intimacy to take place and encouraged the hopes of the youthful lovers, while in his heart he had formed far other plans. He loathed the idea that his daughter should be united to a Christian, but he feared the **resentment** of Felix if he should appear **lukewarm**, for he knew that he was still in the power of his deliverer if he should choose to **betray** him to the Italian state which they inhabited. He **revolved** a thousand plans by which he should be enabled to prolong the deceit until it might be no longer necessary, and secretly to take his daughter with him when he departed. His plans were **facilitated** by the news which arrived from Paris.

"The government of France were greatly **enraged** at the escape of their victim and **spared** no pains to detect and punish his deliverer. The plot of Felix was quickly discovered, and De Lacey and Agatha were thrown into prison. The news reached Felix and roused him from his dream of pleasure. His blind and aged father and his gentle sister lay in a **noisome** dungeon while he enjoyed the free air and the society of her whom he loved. This idea was torture to him. He quickly arranged with the Turk that if the latter should find a favourable opportunity for escape before Felix could return to Italy, Safie should remain as a boarder at a **convent** at Leghorn; and then, quitting the lovely Arabian, he hastened to Paris and **delivered** himself up to the vengeance of the law, hoping to free De Lacey and Agatha by this proceeding.

"He did not succeed. They remained confined for five months before the trial took place, the result of which deprived them of their fortune and condemned them to a perpetual **exile** from their native country.

"They found a miserable asylum in the cottage in Germany, where I discovered them. Felix soon learned that the **treacherous** Turk, for whom he and his family endured such unheard-of oppression, on discovering that his deliverer was thus reduced to poverty and ruin, became a traitor to good feeling and honour and had quitted Italy with his daughter, insultingly sending Felix a **pittance** of money to aid him, as he said, in some plan of future maintenance.

"Such were the events that preyed on the heart of Felix and rendered him, when I first saw him, the most miserable of his family. He could have endured poverty, and while this distress had been the **meed** of his virtue, he gloried in it; but the **ingratitude** of the Turk and the loss of his beloved Safie were misfortunes more bitter and **irreparable**. The arrival of the Arabian now infused new life into his soul.

"When the news reached Leghorn that Felix was deprived of his wealth and rank, the merchant commanded his daughter to think no more of her lover, but to prepare to return to her native country. The generous nature of Safie was **outraged** by this command; she attempted to **expostulate** with her father, but he left her angrily, **reiterating** his tyrannical **mandate**.

"A few days after, the Turk entered his daughter's apartment and told her hastily that he had reason to believe that his residence at Leghorn had been **divulged** and that he should speedily be delivered up to the French government; he had consequently hired a vessel to convey him to Constantinople, for which city he should sail in a few hours. He intended to leave his daughter under the care of a confidential servant, to follow at her leisure with the greater part of his property, which had not yet arrived at Leghorn.

"When alone, Safie resolved in her own mind the plan of conduct that it would **become** her to pursue in this emergency. A residence in Turkey was **abhorrent** to her; her religion and her feelings were alike **averse** to it. By some papers of her father which fell into her hands

---

outrage [áutrèidʒ] v.
화나게 하다, 격분하게 하다
expostulate [ikspástʃulèit / -pós-] v.
충고하다, 설교하다
reiterate [ri:ítərèit] v.
되풀이하다
mandate [mǽndeit] n.
명령, 지령

divulge [diváldʒ, dai-] v.
누설하다, 밝히다, 폭로하다

become [bikám] v.
~에 어울리다, ~에 맞다
abhorrent [æbhɔ́:rənt, -hár-] adj. 몹시 싫은, 질색인
averse [əvə́:rs] adj
몹시 싫어하는

at length:
드디어, 마침내
attendant [əténdənt] n.
돌보는 사람, 시중드는 사람; 하인, 수행원

she heard of the exile of her lover and learnt the name of the spot where he then resided. She hesitated some time, but **at length** she formed her determination. Taking with her some jewels that belonged to her and a sum of money, she quitted Italy with an **attendant**, a native of Leghorn, but who understood the common language of Turkey, and departed for Germany.

"She arrived in safety at a town about twenty leagues from the cottage of De Lacey, when her attendant fell dangerously ill. Safie nursed her with the most devoted affection, but the poor girl died, and the Arabian was left alone, unacquainted with the language of the country and utterly ignorant of the customs of the world. She fell, however, into good hands. The Italian had mentioned the name of the spot for which they were bound, and after her death the woman of the house in which they had lived took care that Safie should arrive in safety at the cottage of her lover."

Chapter 15

deprecate [déprikèit] v.
비난하다, 경시하다
vice [vais] n.
악덕, 사악, 부도덕

incite [insáit] v.
자극하다, 격려하다, 선동하다

"Such was the history of my beloved cottagers. It impressed me deeply. I learned, from the views of social life which it developed, to admire their virtues and to **deprecate** the **vices** of mankind.

"As yet I looked upon crime as a distant evil, benevolence and generosity were ever present before me, **inciting** within me a desire to become an actor in the busy scene where so many admirable qualities were called forth and displayed. But in giving an account of the progress of my intellect, I must not omit a circumstance which occurred in the beginning of the month of August of the same year.

"One night during my accustomed visit to

leathern [léðə:rn] adj.
가죽의, 가죽으로 된
portmanteau [pɔ:rtmǽntou] n.
가죽 트렁크

dejection [didʒékʃən] n.
의기소침, 낙담
canvass [kǽnvəs] v.
점검하다, 검토하다, 토론하다
accord [əkɔ́:rd] v.
일치하다, 조화하다

the neighbouring wood where I collected my own food and brought home firing for my protectors, I found on the ground a **leathern portmanteau** containing several articles of dress and some books. I eagerly seized the prize and returned with it to my hovel. Fortunately the books were written in the language, the elements of which I had acquired at the cottage; they consisted of *Paradise Lost*, a volume of Plutarch's *Lives*, and the *Sorrows of Werter*. The possession of these treasures gave me extreme delight; I now continually studied and exercised my mind upon these histories, whilst my friends were employed in their ordinary occupations.

"I can hardly describe to you the effect of these books. They produced in me an infinity of new images and feelings, that sometimes raised me to ecstasy, but more frequently sunk me into the lowest **dejection**. In the *Sorrows of Werter*, besides the interest of its simple and affecting story, so many opinions are **canvassed** and so many lights thrown upon what had hitherto been to me obscure subjects that I found in it a never-ending source of speculation and astonishment. The gentle and domestic manners it described, combined with lofty sentiments and feelings, which had for their object something out of self, **accorded** well

pretension [priténʃən] n.
가장, 허식
disquisition [dìskwəzíʃən] n.
조사, 연구

unformed [ʌnfɔ́:rmd] adj.
아직 형체를 이루지 않은; 미발달의; 미숙한
lament [ləmént] v.
슬퍼하다, 비탄하다, 애도하다
annihilation [ənàiəléiʃən] n.
멸망, 소멸
hideous [hídiəs] adj.
무서운, 몹시 추한, 극악 무도한
whence [hwens] adv.
어디에서, 어디로부터
recur [rikə́:r] v.
되돌아가다, 되풀이되다

founder [fáundə:r] n.
설립자, 창시자

with my experience among my protectors and with the wants which were for ever alive in my own bosom. But I thought Werter himself a more divine being than I had ever beheld or imagined; his character contained no **pretension**, but it sank deep. The **disquisitions** upon death and suicide were calculated to fill me with wonder. I did not pretend to enter into the merits of the case, yet I inclined towards the opinions of the hero, whose extinction I wept, without precisely understanding it.

"As I read, however, I applied much personally to my own feelings and condition. I found myself similar yet at the same time strangely unlike to the beings concerning whom I read and to whose conversation I was a listener. I sympathised with and partly understood them, but I was **unformed** in mind; I was dependent on none and related to none. 'The path of my departure was free,' and there was none to **lament** my **annihilation**. My person was **hideous** and my stature gigantic. What did this mean? Who was I? What was I? **Whence** did I come? What was my destination? These questions continually **recurred**, but I was unable to solve them.

"The volume of Plutarch's *Lives* which I possessed contained the histories of the first **founders** of the ancient republics. This book

surpass [sərpǽs, -pάːs] v.
~보다 낫다, 능가하다, 뛰어나다
unacquainted [ʌ̀nəkwéintid]
adj. 모르는, 낯선, 생소한
assemblage [əsémblidʒ] n.
모임, 무리, 집단
ardour [άːrdər] n.
열정, 열의
lawgiver [lɔ́ːgìvəːr] n.
입법자, 법률 제정자
patriarchal [pèitriάːrkəl] adj.
족장의, 원로의, 존경할 만한

Who was I? What was I? Whence did I come? What was my destination?

had a far different effect upon me from the *Sorrows of Werter*. I learned from Werter's imaginations despondency and gloom, but Plutarch taught me high thoughts; he elevated me above the wretched sphere of my own reflections, to admire and love the heroes of past ages. Many things I read **surpassed** my understanding and experience. I had a very confused knowledge of kingdoms, wide extents of country, mighty rivers, and boundless seas. But I was perfectly **unacquainted** with towns and large **assemblages** of men. The cottage of my protectors had been the only school in which I had studied human nature, but this book developed new and mightier scenes of action. I read of men concerned in public affairs, governing or massacring their species. I felt the greatest **ardour** for virtue rise within me, and abhorrence for vice, as far as I understood the signification of those terms, relative as they were, as I applied them, to pleasure and pain alone. Induced by these feelings, I was of course led to admire peaceable **lawgivers**, Numa, Solon, and Lycurgus, in preference to Romulus and Theseus. The **patriarchal** lives of my protectors caused these impressions to take a firm hold on my mind; perhaps, if my first introduction to humanity had been made by a young soldier, burning for glory and slaughter, I

imbue [imbjúː] v.
감염시키다, 감화시키다, 불어넣다
omnipotent [ɑmnípətənt / ɔm-]
adj. 전능의
converse [kənvə́ːrs] v.
대화하다
emblem [émbləm] n.
상징, 표상
bliss [blis] n.
(더 없는) 행복, 희열
gall [gɔːl] n.
불쾌, 증오, 원한

Many times I considered Satan as the fitter emblem of my condition, for often, like him, when I viewed the bliss of my protectors, the bitter gall of envy rose within me.

decipher [disáifər] v.
풀다, 판독하다

should have been **imbued** with different sensations.

"But *Paradise Lost* excited different and far deeper emotions. I read it, as I had read the other volumes which had fallen into my hands, as a true history. It moved every feeling of wonder and awe that the picture of an **omnipotent** God warring with his creatures was capable of exciting. I often referred the several situations, as their similarity struck me, to my own. Like Adam, I was apparently united by no link to any other being in existence; but his state was far different from mine in every other respect. He had come forth from the hands of God a perfect creature, happy and prosperous, guarded by the especial care of his Creator; he was allowed to **converse** with and acquire knowledge from beings of a superior nature, but I was wretched, helpless, and alone. Many times I considered Satan as the fitter **emblem** of my condition, for often, like him, when I viewed the **bliss** of my protectors, the bitter **gall** of envy rose within me.

"Another circumstance strengthened and confirmed these feelings. Soon after my arrival in the hovel I discovered some papers in the pocket of the dress which I had taken from your laboratory. At first I had neglected them, but now that I was able to **decipher** the characters in which they were written, I began to study them with diligence. It was your journal of the four months that **preceded** my creation. You **minutely** described in these papers every step you took in the progress of your work; this history was mingled with accounts of domestic occurrences. You doubtless recollect these papers. Here they are. Everything is related in them which bears reference to my **accursed** origin; the whole detail of that series of disgusting circumstances which produced it is set in view; the minutest description of my **odious** and loathsome person is given, in language which painted your own horrors and rendered mine **indelible**. I sickened as I read. 'Hateful day when I received life!' I exclaimed in agony. '**Accursed** creator! Why did you form a monster so hideous that even *you* turned from me in disgust? God, in pity, made man beautiful and alluring, after his own image; but my form is a filthy type of yours, more horrid even from the very resemblance. Satan had his companions, fellow devils, to admire and encourage him, but I am solitary and abhorred.'

"These were the reflections of my hours of despondency and solitude; but when I contemplated the virtues of the cottagers, their amiable and benevolent dispositions, I persuaded myself

---

precede [prisíːd] v.
선행하다, 앞서다, 먼저 일어나다
minutely [mainjuːtli, mi-] adv.
세세하게, 상세하게, 정밀하게
accursed [əkə́ːrsid] adj.
저주받은, 불행한
odious [óudiəs] adj.
싫은, 미운, 가증스러운
indelible [indéləbəl] adj.
지울 수 없는
accursed [əkə́ːrsid] adj.
저주받은, 가증스런

'Accursed creator! Why did you form a monster so hideous that even *you* turned from me in disgust?

compassionate [kəmpǽʃənèit] v. 불쌍히 여기다, 동정하다
overlook [òuvərlúk] v. 관대히 봐주다, 눈감아주다
solicit [səlísit] v. 간청하다
sagacity [səgǽsəti] n. 현명함

that when they should become acquainted with my admiration of their virtues they would **compassionate** me and **overlook** my personal deformity. Could they turn from their door one, however monstrous, who **solicited** their compassion and friendship? I resolved, at least, not to despair, but in every way to fit myself for an interview with them which would decide my fate. I postponed this attempt for some months longer, for the importance attached to its success inspired me with a dread lest I should fail. Besides, I found that my understanding improved so much with every day's experience that I was unwilling to commence this undertaking until a few more months should have added to my **sagacity**.

tumultuous [tju:mʌ́ltʃuəs] adj. 떠들썩한, 거친, 무질서한
outcast [áutkæ̀st / -kɑ̀:st] n. 버림받은 사람, 추방자

"Several changes, in the meantime, took place in the cottage. The presence of Safie diffused happiness among its inhabitants, and I also found that a greater degree of plenty reigned there. Felix and Agatha spent more time in amusement and conversation, and were assisted in their labours by servants. They did not appear rich, but they were contented and happy; their feelings were serene and peaceful, while mine became every day more **tumultuous**. Increase of knowledge only discovered to me more clearly what a wretched **outcast** I was. I cherished hope, it is true, but it vanished when

I beheld my person reflected in water or my shadow in the moonshine, even as that **frail** image and that **inconstant** shade.

"I endeavoured to crush these fears and to **fortify** myself for the trial which in a few months I resolved to undergo; and sometimes I allowed my thoughts, unchecked by reason, to ramble in the fields of Paradise, and dared to fancy amiable and lovely creatures sympathising with my feelings and cheering my gloom; their angelic countenances breathed smiles of **consolation**. But it was all a dream; no Eve **soothed** my sorrows nor shared my thoughts; I was alone. I remembered Adam's **supplication** to his Creator. But where was mine? He had abandoned me, and in the bitterness of my heart I cursed him.

"Autumn passed thus. I saw, with surprise and grief, the leaves decay and fall, and nature again assume the **barren** and **bleak** appearance it had worn when I first beheld the woods and the lovely moon. Yet I did not **heed** the bleakness of the weather; I was better fitted by my **conformation** for the endurance of cold than heat. But my chief delights were the sight of the flowers, the birds, and all the gay apparel of summer; when those deserted me, I turned with more attention towards the cottagers. Their happiness was not decreased by the

---

frail [freil] adj.
허약한, 무른; 덧없는
inconstant [inkánstənt / -kɔ́n-] adj. 변하기 쉬운, 일정치 않은, 변덕스러운
fortify [fɔ́:rtəfài] v.
강하게 하다, 튼튼히 하다
consolation [kànsəléiʃən / kɔ̀n-] n.
위로, 위안
soothe [su:ð] v.
달래다, 진정시키다
supplication [sʌ̀pləkéiʃən] n.
탄원, 애원, 기원

barren [bǽrən] adj.
불모의, 메마른, 쓸모없는
bleak [bli:k] adj.
황량한, 쓸쓸한, 흐린
heed [hi:d] v.
주의하다, 조심하다
conformation [kànfɔ:rméiʃən / kɔ̀n-] n.
구조, 형태

yearn [jə:rn] v.
갈망하다

absence of summer. They loved and sympathised with one another; and their joys, depending on each other, were not interrupted by the casualties that took place around them. The more I saw of them, the greater became my desire to claim their protection and kindness; my heart **yearned** to be known and loved by these amiable creatures; to see their sweet looks directed towards me with affection was the utmost limit of my ambition. I dared not think that they would turn them from me with disdain and horror. The poor that stopped at their door were never driven away. I asked, it is true, for greater treasures than a little food or rest: I required kindness and sympathy; but I did not believe myself utterly unworthy of it.

"The winter advanced, and an entire revolution of the seasons had taken place since I awoke into life. My attention at this time was solely directed towards my plan of introducing myself into the cottage of my protectors. I revolved many projects, but that on which I finally fixed was to enter the dwelling when the blind old man should be alone. I had sagacity enough to discover that the unnatural hideousness of my person was the chief object of horror with those who had formerly beheld me. My voice, although harsh, had nothing terrible in it; I thought, therefore, that if in the absence of his children I could gain the good will and **mediation** of the old De Lacey, I might by his means be tolerated by my younger protectors.

"One day, when the sun shone on the red leaves that strewed the ground and diffused cheerfulness, although it denied warmth, Safie, Agatha, and Felix departed on a long country walk, and the old man, at his own desire, was left alone in the cottage. When his children had departed, he took up his guitar and played several mournful but sweet airs, more sweet and mournful than I had ever heard him play before. At first his countenance was illuminated with pleasure, but as he continued, thoughtfulness and sadness succeeded; at length, laying aside the instrument, he sat absorbed in reflection.

"My heart beat quick; this was the hour and moment of trial, which would decide my hopes or realise my fears. The servants were gone to a neighbouring fair. All was silent in and around the cottage; it was an excellent opportunity; yet, when I proceeded to execute my plan, my limbs failed me and I sank to the ground. Again I rose, and **exerting** all the firmness of which I was master, removed the planks which I had placed before my hovel to conceal my retreat. The fresh air revived me, and with renewed determination I approached the door of their cottage.

"I knocked. 'Who is there?' said the old man. 'Come in.'

"I entered. 'Pardon this intrusion,' said I; 'I am a traveller in **want** of a little rest; you would greatly **oblige** me if you would allow me to remain a few minutes before the fire.'

"'Enter,' said De Lacey, 'and I will try in what manner I can to relieve your wants; but, unfortunately, my children are from home, and as I am blind, I am afraid I shall find it difficult to procure food for you.'

"'Do not trouble yourself, my kind host; I have food; it is warmth and rest only that I need.'

"I sat down, and a silence **ensued**. I knew that every minute was precious to me, yet I remained **irresolute** in what manner to commence the interview, when the old man addressed me. 'By your language, stranger, I suppose you are my countryman; are you French?'

"'No; but I was educated by a French family and understand that language only. I am now going to claim the protection of some friends, whom I sincerely love, and of whose favour I have some hopes.'

"'Are they Germans?'

"'No, they are French. But let us change the subject. I am an unfortunate and deserted creature, I look around and I have no relation or

---

want [wɔ(:)nt, wɑnt] n.
결핍, 부족
oblige [əbláidʒ] v.
은혜를 베풀다, 소원을 들어주다

ensue[ensú:] v.
계속되다, 따라오다
irresolute [irézəlù:t] adj.
망설이는, 우유부단한

outcast [áutkæst / -kɑ̀ːst] n.
버림받은 사람, 추방자

cloud [klaud] v.
흐리게 하다, 더럽히다, 모호하게 하다
detestable [ditéstəbəl] adj.
혐오할, 몹시 싫은

undeceive [Ằndisíːv] v.
미혹을 깨우치다, 깨우쳐 주다, 깨닫게 하다
undertake [Ằndərtéik] v.
떠맡다, 시작하다

friend upon earth. These amiable people to whom I go have never seen me and know little of me. I am full of fears, for if I fail there, I am an **outcast** in the world for ever.'

"'Do not despair. To be friendless is indeed to be unfortunate, but the hearts of men, when unprejudiced by any obvious self-interest, are full of brotherly love and charity. Rely, therefore, on your hopes; and if these friends are good and amiable, do not despair.'

"'They are kind — they are the most excellent creatures in the world; but, unfortunately, they are prejudiced against me. I have good dispositions; my life has been hitherto harmless and in some degree beneficial; but a fatal prejudice **clouds** their eyes, and where they ought to see a feeling and kind friend, they behold only a **detestable** monster.'

"'That is indeed unfortunate; but if you are really blameless, cannot you **undeceive** them?'

"'I am about to **undertake** that task; and it is on that account that I feel so many overwhelming terrors. I tenderly love these friends; I have, unknown to them, been for many months in the habits of daily kindness towards them; but they believe that I wish to injure them, and it is that prejudice which I wish to overcome.'

"'Where do these friends reside?'

"'Near this spot.'

unreservedly [ʌ̀nrizə́:rvdli] adv. 기탄없이, 거리낌없이
confide [kənfáid] v. 비밀을 털어놓다, 개인 일을 이야기하다

instigate [ínstəgèit] v. 부추기다, 선동하다

benefactor [bénəfæ̀ktər] n. 은인, 후원자

"The old man paused and then continued, 'If you will **unreservedly confide** to me the particulars of your tale, I perhaps may be of use in undeceiving them. I am blind and cannot judge of your countenance, but there is something in your words which persuades me that you are sincere. I am poor and an exile, but it will afford me true pleasure to be in any way serviceable to a human creature.'

"'Excellent man! I thank you and accept your generous offer. You raise me from the dust by this kindness; and I trust that, by your aid, I shall not be driven from the society and sympathy of your fellow creatures.'

"'Heaven forbid! Even if you were really criminal, for that can only drive you to desperation, and not **instigate** you to virtue. I also am unfortunate; I and my family have been condemned, although innocent; judge, therefore, if I do not feel for your misfortunes.'

"'How can I thank you, my best and only **benefactor**? From your lips first have I heard the voice of kindness directed towards me; I shall be for ever grateful; and your present humanity assures me of success with those friends whom I am on the point of meeting.'

"'May I know the names and residence of those friends?'

"I paused. This, I thought, was the moment

desert [dizə́ːrt] v.
버리다, 포기하다, 돌보지 않다
trial [trái-əl] n.
시련, 고난, 재난

consternation [kɑ̀nstərnéiʃən / kɔ̀n-] n.
경악, 대경실색
transport [trǽnspɔ̀ːrt] n.
황홀, 도취, 열중
refrain [rifréin] v.
삼가다, 자제하다

of decision, which was to rob me of or bestow happiness on me for ever. I struggled vainly for firmness sufficient to answer him, but the effort destroyed all my remaining strength; I sank on the chair and sobbed aloud. At that moment I heard the steps of my younger protectors. I had not a moment to lose, but seizing the hand of the old man, I cried, 'Now is the time! Save and protect me! You and your family are the friends whom I seek. Do not you **desert** me in the hour of **trial**!'

"'Great God!' exclaimed the old man. 'Who are you?'

"At that instant the cottage door was opened, and Felix, Safie, and Agatha entered. Who can describe their horror and **consternation** on beholding me? Agatha fainted, and Safie, unable to attend to her friend, rushed out of the cottage. Felix darted forward, and with supernatural force tore me from his father, to whose knees I clung, in a **transport** of fury, he dashed me to the ground and struck me violently with a stick. I could have torn him limb from limb, as the lion rends the antelope. But my heart sank within me as with bitter sickness, and I **refrained**. I saw him on the point of repeating his blow, when, overcome by pain and anguish, I quitted the cottage, and in the general tumult escaped unperceived to my hovel."

Chapter 16

wantonly [wɔ́(:)nt-ənli, wán-] adv.
제멋대로, 변덕스럽게, 방자하게

"Cursed, cursed creator! Why did I live? Why, in that instant, did I not extinguish the spark of existence which you had so **wantonly** bestowed? I know not; despair had not yet taken possession of me; my feelings were those of rage and revenge. I could with pleasure have destroyed the cottage and its inhabitants and have glutted myself with their shrieks and misery.

toil [tɔil] n.
사냥감을 잡는 망, 덫, 함정
range [reindʒ] v.
헤매다, 떠돌아다니다

"When night came I quitted my retreat and wandered in the wood; and now, no longer restrained by the fear of discovery, I gave vent to my anguish in fearful howlings. I was like a wild beast that had broken the **toils**, destroying the objects that obstructed me and **ranging** through the wood with a stag-like swiftness. Oh! What a miserable night I passed! The cold stars shone in **mockery**, and the bare trees waved their branches above me; now and then the sweet voice of a bird burst forth amidst the universal stillness. All, **save** I, were at rest or in enjoyment; I, like the **arch-fiend**, bore a hell within me, and finding myself unsympathised with, wished to tear up the trees, spread **havoc** and destruction around me, and then to have sat down and enjoyed the ruin.

"But this was a luxury of sensation that could not endure; I became fatigued with excess of bodily exertion and sank on the damp grass in the sick **impotence** of despair. There was none among the **myriads** of men that existed who would pity or assist me; and should I feel kindness towards my enemies? No; from that moment I declared **everlasting** war against the species, and more than all, against him who had formed me and sent me forth to this **insupportable** misery.

"The sun rose; I heard the voices of men and knew that it was impossible to return to my retreat during that day. Accordingly I hid myself in some thick underwood, determining to devote the ensuing hours to reflection on my situation.

"The pleasant sunshine and the pure air of

---

mockery [mákəri, mɔ́(:)k-] n.
비웃음, 조소
save [seiv] prep.
except, ~을 제외하고
archfiend [á:rtʃfí:nd] n.
악마의 우두머리; 마왕, 사탄
havoc [hǽvək] n.
대황폐, 대파괴

impotence [ímpətəns] n.
무기력, 무능
myriad [míriəd] n.
무수한 사람이나 물건
everlasting [èvərlǽstiŋ, -lɑ́:st-] adj.
영구한, 불후의, 끝없는
insupportable [ìnsəpɔ́:rtəbəl] adj.
참을 수 없는, 견딜 수 없는. 지지할 수 없는

"... from that moment I declared everlasting war against the species, and more than all, against him who had formed me and sent me forth to this insupportable misery."

tranquillity [træŋkwíləti] n.
평정, 평온, 침착
familiarize [fəmíljəràiz] v.
친하게 하다, 익숙케 하다
irretrievable [ìritríːvəbəl] adj.
돌이킬 수 없는, 회복할 수 없는

appease [əpíːz] v.
가라앉히다, 진정시키다

day restored me to some degree of **tranquillity**; and when I considered what had passed at the cottage, I could not help believing that I had been too hasty in my conclusions. I had certainly acted imprudently. It was apparent that my conversation had interested the father in my behalf, and I was a fool in having exposed my person to the horror of his children. I ought to have **familiarised** the old De Lacey to me, and by degrees to have discovered myself to the rest of his family, when they should have been prepared for my approach. But I did not believe my errors to be **irretrievable**, and after much consideration I resolved to return to the cottage, seek the old man, and by my representations win him to my party.

"These thoughts calmed me, and in the afternoon I sank into a profound sleep; but the fever of my blood did not allow me to be visited by peaceful dreams. The horrible scene of the preceding day was for ever acting before my eyes; the females were flying and the enraged Felix tearing me from his father's feet. I awoke exhausted, and finding that it was already night, I crept forth from my hiding-place, and went in search of food.

"When my hunger was **appeased**, I directed my steps towards the well-known path that conducted to the cottage. All there was at peace.

I crept into my hovel and remained in silent expectation of the accustomed hour when the family arose. That hour passed, the sun mounted high in the heavens, but the cottagers did not appear. I trembled violently, apprehending some dreadful misfortune. The inside of the cottage was dark, and I heard no motion; I cannot describe the agony of this suspense.

"Presently two countrymen passed by, but pausing near the cottage, they entered into conversation, using violent **gesticulations**; but I did not understand what they said, as they spoke the language of the country, which differed from that of my protectors. Soon after, however, Felix approached with another man; I was surprised, as I knew that he had not quitted the cottage that morning, and waited anxiously to discover from his **discourse** the meaning of these unusual appearances.

"'Do you consider,' said his companion to him, 'that you will be obliged to pay three months' rent and to lose the produce of your garden? I do not wish to take any unfair advantage, and I beg therefore that you will take some days to consider of your determination.'

"'It is utterly useless,' replied Felix; 'we can never again inhabit your cottage. The life of my father is in the greatest danger, owing to the dreadful circumstance that I have related.

---

gesticulation [ʤestìk-jəléiʃən] n.
(흥분한 듯한) 몸짓, 손짓
discourse [dískɔːrs] n.
회화, 이야기, 담화

reason [ríːz-ən] v.
설득하다, 이야기하다
tenement [ténəmənt] n.
가옥, 주택, 셋방

soothe [suːð] v.
달래다, 진정시키다
spurn [spəːrn] v.
퇴짜놓다, 걷어차다
combustible [kəmbʌ́stəbəl] n.
연소물, 가연물
vestige [véstidʒ] n.
자취, 흔적

My wife and my sister will never recover from their horror. I entreat you not to **reason** with me any more. Take possession of your **tenement** and let me fly from this place.'

"Felix trembled violently as he said this. He and his companion entered the cottage, in which they remained for a few minutes, and then departed. I never saw any of the family of De Lacey more.

"I continued for the remainder of the day in my hovel in a state of utter and stupid despair. My protectors had departed and had broken the only link that held me to the world. For the first time the feelings of revenge and hatred filled my bosom, and I did not strive to control them, but allowing myself to be borne away by the stream, I bent my mind towards injury and death. When I thought of my friends, of the mild voice of De Lacey, the gentle eyes of Agatha, and the exquisite beauty of the Arabian, these thoughts vanished and a gush of tears somewhat **soothed** me. But again when I reflected that they had **spurned** and deserted me, anger returned, a rage of anger, and unable to injure anything human, I turned my fury towards inanimate objects. As night advanced, I placed a variety of **combustibles** around the cottage, and after having destroyed every **vestige** of cultivation in the garden, I waited with forced impatience until the moon had sunk to commence my operations.

"As the night advanced, a fierce wind arose from the woods and quickly dispersed the clouds that had loitered in the heavens; the blast tore along like a mighty avalanche and produced a kind of insanity in my spirits that burst all bounds of reason and reflection. I lighted the dry branch of a tree and danced with fury around the devoted cottage, my eyes still fixed on the western horizon, the edge of which the moon nearly touched. A part of its orb was at length hid, and I waved my brand; it sank, and with a loud scream I fired the straw, and heath, and bushes, which I had collected. The wind fanned the fire, and the cottage was quickly enveloped by the flames, which clung to it and licked it with their forked and destroying tongues.

"As soon as I was convinced that no assistance could save any part of the habitation, I quitted the scene and sought for refuge in the woods.

"And now, with the world before me, **whither** should I bend my steps? I resolved to fly far from the scene of my misfortunes; but to me, hated and despised, every country must be equally horrible. At length the thought of you **crossed my mind**. I learned from your papers that you were my father, my creator; and to

whither [hwíðə:r] adv.
어디로
cross one's mind:
떠오르다, 생각나다

whom could I apply with more fitness than to him who had given me life? Among the lessons that Felix had bestowed upon Safie, geography had not been omitted; I had learned from these the relative situations of the different countries of the earth. You had mentioned Geneva as the name of your native town, and towards this place I resolved to proceed.

"But how was I to direct myself? I knew that I must travel in a southwesterly direction to reach my destination, but the sun was my only guide. I did not know the names of the towns that I was to pass through, nor could I ask information from a single human being; but I did not despair. From you only could I hope for **succour**, although towards you I felt no sentiment but that of hatred. **Unfeeling**, **heartless** creator! You had endowed me with perceptions and passions and then cast me abroad an object for the scorn and horror of mankind. But on you only had I any claim for pity and **redress**, and from you I determined to seek that justice which I vainly attempted to gain from any other being that wore the human form.

"My travels were long and the sufferings I endured intense. It was late in autumn when I quitted the district where I had so long resided. I travelled only at night, fearful of

succor [sʌ́kər] n.
구조, 원조
unfeeling [ʌnfíːliŋ] adj.
느낌이 없는; 무정한, 냉혹한
heartless [háːrtlis] adj.
무정한, 매정한
redress [ríːdres, ridrés] n.
배상, 보상, 구제

encountering the visage of a human being. Nature decayed around me, and the sun became heatless; rain and snow poured around me; mighty rivers were frozen; the surface of the earth was hard and chill, and bare, and I found no shelter. Oh, earth! How often did I **imprecate** curses on the cause of my being! The mildness of my nature had fled, and all within me was turned to gall and bitterness. The nearer I approached to your habitation, the more deeply did I feel the spirit of revenge **enkindled** in my heart. Snow fell, and the waters were hardened, but I rested not. A few incidents now and then directed me, and I possessed a map of the country; but I often wandered wide from my path. The agony of my feelings allowed me no **respite**; no incident occurred from which my rage and misery could not extract its food; but a circumstance that happened when I arrived on the **confines** of Switzerland, when the sun had recovered its warmth and the earth again began to look green, confirmed in an especial manner the bitterness and horror of my feelings.

"I generally rested during the day and travelled only when I was secured by night from the view of man. One morning, however, finding that my path lay through a deep wood, I ventured to continue my journey after the sun had

---

imprecate [ímprikèit] v.
(재앙 등을) 빌다, 저주하다
enkindle [enkíndl] v.
(불을) 붙이다, 태우다, 타오르게 하다
respite [réspit] n.
연기, 유예, 휴식
confine [kánfain / kɔ́n-] n.
경계, 국경

bedew [bidjúː] v.
이슬(눈물)로 적시다

risen; the day, which was one of the first of spring, cheered even me by the loveliness of its sunshine and the balminess of the air. I felt emotions of gentleness and pleasure, that had long appeared dead, revive within me. Half surprised by the novelty of these sensations, I allowed myself to be borne away by them, and forgetting my solitude and deformity, dared to be happy. Soft tears again **bedewed** my cheeks, and I even raised my humid eyes with thankfulness towards the blessed sun, which bestowed such joy upon me.

"I continued to wind among the paths of the wood, until I came to its boundary, which was skirted by a deep and rapid river, into which many of the trees bent their branches, now budding with the fresh spring. Here I paused, not exactly knowing what path to pursue, when I heard the sound of voices, that induced me to conceal myself under the shade of a cypress. I was scarcely hid when a young girl came running towards the spot where I was concealed, laughing, as if she ran from someone in sport. She continued her course along the precipitous sides of the river, when suddenly her foot slipped, and she fell into the rapid stream. I rushed from my hiding-place and with extreme labour, from the force of the current, saved her and dragged her to shore.

rustic [rʌ́stik] n.
시골 사람, 농부

She was senseless, and I endeavoured by every means in my power to restore animation, when I was suddenly interrupted by the approach of a **rustic**, who was probably the person from whom she had playfully fled. On seeing me, he darted towards me, and tearing the girl from my arms, hastened towards the deeper parts of the wood. I followed speedily, I hardly knew why; but when the man saw me draw near, he aimed a gun, which he carried, at my body and fired. I sank to the ground, and my injurer, with increased swiftness, escaped into the wood.

"This was then the reward of my benevolence! I had saved a human being from destruction, and as a **recompense** I now **writhed** under the miserable pain of a wound which shattered the flesh and bone. The feelings of kindness and gentleness which I had **entertained** but a few moments before **gave place to** hellish rage and gnashing of teeth. Inflamed by pain, I vowed eternal hatred and vengeance to all mankind. But the agony of my wound overcame me; my pulses paused, and I fainted.

recompense [rékəmpèns] n.
보수, 보답
writhe [raið] v.
몸부림치다, 괴로워하다, 고민하다
entertain [èntərtéin] v.
마음에 품다, 생각하다
give place to:
~으로 바뀌다

Inflamed by pain, I vowed eternal hatred and vengeance to all mankind.

"For some weeks I led a miserable life in the woods, endeavouring to cure the wound which I had received. The ball had entered my shoulder, and I knew not whether it had remained there or passed through; at any rate I had no means of extracting it. My sufferings were

augment [ɔ:gmént] v.
늘리다, 증대하다
oppressive [əprésiv] adj.
도가 지나친, 불쾌하게 하는

alleviate [əlí:vièit] v.
경감하다, 완화하다, 누그러뜨리다

toil [tɔil] n.
힘드는 일, 수고, 노고

prospect [práspekt / prɔ́s-] n.
조망, 전망, 경치
stupendous [stju:péndəs] adj.
엄청난, 놀란 만한, 굉장한

augmented also by the **oppressive** sense of the injustice and ingratitude of their infliction. My daily vows rose for revenge — a deep and deadly revenge, such as would alone compensate for the outrages and anguish I had endured.

"After some weeks my wound healed, and I continued my journey. The labours I endured were no longer to be **alleviated** by the bright sun or gentle breezes of spring; all joy was but a mockery which insulted my desolate state and made me feel more painfully that I was not made for the enjoyment of pleasure.

"But my **toils** now drew near a close, and in two months from this time I reached the environs of Geneva.

"It was evening when I arrived, and I retired to a hiding-place among the fields that surround it to meditate in what manner I should apply to you. I was oppressed by fatigue and hunger and far too unhappy to enjoy the gentle breezes of evening or the **prospect** of the sun setting behind the **stupendous** mountains of Jura.

"At this time a slight sleep relieved me from the pain of reflection, which was disturbed by the approach of a beautiful child, who came running into the recess I had chosen, with all the sportiveness of infancy. Suddenly, as I gazed on him, an idea seized me that this little creature was unprejudiced and had lived too short a time to have **imbibed** a horror of deformity. If, therefore, I could seize him and educate him as my companion and friend, I should not be so desolate in this peopled earth.

"Urged by this impulse, I seized on the boy as he passed and drew him towards me. As soon as he beheld my form, he placed his hands before his eyes and uttered a shrill scream; I drew his hand forcibly from his face and said, 'Child, what is the meaning of this? I do not intend to hurt you; listen to me.'

"He struggled violently. 'Let me go,' he cried; 'monster! Ugly wretch! You wish to eat me and tear me to pieces. You are an **ogre**. Let me go, or I will tell my papa.'

"'Boy, you will never see your father again; you must come with me.'

"'Hideous monster! Let me go. My papa is a **syndic** — he is M. Frankenstein — he will punish you. You dare not keep me.'

"'Frankenstein! You belong then to my enemy — to him towards whom I have sworn eternal revenge; you shall be my first victim.'

"The child still struggled and loaded me with epithets which carried despair to my heart; I grasped his throat to silence him, and in a moment he lay dead at my feet.

"I gazed on my victim, and my heart swelled

---

imbibe [imbáib] v.
(사상 등을) 받아들이다, 동화하다

ogre [óugər] n.
괴물, 도깨비

syndic [síndik] n.
지방 행정관

with exultation and hellish triumph; clapping my hands, I exclaimed, 'I too can create desolation; my enemy is not invulnerable; this death will carry despair to him, and a thousand other miseries shall torment and destroy him.'

"As I fixed my eyes on the child, I saw something glittering on his breast. I took it; it was a portrait of a most lovely woman. **In spite of** my **malignity**, it softened and attracted me. For a few moments I gazed with delight on her dark eyes, fringed by deep lashes, and her lovely lips; but presently my rage returned; I remembered that I was for ever deprived of the delights that such beautiful creatures could bestow and that she whose resemblance I contemplated would, in regarding me, have changed that air of divine **benignity** to one expressive of disgust and **affright**.

"Can you wonder that such thoughts **transported** me with rage? I only wonder that at that moment, instead of **venting** my sensations in exclamations and agony, I did not rush among mankind and perish in the attempt to destroy them.

"While I was overcome by these feelings, I left the spot where I had committed the murder, and seeking a more secluded hiding-place, I entered a barn which had appeared to me to be empty. A woman was sleeping on some straw;

she was young, not indeed so beautiful as her whose portrait I held, but of an agreeable aspect and blooming in the loveliness of youth and health. Here, I thought, is one of those whose joy-imparting smiles are bestowed on all but me. And then I bent over her and whispered, 'Awake, fairest, thy lover is near—he who would give his life but to obtain one look of affection from thine eyes; my beloved, awake!'

"The sleeper **stirred**; a thrill of terror ran through me. Should she indeed awake, and see me, and curse me, and **denounce** the murderer? Thus would she assuredly act if her darkened eyes opened and she beheld me. The thought was madness; it stirred the **fiend** within me—not I, but she, shall suffer; the murder I have committed because I am for ever robbed of all that she could give me, she shall atone. The crime had its source in her; be hers the punishment! Thanks to the lessons of Felix and the **sanguinary** laws of man, I had learned now to work mischief. I bent over her and placed the portrait securely in one of the folds of her dress. She moved again, and I fled.

"For some days I **haunted** the spot where these scenes had taken place, sometimes wishing to see you, sometimes resolved to quit the world and its miseries for ever. At length I wandered towards these mountains, and have

---

stir [stə:r] v.
움직이다, 뒤척이다
denounce [dináuns] v.
고발하다, 고소하다
fiend [fi:nd] n.
마귀, 악령, 악한
sanguinary [sǽŋgwənèri / -nəri] adj.
피비린내나는, 살벌한, 포악한

haunt [hɔ:nt, hɑ:nt] v.
종종 방문하다, 빈번히 들르다

consume [kənsúːm] v.
마음을 빼앗다, 열중시키다, 사로잡다
gratify [grǽtəfài] v.
기쁘게 하다, 만족시키다
comply [kəmplái] v.
따르다, 응하다
requisition [rèkwəzíʃ-ən] n.
요구, 청구
associate [əsóuʃièit] v.
교제하다, 사귀다
deformed [difɔ́ːrmd] adj.
볼품없는, 불구의, 기형의

ranged through their immense recesses, **consumed** by a burning passion which you alone can **gratify**. We may not part until you have promised to **comply** with my **requisition**. I am alone and miserable; man will not **associate** with me; but one as **deformed** and horrible as myself would not deny herself to me. My companion must be of the same species and have the same defects. This being you must create."

"... My companion must be of the same species and have the same defects. This being you must create."

Chapter 17

proposition [pràpəzíʃən / pràp-] n.
제안, 발의, 건의
concede [kənsí:d] v.
인정하다, 시인하다, 양보하다

The being finished speaking and fixed his looks upon me in the expectation of a reply. But I was bewildered, perplexed, and unable to arrange my ideas sufficiently to understand the full extent of his **proposition**. He continued, "You must create a female for me with whom I can live in the interchange of those sympathies necessary for my being. This you alone can do, and I demand it of you as a right which you must not refuse to **concede**."

kindle [kíndl] v.
불을 붙이다, 타오르게 하다, 선동하다
anew [ənjú:] adv.
다시, 새로이
suppress [səprés] v.
억누르다, 참다

The latter part of his tale had **kindled anew** in me the anger that had died away while he narrated his peaceful life among the cottagers, and as he said this I could no longer **suppress** the rage that burned within me.

extort [ikstɔ́:rt] v.
억지로 빼앗다, 강탈하다, 강요하다
desolate [désəlèit] v.
황폐하게 하다, 살지 못하게 하다

reason [rí:z-ən] v.
설득하다, 이야기하다
malicious [məlíʃəs] adj.
악의적인, 심술궂은
shun [ʃʌn] v.
피하다, 비키다, 멀리하다
tear [tɛə:r] v.
찢다, 째다, 잡아뜯다
precipitate [prisípətèit] v.
곤두박이치게 하다, 떨어뜨리다
insurmountable [ìnsər-máuntəbəl] adj.
극복할 수 없는, 넘을 수 없는
abject [ǽbdʒekt] adj.
영락한, 비참한, 비열한
inextinguishable [ìnikstíŋ-wiʃəbəl] adj.
끌 수 없는, 억누를 수 없는, 멈출 수 없는

"I do refuse it," I replied; "and no torture shall ever **extort** a consent from me. You may render me the most miserable of men, but you shall never make me base in my own eyes. Shall I create another like yourself, whose joint wickedness might **desolate** the world. Begone! I have answered you; you may torture me, but I will never consent."

"You are in the wrong," replied the fiend; "and instead of threatening, I am content to **reason** with you. I am **malicious** because I am miserable. Am I not **shunned** and hated by all mankind? You, my creator, would **tear** me to pieces and triumph; remember that, and tell me why I should pity man more than he pities me? You would not call it murder if you could **precipitate** me into one of those ice-rifts and destroy my frame, the work of your own hands. Shall I respect man when he condemns me? Let him live with me in the interchange of kindness, and instead of injury I would bestow every benefit upon him with tears of gratitude at his acceptance. But that cannot be; the human senses are **insurmountable** barriers to our union. Yet mine shall not be the submission of **abject** slavery. I will revenge my injuries; if I cannot inspire love, I will cause fear, and chiefly towards you my arch-enemy, because my creator, do I swear **inextinguishable** hatred.

fiendish [fíːndiʃ] adj.
악마 같은, 극악무도한
contortion [kəntɔ́ːrʃən] n.
뒤틀림, 일그러짐
detrimental [dètrəméntl] adj.
유해한, 손해되는
bliss [blis] n.
천상의 기쁨; 천국, 낙원
gratification [græ̀təfikéiʃən] n.
만족, 기쁨
content [kəntént] v.
만족시키다, (~에) 만족하다

"... Yet mine shall not be the submission of abject slavery. I will revenge my injuries; if I cannot inspire love, I will cause fear, and chiefly towards you my arch-enemy, ..."

Have a care; I will work at your destruction, nor finish until I desolate your heart, so that you shall curse the hour of your birth."

A **fiendish** rage animated him as he said this; his face was wrinkled into **contortions** too horrible for human eyes to behold; but presently he calmed himself and proceeded— "I intended to reason. This passion is **detrimental** to me, for you do not reflect that *you* are the cause of its excess. If any being felt emotions of benevolence towards me, I should return them a hundred and a hundredfold; for that one creature's sake I would make peace with the whole kind! But I now indulge in dreams of **bliss** that cannot be realised. What I ask of you is reasonable and moderate; I demand a creature of another sex, but as hideous as myself; the **gratification** is small, but it is all that I can receive, and it shall **content** me. It is true, we shall be monsters, cut off from all the world; but on that account we shall be more attached to one another. Our lives will not be happy, but they will be harmless and free from the misery I now feel. Oh! My creator, make me happy; let me feel gratitude towards you for one benefit! Let me see that I excite the sympathy of some existing thing; do not deny me my request!"

I was moved. I shuddered when I thought

of the possible consequences of my consent, but I felt that there was some justice in his argument. His tale and the feelings he now expressed proved him to be a creature of fine sensations, and did I not as his maker owe him all the portion of happiness that it was in my power to bestow? He saw my change of feeling and continued,

"If you consent, neither you nor any other human being shall ever see us again; I will go to the vast wilds of South America. My food is not that of man; I do not destroy the lamb and the kid to **glut** my appetite; acorns and berries afford me sufficient nourishment. My companion will be of the same nature as myself and will be content with the same **fare**. We shall make our bed of dried leaves; the sun will shine on us as on man and will ripen our food. The picture I present to you is peaceful and human, and you must feel that you could deny it only in the **wantonness** of power and cruelty. **Pitiless** as you have been towards me, I now see compassion in your eyes; let me seize the favourable moment and persuade you to promise what I so ardently desire."

"You propose," replied I, "to fly from the habitations of man, to dwell in those wilds where the beasts of the field will be your only companions. How can you, who long for the love and sympathy of man, **persevere** in this exile? You will return and again seek their kindness, and you will meet with their **detestation**; your evil passions will be renewed, and you will then have a companion to aid you in the task of destruction. This may not be; cease to argue the point, for I cannot consent."

"How **inconstant** are your feelings! But a moment ago you were moved by my representations, and why do you again harden yourself to my complaints? I swear to you, by the earth which I inhabit, and by you that made me, that with the companion you bestow, I will **quit** the neighbourhood of man and dwell, as it may chance, in the most savage of places. My evil passions will have fled, for I shall meet with sympathy! My life will flow quietly away, and in my dying moments I shall not curse my maker."

His words had a strange effect upon me. I **compassionated** him and sometimes felt a wish to **console** him, but when I looked upon him, when I saw the filthy mass that moved and talked, my heart sickened and my feelings were altered to those of horror and hatred. I tried to **stifle** these sensations; I thought that as I could not sympathise with him, I had no right to **withhold** from him the small portion of happiness which was yet in my power to bestow.

"You swear," I said, "to be harmless; but have you not already shown a degree of **malice** that should reasonably make me **distrust** you? May not even this be a **feint** that will increase your triumph by affording a wider **scope** for your revenge?"

"How is this? I must not be trifled with, and I demand an answer. If I have no ties and no affections, hatred and vice must be my **portion**; the love of another will destroy the cause of my crimes, and I shall become a thing of whose existence everyone will be ignorant. My vices are the children of a forced solitude that I abhor, and my virtues will necessarily arise when I live in **communion** with an equal. I shall feel the affections of a sensitive being and become linked to the chain of existence and events from which I am now excluded."

I paused some time to reflect on all he had related and the various arguments which he had employed. I thought of the promise of virtues which he had displayed on the opening of his existence and the subsequent **blight** of all kindly feeling by the loathing and scorn which his protectors had **manifested** towards him. His power and threats were not omitted in my calculations; a creature who could exist in the ice-caves of the glaciers and hide himself from pursuit among the ridges of **inaccessible precipices** was a being possessing faculties it would be vain to **cope** with. After a long pause of reflection I concluded that the justice due both to him and my fellow creatures demanded of me that I should **comply** with his request. Turning to him, therefore, I said,

"I consent to your demand, on your solemn oath to quit Europe for ever, and every other place in the neighbourhood of man, as soon as I shall deliver into your hands a female who will accompany you in your exile."

"I swear," he cried, "by the sun, and by the blue sky of heaven, and by the fire of love that burns my heart, that if you grant my prayer, while they exist you shall never behold me again. Depart to your home and commence your labours; I shall watch their progress with unutterable anxiety; and fear not but that when you are ready I shall appear."

Saying this, he suddenly quitted me, fearful, perhaps, of any change in my sentiments. I saw him descend the mountain with greater speed than the flight of an eagle, and quickly lost among the **undulations** of the sea of ice.

His tale had occupied the whole day, and the sun was upon the verge of the horizon when he departed. I knew that I ought to hasten my descent towards the valley, as I should soon

solemnity [səlémnəti] n.
장엄, 엄숙, 근엄
stir [stəːr] v.
(감정 등을) 움직이다, 불러일으키다
nought [nɔːt, nɑːt] n.
제로, 무(無)

weigh on/upon:
슬프게 하다, 우울하게 하다, 걱정하게 하다
siroc [sirák / -rók] n.
열풍(아프리카에서 남유럽으로 몰아쳐 오는 바람); 강열풍
consume [kənsúːm] v.
없애다, 파괴하다, 소멸시키다

be encompassed in darkness; but my heart was heavy, and my steps slow. The labour of winding among the little paths of the mountain and fixing my feet firmly as I advanced perplexed me, occupied as I was by the emotions which the occurrences of the day had produced. Night was far advanced when I came to the halfway resting-place and seated myself beside the fountain. The stars shone at intervals as the clouds passed from over them; the dark pines rose before me, and every here and there a broken tree lay on the ground; it was a scene of wonderful **solemnity** and **stirred** strange thoughts within me. I wept bitterly, and clasping my hands in agony, I exclaimed, "Oh! Stars and clouds and winds, ye are all about to mock me; if ye really pity me, crush sensation and memory; let me become as **nought**; but if not, depart, depart, and leave me in darkness."

These were wild and miserable thoughts, but I cannot describe to you how the eternal twinkling of the stars **weighed upon** me and how I listened to every blast of wind as if it were a dull ugly **siroc** on its way to **consume** me.

Morning dawned before I arrived at the village of Chamounix; I took no rest, but returned immediately to Geneva. Even in my own heart I could give no expression to my

haggard [hǽgərd] adj.
수척한, 초췌한
ban [bæn] n.
저주, 파문
adoration [æ̀dəréiʃən] n.
예배, 숭배, 동경

sensations — they weighed on me with a mountain's weight and their excess destroyed my agony beneath them. Thus I returned home, and entering the house, presented myself to the family. My **haggard** and wild appearance awoke intense alarm, but I answered no question, scarcely did I speak. I felt as if I were placed under a **ban** — as if I had no right to claim their sympathies — as if never more might I enjoy companionship with them. Yet even thus I loved them to **adoration**; and to save them, I resolved to dedicate myself to my most abhorred task. The prospect of such an occupation made every other circumstance of existence pass before me like a dream, and that thought only had to me the reality of life.

Chapter 18

recommence [rìːkəméns] v.
재개하다, 다시 시작하다
repugnance [ripʌ́gnəns] n.
질색, 강한 반감
enjoin [endʒɔ́in] v.
요구하다
disquisition [dìskwəzíʃən] n.
조사, 연구
material [mətíːəriəl] adj.
중요한
cling [kliŋ] v.
집착하다, 매달리다
pretence [priténs] n.
구실, 핑계

Day after day, week after week, passed away on my return to Geneva; and I could not collect the courage to **recommence** my work. I feared the vengeance of the disappointed fiend, yet I was unable to overcome my **repugnance** to the task which was **enjoined** me. I found that I could not compose a female without again devoting several months to profound study and laborious **disquisition**. I had heard of some discoveries having been made by an English philosopher, the knowledge of which was **material** to my success, and I sometimes thought of obtaining my father's consent to visit England for this purpose; but I **clung** to every **pretence** of delay and shrank from taking

eradicate [irǽdəkèit] v.
근절하다, 박멸하다
overcast [òuvərkǽst, -káːst] v.
구름으로 덮다, 흐리게 하다,
어둡게 하다
listless [lístlis] adj.
무관심한, 늘어진, 굼뜬
composure [kəmpóuʒər] n.
침착, 평정
salutation [sæ̀ljətéiʃ-ən] n.
인사

conjecture [kəndʒéktʃər] n.
추측, 추리
as to ~:
~에 관하여

the first step in an undertaking whose immediate necessity began to appear less absolute to me. A change indeed had taken place in me; my health, which had hitherto declined, was now much restored; and my spirits, when unchecked by the memory of my unhappy promise, rose proportionably. My father saw this change with pleasure, and he turned his thoughts towards the best method of **eradicating** the remains of my melancholy, which every now and then would return by fits, and with a devouring blackness **overcast** the approaching sunshine. At these moments I took refuge in the most perfect solitude. I passed whole days on the lake alone in a little boat, watching the clouds and listening to the rippling of the waves, silent and **listless**. But the fresh air and bright sun seldom failed to restore me to some degree of **composure**, and on my return I met the **salutations** of my friends with a readier smile and a more cheerful heart.

It was after my return from one of these rambles that my father, calling me aside, thus addressed me, "I am happy to remark, my dear son, that you have resumed your former pleasures and seem to be returning to yourself. And yet you are still unhappy and still avoid our society. For some time I was lost in **conjecture as to** the cause of this, but yesterday an idea

conjure [kándʒər, kʌ́n-] v.
간청하다, 탄원하다, 부탁하다
avow [əváu] v.
인정하다
reserve [rizə́:rv] n.
삼감, 자제, 신중함
treble [tréb-əl] adj.
3배[겹, 중]의
exordium [igzɔ́:rdiəm, iksɔ́:r-] n.
첫머리, 서두
look forward to:
기대하다, 예상하다, 기다리다
occasion [əkéiʒən] v.
~을 야기하다, ~의 원인이 되다
poignant [pɔ́injənt] adj.
매서운, 통렬한

struck me, and if it is well founded, I **conjure** you to **avow** it. **Reserve** on such a point would be not only useless, but draw down **treble** misery on us all."

I trembled violently at his **exordium**, and my father continued —

"I confess, my son, that I have always **looked forward to** your marriage with our dear Elizabeth as the tie of our domestic comfort and the stay of my declining years. You were attached to each other from your earliest infancy; you studied together, and appeared, in dispositions and tastes, entirely suited to one another. But so blind is the experience of man that what I conceived to be the best assistants to my plan may have entirely destroyed it. You, perhaps, regard her as your sister, without any wish that she might become your wife. Nay, you may have met with another whom you may love; and considering yourself as bound in honour to Elizabeth, this struggle may **occasion** the **poignant** misery which you appear to feel."

"My dear father, reassure yourself. I love my cousin tenderly and sincerely. I never saw any woman who excited, as Elizabeth does, my warmest admiration and affection. My future hopes and prospects are entirely bound up in the expectation of our union."

"The expression of your sentiments of this

subject, my dear Victor, gives me more pleasure than I have for some time experienced. If you feel thus, we shall assuredly be happy, however present events may cast a gloom over us. But it is this gloom which appears to have taken so strong a hold of your mind that I wish to **dissipate**. Tell me, therefore, whether you object to an immediate **solemnisation** of the marriage. We have been unfortunate, and recent events have drawn us from that everyday tranquillity **befitting** my years and **infirmities**. You are younger; yet I do not suppose, possessed as you are of a competent fortune, that an early marriage would at all interfere with any future plans of honour and utility that you may have formed. Do not suppose, however, that I wish to dictate happiness to you or that a delay on your part would cause me any serious uneasiness. Interpret my words with **candour** and answer me, I **conjure** you, with confidence and sincerity."

I listened to my father in silence and remained for some time incapable of offering any reply. I revolved rapidly in my mind a multitude of thoughts and endeavoured to arrive at some conclusion. Alas! To me the idea of an immediate union with my Elizabeth was one of horror and dismay. I was bound by a solemn promise which I had not yet fulfilled

---

dissipate [dísəpèit] v.
흩뜨리다, 일소하다
solemnization [sὰləm-nizéiʃən / sɔ̀ləm-] n.
식을 올림, 예식 거행
befit [bifít] v.
걸맞다, 어울리다
infirmity [infə́:rməti] n.
허약, 쇠약, 병약
candor, candour [kǽndər] n.
공정, 정직, 솔직
conjure [kándʒər, kʌ́n-] v.
탄원하다, 부탁하다

manifold [mǽnəfòuld] adj.
다양한, 여러 가지의
impend [impénd] v.
임박하다, 바야흐로 일어나려 하다, 드리워지다
devoted [divóutid] adj.
충실한, 헌신적인
engagement [engéidʒmənt] n.
약속, 맹세, 계약

indispensable [ìndispénsəbəl] adj.
불가결의, 절대 필요한
dilatory [dílətɔ̀:ri / -təri] adj.
더딘, 꾸물거리는, 시간을 끄는
insurmountable [ìnsərmáuntəbəl] adj.
극복할 수 없는, 넘을 수 없는
aversion [əvə́:rʒən / -ʃən] n.
혐오, 반감
loathsome [lóuðsəm] adj.
싫은, 지긋지긋한, 불쾌한
harrowing [hǽrouiŋ] adj.
비참한, 괴로운
unearthly [ʌnə́:rθli] adj.
이 세상의 것이 아닌, 초자연적인, 괴상한
absent [ǽbsént] v.
자리를 비우다, 결석하다

and dared not break, or if I did, what **manifold** miseries might not **impend** over me and my **devoted** family! Could I enter into a festival with this deadly weight yet hanging round my neck and bowing me to the ground? I must perform my **engagement** and let the monster depart with his mate before I allowed myself to enjoy the delight of a union from which I expected peace.

I remembered also the necessity imposed upon me of either journeying to England or entering into a long correspondence with those philosophers of that country whose knowledge and discoveries were of **indispensable** use to me in my present undertaking. The latter method of obtaining the desired intelligence was **dilatory** and unsatisfactory; besides, I had an **insurmountable aversion** to the idea of engaging myself in my **loathsome** task in my father's house while in habits of familiar intercourse with those I loved. I knew that a thousand fearful accidents might occur, the slightest of which would disclose a tale to thrill all connected with me with horror. I was aware also that I should often lose all self-command, all capacity of hiding the **harrowing** sensations that would possess me during the progress of my **unearthly** occupation. I must **absent** myself from all I loved while thus employed. Once commenced, it would quickly be achieved, and I might be restored to my family in peace and happiness. My promise fulfilled, the monster would depart for ever. Or (so my fond fancy imaged) some accident might meanwhile occur to destroy him and put an end to my slavery for ever.

These feelings dictated my answer to my father. I expressed a wish to visit England, but concealing the true reasons of this request, I **clothed** my desires under a **guise** which excited no suspicion, while I urged my desire with an **earnestness** that easily induced my father to comply. After so long a period of an absorbing melancholy that resembled madness in its intensity and effects, he was glad to find that I was capable of taking pleasure in the idea of such a journey, and he hoped that change of scene and varied amusement would, before my return, have restored me entirely to myself.

The duration of my absence was left to my own choice; a few months, or at most a year, was the period contemplated. One **paternal** kind **precaution** he had taken to ensure my having a companion. Without previously communicating with me, he had, **in concert** with Elizabeth, arranged that Clerval should join me at Strasbourg. This interfered with the solitude I **coveted** for the **prosecution** of my task;

impediment [impédəmənt] n.
방해, 장애물
maddening [mǽdniŋ] adj
미치게 하는, 화나게 하는

averse [əvə́:rs] adj.
싫어하는, 반대하는
unparalleled [ʌnpǽrəlèld] adj.
비길 데 없는
enfranchise [enfrǽntʃaiz] v.
해방하다, 자유롭게 하다

haunt [hɔ:nt, hɑ:nt] v.
괴롭히다, 끊임없이 떠오르다

yet at the commencement of my journey the presence of my friend could in no way be an **impediment**, and truly I rejoiced that thus I should be saved many hours of lonely, **maddening** reflection. Nay, Henry might stand between me and the intrusion of my foe. If I were alone, would he not at times force his abhorred presence on me to remind me of my task or to contemplate its progress?

To England, therefore, I was bound, and it was understood that my union with Elizabeth should take place immediately on my return. My father's age rendered him extremely **averse** to delay. For myself, there was one reward I promised myself from my detested toils — one consolation for my **unparalleled** sufferings; it was the prospect of that day when, **enfranchised** from my miserable slavery, I might claim Elizabeth and forget the past in my union with her.

I now made arrangements for my journey, but one feeling **haunted** me which filled me with fear and agitation. During my absence I should leave my friends unconscious of the existence of their enemy and unprotected from his attacks, exasperated as he might be by my departure. But he had promised to follow me wherever I might go, and would he not accompany me to England? This imagination was dreadful in itself, but **soothing inasmuch as** it supposed the safety of my friends. I was agonised with the idea of the possibility that the reverse of this might happen. But through the whole period during which I was the slave of my creature I allowed myself to be governed by the impulses of the moment; and my present sensations strongly **intimated** that the fiend would follow me and **exempt** my family from the danger of his **machinations**.

It was in the latter end of September that I again quitted my native country. My journey had been my own suggestion, and Elizabeth therefore **acquiesced**, but she was filled with **disquiet** at the idea of my suffering, away from her, the **inroads** of misery and grief. It had been her care which provided me a companion in Clerval — and yet a man is blind to a thousand minute circumstances which call forth a woman's **sedulous** attention. She longed to bid me hasten my return; a thousand conflicting emotions rendered her **mute** as she bade me a tearful, silent farewell.

I threw myself into the carriage that was to convey me away, hardly knowing whither I was going, and careless of what was passing around. I remembered only, and it was with a bitter anguish that I reflected on it, to order that my chemical instruments should be packed

---

soothing [súːðiŋ] adj.
진정시키는, 누그러뜨리는
inasmuch as [ìnəzmʌ́tʃ-] conj.
~이므로, ~하므로
intimate [íntəmèit] v.
넌지시 비추다, 암시하다
exempt [igzémpt] v.
면제하다, 면해주다
machination [mæ̀kənéiʃ-ən] n.
책동, 간계, 음모

acquiesce [æ̀kwiés] v.
묵묵히 따르다, 묵인하다, 동의하다
disquiet [diskwáiət] n.
불안, 동요, 걱정
inroad [ínròud] n.
침입, 전진
sedulous [sédʒuləs] adj.
정성을 다하는, 공들인
mute [mjuːt] adj.
무언의, 말이 없는

unobserving [ʌ̀nəbzə́:rviŋ] adj.
부주의한, 무관심한
bourne [buə:rn, bɔ:rn] n.
목적지, 도달점

listless [lístlis] adj.
무관심한, 늘어진, 굼뜬
indolence [índələns] n.
나태, 게으름
traverse [trǽvə:rs, trəvə́:rs] v.
가로지르다, 횡단하다
wherefore [hwέə:rfɔ̀:r] adv.
(의문사) 무엇 때문에, 왜
avenue [ǽvənjù:] n.
(어떤 목적을 달성하기 위한)
수단, 방법, 길

to go with me. Filled with dreary imaginations, I passed through many beautiful and majestic scenes, but my eyes were fixed and **unobserving**. I could only think of the **bourne** of my travels and the work which was to occupy me whilst they endured.

After some days spent in **listless indolence**, during which I **traversed** many leagues, I arrived at Strasbourg, where I waited two days for Clerval. He came. Alas, how great was the contrast between us! He was alive to every new scene, joyful when he saw the beauties of the setting sun, and more happy when he beheld it rise and recommence a new day. He pointed out to me the shifting colours of the landscape and the appearances of the sky. "This is what it is to live," he cried; "now I enjoy existence! But you, my dear Frankenstein, **wherefore** are you desponding and sorrowful!" In truth, I was occupied by gloomy thoughts and neither saw the descent of the evening star nor the golden sunrise reflected in the Rhine. And you, my friend, would be far more amused with the journal of Clerval, who observed the scenery with an eye of feeling and delight, than in listening to my reflections. I, a miserable wretch, haunted by a curse that shut up every **avenue** to enjoyment.

We had agreed to descend the Rhine in a

boat from Strasbourg to Rotterdam, whence we might take shipping for London. During this voyage we passed many **willowy** islands and saw several beautiful towns. We stayed a day at Mannheim, and on the fifth from our departure from Strasbourg, arrived at Mainz. The course of the Rhine below Mainz becomes much more **picturesque**. The river descends rapidly and winds between hills, not high, but steep, and of beautiful forms. We saw many ruined castles standing on the edges of precipices, surrounded by black woods, high and inaccessible. This part of the Rhine, indeed, presents a singularly **variegated** landscape. In one spot you view rugged hills, ruined castles overlooking tremendous precipices, with the dark Rhine rushing beneath; and on the sudden turn of a **promontory**, flourishing **vineyards** with green sloping banks and a meandering river and populous towns occupy the scene.

We travelled at the time of the **vintage** and heard the song of the labourers as we glided down the stream. Even I, depressed in mind, and my spirits continually agitated by gloomy feelings, even I was pleased. I lay at the bottom of the boat, and as I gazed on the cloudless blue sky, I seemed to drink in a tranquillity to which I had long been a stranger. And if these

---

willowy [wíloui] adj.
버들이 무성한
picturesque [pìktʃərésk] adj.
그림같은, 아름다운
variegated [véəriəgèitid] adj.
변화가 많은, 다채로운
promontory [práməntɔ̀:ri / prɔ́məntəri] n.
곶, 갑(岬)
vineyard [vínjərd] n.
포도원

vintage [víntidʒ] n.
포도 수확(기)

were my sensations, who can describe those of Henry? He felt as if he had been transported to fairy-land and enjoyed a happiness seldom tasted by man. "I have seen," he said, "the most beautiful scenes of my own country; I have visited the lakes of Lucerne and Uri, where the snowy mountains descend almost perpendicularly to the water, casting black and impenetrable shades, which would cause a gloomy and mournful appearance **were it not** for the most **verdant** islands that relieve the eye by their gay appearance; I have seen this lake agitated by a tempest, when the wind tore up whirlwinds of water and gave you an idea of what the **water-spout** must be on the great ocean; and the waves dash with fury the base of the mountain, where the priest and his mistress were overwhelmed by an avalanche and where their dying voices are still said to be heard amid the pauses of the nightly wind; I have seen the mountains of La Valais, and the Pays de Vaud; but this country, Victor, pleases me more than all those wonders. The mountains of Switzerland are more **majestic** and strange, but there is a charm in the banks of this divine river that I never before saw equalled. Look at that castle which overhangs **yon** precipice; and that also on the island, almost concealed amongst the **foliage** of those lovely trees; and

---

were it not:
if it were not
verdant [və́:rdənt] adj.
푸릇푸릇한, 푸른 잎이 무성한, 신록의
waterspout [wɔ́:tə:rspàut] n.
바다 회오리, 물기둥, 용오름
majestic [mədʒéstik] adj.
장엄한, 위엄 있는, 웅대한
yon [jɑn / jɔn] adj.
저 곳의, 저쪽의
foliage [fóuliidʒ] n.
녹음, 산림

now that group of labourers coming from among their vines; and that village half hid in the recess of the mountain. Oh, surely the spirit that inhabits and guards this place has a soul more in harmony with man than those who pile the glacier or retire to the inaccessible peaks of the mountains of our own country."

Clerval! Beloved friend! Even now it delights me to record your words and to **dwell on** the praise of which you are so eminently deserving. He was a being formed in the "very poetry of nature." His wild and enthusiastic imagination was **chastened** by the sensibility of his heart. His soul overflowed with ardent affections, and his friendship was of that devoted and wondrous nature that the worldly-minded teach us to look for only in the imagination. But even human sympathies were not sufficient to satisfy his eager mind. The scenery of external nature, which others regard only with admiration, he loved with ardour:

>The sounding cataract
>Haunted him like a passion: the tall rock,
>The mountain, and the deep and gloomy wood,
>Their colours and their forms, were then to him
>An appetite; a feeling, and a love,

dwell on:
깊이 생각하다, 상세히 말하다
chasten [tʃéisən] v.
다듬다, 순화시키다

> That had no need of a remoter charm,
> By thought supplied, or any interest
> Unborrow'd from the eye.*

And where does he now exist? Is this gentle and lovely being lost for ever? Has this mind, so **replete** with ideas, imaginations fanciful and magnificent, which formed a world, whose existence depended on the life of its creator — has this mind perished? Does it now only exist in my memory? No, it is not thus; your form so divinely wrought, and beaming with beauty, has decayed, but your spirit still visits and consoles your unhappy friend.

Pardon this gush of sorrow; these **ineffectual** words are but a slight **tribute** to the **unexampled** worth of Henry, but they soothe my heart, overflowing with the anguish which his remembrance creates. I will proceed with my tale.

Beyond Cologne we descended to the plains of Holland; and we resolved to **post** the remainder of our way, for the wind was contrary and the stream of the river was too gentle to aid us.

Our journey here lost the interest arising from beautiful scenery, but we arrived in a few days at Rotterdam, whence we proceeded by sea to England. It was on a clear morning, in

---

* Wordsworth's "Tintern Abbey" [author's footnote].

the latter days of December, that I first saw the white cliffs of Britain. The banks of the Thames presented a new scene; they were flat but fertile, and almost every town was marked by the remembrance of some story. We saw Tilbury Fort and remembered the Spanish Armada, Gravesend, Woolwich, and Greenwich — places which I had heard of even in my country.

At length we saw the numerous steeples of London, St. Paul's towering above all, and the Tower famed in English history.

Chapter 19

London was our present point of rest; we determined to remain several months in this wonderful and celebrated city. Clerval desired the intercourse of the men of genius and talent who flourished at this time, but this was with me a secondary object; I was principally occupied with the means of obtaining the information necessary for the completion of my promise and quickly availed myself of the letters of introduction that I had brought with me, addressed to the most distinguished natural philosophers.

If this journey had taken place during my days of study and happiness, it would have afforded me inexpressible pleasure. But a

blight had come over my existence, and I only visited these people for the sake of the information they might give me on the subject in which my interest was so terribly profound. Company was **irksome** to me; when alone, I could fill my mind with the sights of heaven and earth; the voice of Henry soothed me, and I could thus cheat myself into a **transitory** peace. But busy, uninteresting, joyous faces brought back despair to my heart. I saw an insurmountable barrier placed between me and my fellow men; this barrier was sealed with the blood of William and Justine, and to reflect on the events connected with those names filled my soul with anguish.

But in Clerval I saw the image of my former self; he was **inquisitive** and anxious to gain experience and instruction. The difference of manners which he observed was to him an inexhaustible source of instruction and amusement. He was also pursuing an object he had long had in view. His design was to visit India, in the belief that he had in his knowledge of its various languages, and in the views he had taken of its society, the means of materially assisting the progress of European colonization and trade. In Britain only could he **further** the execution of his plan. He was for ever busy, and the only **check** to his enjoyments was my

debar [dibá:r] v.
내쫓다, 제외하다, 금하다
undisturbed [Àndistá:rbd] adj.
방해되지 않은, 평온한
allege [əlédʒ] v.
(변명으로) 내세우다, 구실로 삼다
palpitate [pǽlpətèit] v.
몹시 고동치다, 두근거리다

allurement [əlúərmənt] n.
매력, 유혹

sorrowful and dejected mind. I tried to conceal this as much as possible, that I might not **debar** him from the pleasures natural to one who was entering on a new scene of life, **undisturbed** by any care or bitter recollection. I often refused to accompany him, **alleging** another engagement, that I might remain alone. I now also began to collect the materials necessary for my new creation, and this was to me like the torture of single drops of water continually falling on the head. Every thought that was devoted to it was an extreme anguish, and every word that I spoke in allusion to it caused my lips to quiver, and my heart to **palpitate**.

After passing some months in London, we received a letter from a person in Scotland who had formerly been our visitor at Geneva. He mentioned the beauties of his native country and asked us if those were not sufficient **allurements** to induce us to prolong our journey as far north as Perth, where he resided. Clerval eagerly desired to accept this invitation, and I, although I abhorred society, wished to view again mountains and streams and all the wondrous works with which Nature adorns her chosen dwelling-places.

We had arrived in England at the beginning of October, and it was now February. We accordingly determined to commence our journey

expiration [èkspəréiʃən] n.
종결, 만료, 만기
nook [nuk] n.
구석, 외진 곳, 벽지

ramble [rǽmb-əl] v.
거닐다, 서성이다, 산책하다
novelty [náv-əlti / nɔ́v-] n.
신기함, 진기함, 새로움

forsake [fə:rséik] v.
내버리다, 떠나다, 포기하다
insolent [ínsələnt] adj.
뻐기는, 거만한, 무례한

towards the north at the **expiration** of another month. In this expedition we did not intend to follow the great road to Edinburgh, but to visit Windsor, Oxford, Matlock, and the Cumberland lakes, resolving to arrive at the completion of this tour about the end of July. I packed up my chemical instruments and the materials I had collected, resolving to finish my labours in some obscure **nook** in the northern highlands of Scotland.

We quitted London on the 27th of March and remained a few days at Windsor, **rambling** in its beautiful forest. This was a new scene to us mountaineers; the majestic oaks, the quantity of game, and the herds of stately deer were all **novelties** to us.

From thence we proceeded to Oxford. As we entered this city, our minds were filled with the remembrance of the events that had been transacted there more than a century and a half before. It was here that Charles I had collected his forces. This city had remained faithful to him, after the whole nation had **forsaken** his cause to join the standard of Parliament and liberty. The memory of that unfortunate king and his companions, the amiable Falkland, the **insolent** Goring, his queen, and son, gave a peculiar interest to every part of the city which they might be supposed to

Isis [áisis] n.
아이시스 강. 영국 Oxford에서의 Thames 강의 명칭
meadow [médou] n.
목초지, 초원
verdure [vá:rdʒər] n.
(초목의) 푸르름, 신록
embosom [embú(:)zəm] v.
품에 안다, 둘러싸다

embitter [imbítər] v.
더 쓰게 하다, 몹시 기분나쁘게 하다, 한층 더 비참하게 하다
discontent [dìskəntént] n.
불만, 불평
ennui [á:nwí:, -́-; F. ãnɥi] n.
권태, 지루함
elasticity [ilæstísəti, ì:læs-] n.
곧 회복하는 힘; 유연성, 명랑함
bolt [boult] n.
전광, 번개
intolerable [intálərəbəl / -tɔ́l-] adj. 견딜 수 없는, 참을 수 없는

have inhabited. The spirit of elder days found a dwelling here, and we delighted to trace its footsteps. If these feelings had not found an imaginary gratification, the appearance of the city had yet in itself sufficient beauty to obtain our admiration. The colleges are ancient and picturesque; the streets are almost magnificent; and the lovely **Isis**, which flows beside it through **meadows** of exquisite **verdure**, is spread forth into a placid expanse of waters, which reflects its majestic assemblage of towers, and spires, and domes, **embosomed** among aged trees.

I enjoyed this scene, and yet my enjoyment was **embittered** both by the memory of the past and the anticipation of the future. I was formed for peaceful happiness. During my youthful days **discontent** never visited my mind, and if I was ever overcome by *ennui*, the sight of what is beautiful in nature or the study of what is excellent and sublime in the productions of man could always interest my heart and communicate **elasticity** to my spirits. But I am a blasted tree; the **bolt** has entered my soul; and I felt then that I should survive to exhibit what I shall soon cease to be — a miserable spectacle of wrecked humanity, pitiable to others and **intolerable** to myself.

We passed a considerable period at Oxford,

epoch [épək / íːpɔk] n.
시대, 시기
patriot [péitriət, -àt / pǽtriət] n.
애국자, 우국지사
remembrancer [rimémbr-ənsəːr] n.
생각나게 하는 사람(것), 기념품, 추억거리

rambling among its environs and endeavouring to identify every spot which might relate to the most animating **epoch** of English history. Our little voyages of discovery were often prolonged by the successive objects that presented themselves. We visited the tomb of the illustrious Hampden and the field on which that **patriot** fell. For a moment my soul was elevated from its debasing and miserable fears to contemplate the divine ideas of liberty and self-sacrifice of which these sights were the monuments and the **remembrancers**. For an instant I dared to shake off my chains and look around me with a free and lofty spirit, but the iron had eaten into my flesh, and I sank again, trembling and hopeless, into my miserable self.

We left Oxford with regret and proceeded to Matlock, which was our next place of rest. The country in the neighbourhood of this village resembled, to a greater degree, the scenery of Switzerland; but everything is on a lower scale, and the green hills want the crown of distant white Alps which always attend on the piny mountains of my native country. We visited the wondrous cave and the little cabinets of natural history, where the curiosities are disposed in the same manner as in the collections at Servox and Chamounix. The latter name made me tremble when pronounced by Henry, and

I hastened to quit Matlock, with which that terrible scene was thus associated.

From Derby, still journeying northwards, we passed two months in Cumberland and Westmorland. I could now almost fancy myself among the Swiss mountains. The little patches of snow which yet lingered on the northern sides of the mountains, the lakes, and the dashing of the rocky streams were all familiar and dear sights to me. Here also we made some **acquaintances**, who almost **contrived** to cheat me into happiness. The delight of Clerval was proportionably greater than mine; his mind expanded in the company of men of talent, and he found in his own nature greater capacities and resources than he could have imagined himself to have possessed while he associated with his inferiors. "I could pass my life here," said he to me; "and among these mountains I should scarcely **regret** Switzerland and the Rhine."

But he found that a traveller's life is one that includes much pain amidst its enjoyments. His feelings are for ever **on the stretch**; and when he begins to sink into **repose**, he finds himself obliged to quit that on which he rests in pleasure for something new, which again engages his attention, and which also he **forsakes** for other novelties.

wreak [ri:k] v.
(벌, 복수 등을) 가하다, (분노 등을) 터뜨리다
expedite [ékspədàit] v. 재촉하다, 진척시키다, 촉진하다
remissness [rimisnis] n. 태만함, 무기력함

We had scarcely visited the various lakes of Cumberland and Westmorland and conceived an affection for some of the inhabitants when the period of our appointment with our Scotch friend approached, and we left them to travel on. For my own part I was not sorry. I had now neglected my promise for some time, and I feared the effects of the daemon's disappointment. He might remain in Switzerland and **wreak** his vengeance on my relatives. This idea pursued me and tormented me at every moment from which I might otherwise have snatched repose and peace. I waited for my letters with feverish impatience; if they were delayed I was miserable and overcome by a thousand fears; and when they arrived and I saw the superscription of Elizabeth or my father, I hardly dared to read and ascertain my fate. Sometimes I thought that the fiend followed me and might **expedite** my **remissness** by murdering my companion. When these thoughts possessed me, I would not quit Henry for a moment, but followed him as his shadow, to protect him from the fancied rage of his destroyer. I felt as if I had committed some great crime, the consciousness of which haunted me. I was guiltless, but I had indeed drawn down a horrible curse upon my head, as mortal as that of crime.

I visited Edinburgh with languid eyes and

antiquity [æntíkwəti] n.
오래됨, 고색, 고아

rendezvous [rándivù: / rón-] n.
만날 약속; 약속에 의한 회합
motion [móuʃ-ən] n.
활동, 이동
congenial [kəndʒí:njəl] adj.
마음에 맞는

dissuade [diswéid] v.
단념시키다, 만류하다
remonstrate [rimánstreit, rémənstrèit / rimónstreit] v.
타이르다, 충고하다

mind; and yet that city might have interested the most unfortunate being. Clerval did not like it so well as Oxford, for the **antiquity** of the latter city was more pleasing to him. But the beauty and regularity of the new town of Edinburgh, its romantic castle and its environs, the most delightful in the world, Arthur's Seat, St. Bernard's Well, and the Pentland Hills, compensated him for the change and filled him with cheerfulness and admiration. But I was impatient to arrive at the termination of my journey.

We left Edinburgh in a week, passing through Coupar, St. Andrew's, and along the banks of the Tay, to Perth, where our friend expected us. But I was in no mood to laugh and talk with strangers or enter into their feelings or plans with the good humour expected from a guest; and accordingly I told Clerval that I wished to make the tour of Scotland alone. "Do you," said I, "enjoy yourself, and let this be our **rendezvous**. I may be absent a month or two; but do not interfere with my **motions**, I entreat you; leave me to peace and solitude for a short time; and when I return, I hope it will be with a lighter heart, more **congenial** to your own temper."

Henry wished to **dissuade** me, but seeing me bent on this plan, ceased to **remonstrate**.

He entreated me to write often. "I had rather be with you," he said, "in your solitary rambles, than with these Scotch people, whom I do not know; hasten, then, my dear friend, to return, that I may again feel myself somewhat at home, which I cannot do in your absence."

Having parted from my friend, I determined to visit some remote spot of Scotland and finish my work in solitude. I did not doubt but that the monster followed me and would discover himself to me when I should have finished, that he might receive his companion.

With this resolution I traversed the northern highlands and fixed on one of the remotest of the Orkneys as the scene of my labours. It was a place fitted for such a work, being hardly more than a rock whose high sides were continually beaten upon by the waves. The soil was barren, scarcely affording **pasture** for a few miserable cows, and oatmeal for its inhabitants, which consisted of five persons, whose **gaunt** and **scraggy** limbs gave **tokens** of their miserable **fare**. Vegetables and bread, when they indulged in such luxuries, and even fresh water, was to be procured from the mainland, which was about five miles distant.

On the whole island there were but three miserable huts, and one of these was vacant when I arrived. This I hired. It contained but

---

pasture [pǽstʃər, pάːs-] n.
목초지, 목장
gaunt [gɔːnt] adj.
여윈, 수척한
scraggy [skrǽgi] adj.
바싹 마른, 들쭉날쭉한
token [tóuk-ən] n.
표시, 상징, 증거
fare [fɛər] n.
음식, 요리

penury [pénjəri] n.
빈곤, 궁핍
benumb [binʌ́m] v.
감각을 잃게 하다, 마비시키다
squalid [skwɑ́lid / skwɔ́l-] adj.
더러운, 누추한
blunt [blʌnt] v.
무디게 하다, 약하게 하다

monotonous [mənɑ́tənəs / -nɔ́t-] adj.
단조로운, 지루한

two rooms, and these exhibited all the squalidness of the most miserable **penury**. The thatch had fallen in, the walls were unplastered, and the door was off its hinges. I ordered it to be repaired, bought some furniture, and took possession, an incident which would doubtless have occasioned some surprise had not all the senses of the cottagers been **benumbed** by want and **squalid** poverty. As it was, I lived ungazed at and unmolested, hardly thanked for the pittance of food and clothes which I gave, so much does suffering **blunt** even the coarsest sensations of men.

In this retreat I devoted the morning to labour; but in the evening, when the weather permitted, I walked on the stony beach of the sea to listen to the waves as they roared and dashed at my feet. It was a **monotonous** yet ever-changing scene. I thought of Switzerland; it was far different from this desolate and appalling landscape. Its hills are covered with vines, and its cottages are scattered thickly in the plains. Its fair lakes reflect a blue and gentle sky, and when troubled by the winds, their tumult is but as the play of a lively infant when compared to the roarings of the giant ocean.

In this manner I distributed my occupations when I first arrived, but as I proceeded in my

frenzy [frénzi] n.
격분, 광란

unequal [ʌníːkwəl] adj.
고르지 못한, 한결같지 않은, 불규칙한

persecutor [pə́ːrsikjùːtər] n.
박해자, 학대자

tremulous [trémjələs] adj.
떨리는, 떠는, 겁많은

labour, it became every day more horrible and irksome to me. Sometimes I could not prevail on myself to enter my laboratory for several days, and at other times I toiled day and night in order to complete my work. It was, indeed, a filthy process in which I was engaged. During my first experiment, a kind of enthusiastic **frenzy** had blinded me to the horror of my employment; my mind was intently fixed on the consummation of my labour, and my eyes were shut to the horror of my proceedings. But now I went to it in cold blood, and my heart often sickened at the work of my hands.

Thus situated, employed in the most detestable occupation, immersed in a solitude where nothing could for an instant call my attention from the actual scene in which I was engaged, my spirits became **unequal**; I grew restless and nervous. Every moment I feared to meet my **persecutor**. Sometimes I sat with my eyes fixed on the ground, fearing to raise them lest they should encounter the object which I so much dreaded to behold. I feared to wander from the sight of my fellow creatures lest when alone he should come to claim his companion.

In the mean time I worked on, and my labour was already considerably advanced. I looked towards its completion with a **tremulous** and

obscure [əbskjúər] adj. 분명치 않은, 불명료한
foreboding [fɔːrbóudiŋ] n. (불길한) 예감, 전조, 조짐

eager hope, which I dared not trust myself to question but which was intermixed with **obscure forebodings** of evil that made my heart sicken in my bosom.

Chapter 20

unremitting [ʌnrimítiŋ] adj.
간단 없는, 끊임 없는
train [trein] n.
연속, 과정, 맥락
reflection [riflékʃ-ən] n.
성찰, 생각, 사상
barbarity [bɑːrbǽrəti] n.
야만, 만행
desolate [désəlèit] v.
황폐하게 하다, 슬프게 하다,
비참하게 하다
remorse [rimɔ́ːrs] n.
후회, 양심의 가책
disposition [dìspəzíʃən] n.
기질, 성미, 성격

I sat one evening in my laboratory; the sun had set, and the moon was just rising from the sea; I had not sufficient light for my employment, and I remained idle, in a pause of consideration of whether I should leave my labour for the night or hasten its conclusion by an **unremitting** attention to it. As I sat, a **train** of **reflection** occurred to me which led me to consider the effects of what I was now doing. Three years before, I was engaged in the same manner and had created a fiend whose unparalleled **barbarity** had **desolated** my heart and filled it for ever with the bitterest **remorse**. I was now about to form another being of whose **dispositions** I was alike ignorant; she might

malignant [məlígnənt] adj.
해로운, 악의에 찬
quit [kwit] v.
떠나다, 물러나다
comply [kəmplái] v.
따르다, 응하다
compact [kámpækt / kóm-] n.
계약, 맹약
exasperate [igzǽspərèit] v.
격노하다, 분개하다
provocation [pràvəkéiʃən / pròv-] n.
성나게 함; 성남, 분개

propagate [prápəgèit / próp-] v.
번식시키다, 늘리다
precarious [prikéəriəs] adj.
불확실한, 불안정한, 위험한
inflict [inflíkt] v.
(고통, 타격) 등을 가하다, 입히다
everlasting [èvərlǽstiŋ, -lɑ́:st-] adj.
영구한, 불후의, 끝없는
sophism [sáfiz-əm / sɔ́f-] n.
궤변, 억지 이론

become ten thousand times more **malignant** than her mate and delight, for its own sake, in murder and wretchedness. He had sworn to **quit** the neighbourhood of man and hide himself in deserts, but she had not; and she, who in all probability was to become a thinking and reasoning animal, might refuse to **comply** with a **compact** made before her creation. They might even hate each other; the creature who already lived loathed his own deformity, and might he not conceive a greater abhorrence for it when it came before his eyes in the female form? She also might turn with disgust from him to the superior beauty of man; she might quit him, and he be again alone, **exasperated** by the fresh **provocation** of being deserted by one of his own species.

Even if they were to leave Europe and inhabit the deserts of the new world, yet one of the first results of those sympathies for which the daemon thirsted would be children, and a race of devils would be **propagated** upon the earth who might make the very existence of the species of man a condition **precarious** and full of terror. Had I right, for my own benefit, to **inflict** this curse upon **everlasting** generations? I had before been moved by the **sophisms** of the being I had created; I had been struck senseless by his fiendish threats; but now, for the first time, the wickedness of my promise burst upon me; I shuddered to think that future ages might curse me as their **pest**, whose selfishness had not hesitated to **buy** its own peace at the price, perhaps, of the existence of the whole human race.

I trembled and my heart failed within me, when, on looking up, I saw by the light of the moon the daemon at the **casement**. A ghastly grin wrinkled his lips as he gazed on me, where I sat fulfilling the task which he had allotted to me. Yes, he had followed me in my travels; he had **loitered** in forests, hid himself in caves, or taken refuge in wide and desert **heaths**; and he now came to mark my progress and claim the fulfilment of my promise.

As I looked on him, his countenance expressed the utmost extent of malice and treachery. I thought with a sensation of madness on my promise of creating another like to him, and trembling with passion, tore to pieces the thing on which I was engaged. The wretch saw me destroy the creature on whose future existence he depended for happiness, and with a howl of devilish despair and revenge, withdrew.

I left the room, and locking the door, made a solemn vow in my own heart never to resume my labours; and then, with trembling steps, I

reverie [rév-əri] n.
공상, 몽상

now and then:
때때로, 이따금
waft [wɑːft, wæft] v.
감돌게 하다, 가볍게 나르다
profundity [prəfʌ́ndəti] n.
깊음, 심오함

presentiment [prizéntəmənt] n. 예감, 육감
helplessness [hélplisnis] n. 어떻게도 할 수 없음, 무기력, 무력함
impending [impéndiŋ] adj. 임박한, 곧 일어날 듯한
root [ruːt, rut] v.
뿌리박게 하다, 얼어붙게 하다

sought my own apartment. I was alone; none were near me to dissipate the gloom and relieve me from the sickening oppression of the most terrible **reveries**.

Several hours passed, and I remained near my window gazing on the sea; it was almost motionless, for the winds were hushed, and all nature reposed under the eye of the quiet moon. A few fishing vessels alone specked the water, and **now and then** the gentle breeze **wafted** the sound of voices as the fishermen called to one another. I felt the silence, although I was hardly conscious of its extreme **profundity**, until my ear was suddenly arrested by the paddling of oars near the shore, and a person landed close to my house.

In a few minutes after, I heard the creaking of my door, as if some one endeavoured to open it softly. I trembled from head to foot; I felt a **presentiment** of who it was and wished to rouse one of the peasants who dwelt in a cottage not far from mine; but I was overcome by the sensation of **helplessness**, so often felt in frightful dreams, when you in vain endeavour to fly from an **impending** danger, and was **rooted** to the spot.

Presently I heard the sound of footsteps along the passage; the door opened, and the wretch whom I dreaded appeared. Shutting the door, he approached me and said in a smothered voice,

"You have destroyed the work which you began; what is it that you intend? Do you dare to break your promise? I have endured toil and misery; I left Switzerland with you; I crept along the shores of the Rhine, among its willow islands and over the summits of its hills. I have dwelt many months in the heaths of England and among the deserts of Scotland. I have endured **incalculable** fatigue, and cold, and hunger; do you dare destroy my hopes?"

"**Begone**! I do break my promise; never will I create another like yourself, equal in deformity and wickedness."

"Slave, I before **reasoned** with you, but you have proved yourself unworthy of my **condescension**. Remember that I have power; you believe yourself miserable, but I can make you so wretched that the light of day will be hateful to you. You are my creator, but I am your master; obey!"

"The hour of my **irresolution** is past, and the **period** of your power is arrived. Your threats cannot move me to do an act of wickedness; but they **confirm** me in a determination of not creating you a companion in vice. Shall I, in cool blood, set loose upon the earth a daemon whose delight is in death and wretchedness?

Begone! I am firm, and your words will only exasperate my rage."

The monster saw my determination in my face and gnashed his teeth in the **impotence** of anger. "Shall each man," cried he, "find a wife for his bosom, and each beast have his mate, and I be alone? I had feelings of affection, and they were **requited** by detestation and scorn. Man! You may hate, but beware! Your hours will pass in dread and misery, and soon the **bolt** will fall which must **ravish** from you your happiness for ever. Are you to be happy while I **grovel** in the intensity of my wretchedness? You can blast my other passions, but revenge remains — revenge, henceforth dearer than light or food! I may die, but first you, my tyrant and tormentor, shall curse the sun that gazes on your misery. Beware, for I am fearless and therefore powerful. I will watch with the **wiliness** of a snake, that I may sting with its **venom**. Man, you shall **repent** of the injuries you inflict."

"Devil, cease; and do not poison the air with these sounds of **malice**. I have declared my resolution to you, and I am no coward to bend beneath words. Leave me; I am **inexorable**."

"It is well. I go; but remember, I shall be with you on your wedding-night."

I started forward and exclaimed, "Villain!

death warrant:
사형 집행 영장

precipitation [prisìpətéiʃən] n.
화급, 조급, 경솔함
arrowy [ǽroui] adj.
화살 같은, 빠른

conjure up:
(상상으로) 만들어내다, 상기시키다, 출현시키다
close with:
맞붙어 싸우다, 접근전을 펴다
insatiate [inséiʃiət] adj.
만족할 줄 모르는, 탐욕스러운
prospect [práspekt / prɔ́s-] n.
전망, 가능성, 예상, 기대

"You are my creator, but I am your master; obey!"
"The hour of my irresolution is past, and the period of your power is arrived. Your threats cannot move me to do an act of wickedness;

Before you sign my **death-warrant**, be sure that you are yourself safe."

I would have seized him, but he eluded me and quitted the house with **precipitation**. In a few moments I saw him in his boat, which shot across the waters with an **arrowy** swiftness and was soon lost amidst the waves.

All was again silent, but his words rang in my ears. I burned with rage to pursue the murderer of my peace and precipitate him into the ocean. I walked up and down my room hastily and perturbed, while my imagination **conjured up** a thousand images to torment and sting me. Why had I not followed him and **closed with** him in mortal strife? But I had suffered him to depart, and he had directed his course towards the mainland. I shuddered to think who might be the next victim sacrificed to his **insatiate** revenge. And then I thought again of his words — *"I will be with you on your wedding-night."* That, then, was the period fixed for the fulfilment of my destiny. In that hour I should die and at once satisfy and extinguish his malice. The **prospect** did not move me to fear; yet when I thought of my beloved Elizabeth, of her tears and endless sorrow, when she should find her lover so barbarously snatched from her, tears, the first I had shed for many months, streamed from my eyes, and I resolved

contention [kənténʃən] n.
싸움, 투쟁
insuperable [insúːpərəbəl] adj.
이겨낼 수 없는, 극복할 수 없는
steal [stiːl] v.
모르는 사이에 지나가다(오다), 어느새 엄습하다

restless [réstlis] adj.
침착하지 못한, 불안한
specter [spéktəːr] n.
유령, 망령
overpower [òuvərpáuər] v.
(힘으로) 눌러 버리다, 제압하다, 무력하게 하다
composure [kəmpóuʒər] n.
침착, 평정

not to fall before my enemy without a bitter struggle.

The night passed away, and the sun rose from the ocean; my feelings became calmer, if it may be called calmness when the violence of rage sinks into the depths of despair. I left the house, the horrid scene of the last night's **contention**, and walked on the beach of the sea, which I almost regarded as an **insuperable** barrier between me and my fellow creatures; nay, a wish that such should prove the fact **stole** across me. I desired that I might pass my life on that barren rock, wearily, it is true, but uninterrupted by any sudden shock of misery. If I returned, it was to be sacrificed or to see those whom I most loved die under the grasp of a daemon whom I had myself created.

I walked about the isle like a **restless spectre**, separated from all it loved and miserable in the separation. When it became noon, and the sun rose higher, I lay down on the grass and was **overpowered** by a deep sleep. I had been awake the whole of the preceding night, my nerves were agitated, and my eyes inflamed by watching and misery. The sleep into which I now sank refreshed me; and when I awoke, I again felt as if I belonged to a race of human beings like myself, and I began to reflect upon what had passed with greater **composure**; yet

death nell:
죽음을 알리는 종

wear away:
닳아 없애다, (시간을) 보내다

society [səsáiəti] n.
교제, 교우, (남과의) 동석

beseech [bisíːtʃ] v.
청하다, 바라다

still the words of the fiend rang in my ears like a **death-knell**; they appeared like a dream, yet distinct and oppressive as a reality.

The sun had far descended, and I still sat on the shore, satisfying my appetite, which had become ravenous, with an oaten cake, when I saw a fishing-boat land close to me, and one of the men brought me a packet; it contained letters from Geneva, and one from Clerval entreating me to join him. He said that he was **wearing away** his time fruitlessly where he was, that letters from the friends he had formed in London desired his return to complete the negotiation they had entered into for his Indian enterprise. He could not any longer delay his departure; but as his journey to London might be followed, even sooner than he now conjectured, by his longer voyage, he entreated me to bestow as much of my **society** on him as I could spare. He **besought** me, therefore, to leave my solitary isle and to meet him at Perth, that we might proceed southwards together. This letter in a degree recalled me to life, and I determined to quit my island at the expiration of two days.

Yet, before I departed, there was a task to perform, on which I shuddered to reflect; I must pack up my chemical instruments, and for that purpose I must enter the room which had been the scene of my odious work, and I must handle those utensils the sight of which was sickening to me. The next morning, at daybreak, I summoned sufficient courage and unlocked the door of my laboratory. The remains of the half-finished creature, whom I had destroyed, lay scattered on the floor, and I almost felt as if I had mangled the living flesh of a human being. I paused to collect myself and then entered the chamber. With trembling hand I conveyed the instruments out of the room, but I reflected that I ought not to leave the relics of my work to excite the horror and suspicion of the peasants; and I accordingly put them into a basket, with a great quantity of stones, and laying them up, determined to throw them into the sea that very night; and in the meantime I sat upon the beach, employed in cleaning and arranging my chemical apparatus.

Nothing could be more complete than the alteration that had taken place in my feelings since the night of the appearance of the daemon. I had before regarded my promise with a gloomy despair as a thing that, with whatever consequences, must be fulfilled; but I now felt as if a film had been taken from before my eyes and that I for the first time saw clearly. The idea of renewing my labours did not for one instant occur to me; the threat I had heard

atrocious [ətróuʃəs] adj.
극악무도한, 매우 심한
banish [bǽniʃ] v.
멀리하다, 쫓아버리다, 떨쳐버리다

skiff [skif] n.
소형 보트
take advantage of ~:
~을 최대한 활용하다

weighed on my thoughts, but I did not reflect that a voluntary act of mine could avert it. I had resolved in my own mind that to create another like the fiend I had first made would be an act of the basest and most **atrocious** selfishness, and I **banished** from my mind every thought that could lead to a different conclusion.

Between two and three in the morning the moon rose; and I then, putting my basket aboard a little **skiff**, sailed out about four miles from the shore. The scene was perfectly solitary; a few boats were returning towards land, but I sailed away from them. I felt as if I was about the commission of a dreadful crime and avoided with shuddering anxiety any encounter with my fellow creatures. At one time the moon, which had before been clear, was suddenly overspread by a thick cloud, and I **took advantage of** the moment of darkness and cast my basket into the sea; I listened to the gurgling sound as it sank and then sailed away from the spot. The sky became clouded, but the air was pure, although chilled by the northeast breeze that was then rising. But it refreshed me and filled me with such agreeable sensations that I resolved to prolong my stay on the water, and fixing the rudder in a direct position, stretched myself at the bottom of the boat.

keel [ki:l] n.
용골

slenderly [sléndə:rli] adv.
적게, 빈약하게
buffet [bʌ́fit] v.
(연속적으로) 치다, 때리다
prelude [prélju:d, préi-, príː-] n.
(사건 등의) 전조

Clouds hid the moon, everything was obscure, and I heard only the sound of the boat as its **keel** cut through the waves; the murmur lulled me, and in a short time I slept soundly.

I do not know how long I remained in this situation, but when I awoke I found that the sun had already mounted considerably. The wind was high, and the waves continually threatened the safety of my little skiff. I found that the wind was northeast and must have driven me far from the coast from which I had embarked. I endeavoured to change my course but quickly found that if I again made the attempt the boat would be instantly filled with water.

Thus situated, my only resource was to drive before the wind. I confess that I felt a few sensations of terror. I had no compass with me and was so **slenderly** acquainted with the geography of this part of the world that the sun was of little benefit to me. I might be driven into the wide Atlantic and feel all the tortures of starvation or be swallowed up in the immeasurable waters that roared and **buffeted** around me. I had already been out many hours and felt the torment of a burning thirst, a **prelude** to my other sufferings. I looked on the heavens, which were covered by clouds that flew before the wind, only to be replaced by others; I looked upon the sea; it was to be my grave. "Fiend," I exclaimed, "your task is already fulfilled!" I thought of Elizabeth, of my father, and of Clerval — all left behind, on whom the monster might satisfy his sanguinary and merciless passions. This idea plunged me into a reverie so despairing and frightful that even now, when the scene is on the point of closing before me for ever, I shudder to reflect on it.

Some hours passed thus; but by degrees, as the sun declined towards the horizon, the wind died away into a gentle breeze and the sea became free from breakers. But these gave place to a heavy swell; I felt sick and hardly able to hold the rudder, when suddenly I saw a line of high land towards the south.

Almost spent, as I was, by fatigue and the dreadful suspense I endured for several hours, this sudden certainty of life rushed like a flood of warm joy to my heart, and tears gushed from my eyes.

How **mutable** are our feelings, and how strange is that clinging love we have of life even in the excess of misery! I constructed another sail with a part of my dress and eagerly steered my course towards the land. It had a wild and rocky appearance, but as I approached nearer I easily perceived the traces of cultivation. I saw vessels near the shore and found

mutable [mjú:təb-əl] adj.
변하기 쉬운, 변덕스러운

steeple [stíːp-əl] n.
(교회 따위의) 뾰족탑
promontory [prámənt̀ɔːri / prɔ́məntəri] n.
곶, 갑(岬)
debility [dibíləti] n.
약함, 쇠약

myself suddenly transported back to the neighbourhood of civilised man. I carefully traced the windings of the land and hailed a **steeple** which I at length saw issuing from behind a small **promontory**. As I was in a state of extreme **debility**, I resolved to sail directly towards the town, as a place where I could most easily procure nourishment. Fortunately I had money with me. As I turned the promontory I perceived a small neat town and a good harbour, which I entered, my heart bounding with joy at my unexpected escape.

As I was occupied in fixing the boat and arranging the sails, several people crowded towards the spot. They seemed much surprised at my appearance, but instead of offering me any assistance, whispered together with gestures that at any other time might have produced in me a slight sensation of alarm. As it was, I merely remarked that they spoke English, and I therefore addressed them in that language. "My good friends," said I, "will you be so kind as to tell me the name of this town and inform me where I am?"

"You will know that soon enough," replied a man with a hoarse voice.

"Maybe you are come to a place that will not prove much to your taste, but you will not be consulted as to your **quarters**, I promise you."

quarters [kwɔ́ːrtər] n.
숙소, 주거

disconcerted [dìskənsə́:rtid] adj. 당혹한, 당황한, 혼란한
inhospitably [inháspitəbəli] adv. 불친절하게, 황량하게, 적막하게

villain [vílən] n. 악한, 악당

account [əkáunt] n. 변명, 해명, 설명

magistrate [mǽdʒəstrèit, -trit] n. 법관, 판사, 행정관

I was exceedingly surprised on receiving so rude an answer from a stranger, and I was also **disconcerted** on perceiving the frowning and angry countenances of his companions. "Why do you answer me so roughly?" I replied. "Surely it is not the custom of Englishmen to receive strangers so **inhospitably**."

"I do not know," said the man, "what the custom of the English may be, but it is the custom of the Irish to hate **villains**."

While this strange dialogue continued, I perceived the crowd rapidly increase. Their faces expressed a mixture of curiosity and anger, which annoyed and in some degree alarmed me. I inquired the way to the inn, but no one replied. I then moved forward, and a murmuring sound arose from the crowd as they followed and surrounded me, when an ill-looking man approaching tapped me on the shoulder and said, "Come, sir, you must follow me to Mr. Kirwin's to give an **account** of yourself."

"Who is Mr. Kirwin? Why am I to give an account of myself? Is not this a free country?"

"Ay, sir, free enough for honest folks. Mr. Kirwin is a **magistrate**, and you are to give an account of the death of a gentleman who was found murdered here last night."

This answer startled me, but I presently recovered myself. I was innocent; that could

politic [púlitik / pól-] adj.
사려 깊은, 현명한
construe [kənstrúː] v.
해석하다, 추론하다
apprehension [æ̀prihénʃən] n.
불안, 걱정
calamity [kəlǽməti] n.
재난, 불행, 비운
ignominy [ígnəmìni] n.
치욕, 불명예

fortitude [fɔ́ːrtətjùːd] n.
용기, 불굴의 정신, 인내

easily be proved; accordingly I followed my conductor in silence and was led to one of the best houses in the town. I was ready to sink from fatigue and hunger, but being surrounded by a crowd, I thought it **politic** to rouse all my strength, that no physical debility might be **construed** into **apprehension** or conscious guilt. Little did I then expect the **calamity** that was in a few moments to overwhelm me and extinguish in horror and despair all fear of **ignominy** or death.

I must pause here, for it requires all my **fortitude** to recall the memory of the frightful events which I am about to relate, in proper detail, to my recollection.

Chapter 21

severity [sivérəti] n.
엄격, 엄중

I was soon introduced into the presence of the magistrate, an old benevolent man with calm and mild manners. He looked upon me, however, with some degree of **severity**, and then, turning towards my conductors, he asked who appeared as witnesses on this occasion.

depose [dipóuz] v.
증언하다

About half a dozen men came forward; and, one being selected by the magistrate, he **deposed** that he had been out fishing the night before with his son and brother-in-law, Daniel Nugent, when, about ten o'clock, they observed a strong northerly blast rising, and they accordingly put in for port. It was a very dark night, as the moon had not yet risen; they did not land at the harbour, but, as they had been

tackle [tǽk-əl] n.
연장, 도구, 기구

supposition [sʌ̀pəzíʃən] n.
추측, 상상, 가정

accustomed, at a creek about two miles below. He walked on first, carrying a part of the fishing **tackle**, and his companions followed him at some distance. As he was proceeding along the sands, he struck his foot against something and fell at his length on the ground. His companions came up to assist him, and by the light of their lantern they found that he had fallen on the body of a man, who was to all appearance dead. Their first **supposition** was that it was the corpse of some person who had been drowned and was thrown on shore by the waves, but on examination they found that the clothes were not wet and even that the body was not then cold. They instantly carried it to the cottage of an old woman near the spot and endeavoured, but in vain, to restore it to life. It appeared to be a handsome young man, about five and twenty years of age. He had apparently been strangled, for there was no sign of any violence except the black mark of fingers on his neck.

deposition [dèpəzíʃən, dìːp-] n.
(법정 등에서의) 증언

The first part of this **deposition** did not in the least interest me, but when the mark of the fingers was mentioned I remembered the murder of my brother and felt myself extremely agitated; my limbs trembled, and a mist came over my eyes, which obliged me to lean on a chair for support. The magistrate observed me with a keen eye and of course drew an unfavourable **augury** from my manner.

The son confirmed his father's account, but when Daniel Nugent was called he swore positively that just before the fall of his companion, he saw a boat, with a single man in it, at a short distance from the shore; and as far as he could judge by the light of a few stars, it was the same boat in which I had just landed.

A woman deposed that she lived near the beach and was standing at the door of her cottage, waiting for the return of the fishermen, about an hour before she heard of the discovery of the body, when she saw a boat with only one man in it push off from that part of the shore where the corpse was afterwards found.

Another woman confirmed the account of the fishermen having brought the body into her house; it was not cold. They put it into a bed and rubbed it, and Daniel went to the town for an **apothecary**, but life was quite gone.

Several other men were examined concerning my landing, and they agreed that, with the strong north wind that had arisen during the night, it was very probable that I had beaten about for many hours and had been obliged to return nearly to the same spot from which I had departed. Besides, they observed that it appeared that I had brought the body from another place, and it was likely that as I did not appear to know the shore, I might have put into the harbour ignorant of the distance of the town of — from the place where I had deposited the corpse.

Mr. Kirwin, on hearing this evidence, desired that I should be taken into the room where the body lay for **interment**, that it might be observed what effect the sight of it would produce upon me. This idea was probably suggested by the extreme agitation I had exhibited when the mode of the murder had been described. I was accordingly conducted, by the magistrate and several other persons, to the inn. I could not help being struck by the strange coincidences that had taken place during this eventful night; but, knowing that I had been conversing with several persons in the island I had inhabited about the time that the body had been found, I was perfectly tranquil as to the consequences of the affair.

I entered the room where the corpse lay and was led up to the coffin. How can I describe my sensations on beholding it? I feel yet parched with horror, nor can I reflect on that terrible moment without shuddering and agony. The examination, the presence of the magistrate and witnesses, passed like a dream from my memory when I saw the lifeless form

---

interment [intə́ːrmənt] n.
매장

of Henry Clerval stretched before me. I gasped for breath, and throwing myself on the body, I exclaimed, "Have my murderous machinations deprived you also, my dearest Henry, of life? Two I have already destroyed; other victims await their destiny; but you, Clerval, my friend, my benefactor —"

The human frame could no longer support the agonies that I endured, and I was carried out of the room in strong convulsions.

A fever succeeded to this. I lay for two months on the point of death; my ravings, as I afterwards heard, were frightful; I called myself the murderer of William, of Justine, and of Clerval. Sometimes I entreated my attendants to assist me in the destruction of the fiend by whom I was tormented; and at others I felt the fingers of the monster already grasping my neck, and screamed aloud with agony and terror. Fortunately, as I spoke my native language, Mr. Kirwin alone understood me; but my gestures and bitter cries were sufficient to **affright** the other witnesses.

Why did I not die? More miserable than man ever was before, why did I not sink into forgetfulness and rest? Death snatches away many blooming children, the only hopes of their doting parents; how many brides and youthful lovers have been one day in the bloom of health

affright [əfráit] v.
두려워하게 하다, 놀래다

and hope, and the next a prey for worms and the decay of the tomb! Of what materials was I made that I could thus resist so many shocks, which, like the turning of the wheel, continually renewed the torture?

But I was **doomed** to live and in two months found myself as awaking from a dream, in a prison, stretched on a wretched bed, surrounded by **gaolers**, **turnkeys**, bolts, and all the miserable apparatus of a dungeon. It was morning, I remember, when I thus awoke to understanding; I had forgotten the particulars of what had happened and only felt as if some great misfortune had suddenly overwhelmed me; but when I looked around and saw the barred windows and the squalidness of the room in which I was, all **flashed** across my memory and I groaned bitterly.

This sound disturbed an old woman who was sleeping in a chair beside me. She was a hired nurse, the wife of one of the turnkeys, and her countenance expressed all those bad qualities which often characterise that class. The lines of her face were hard and rude, like that of persons accustomed to see without sympathising in sights of misery. Her tone expressed her entire **indifference**; she addressed me in English, and the voice struck me as one that I had heard during my sufferings.

---

doom [du:m] v.
~할 운명에 있다
gaoler [dʒeilər] n.
교도관, 간수
turnkey [tə́:rnkì:] n.
옥지기, 교도관
flash [flæʃ] v.
번개처럼 스치다, 문뜩 떠오르다

indifference [indífərəns] n.
무관심, 냉담함

"Are you better now, sir?" said she.

I replied in the same language, with a feeble voice, "I believe I am; but if it be all true, if indeed I did not dream, I am sorry that I am still alive to feel this misery and horror."

"For that matter," replied the old woman, "if you mean about the gentleman you murdered, I believe that it were better for you if you were dead, for I fancy it will go hard with you! However, that's none of my business; I am sent to nurse you and get you well; I do my duty with a safe conscience; it were well if everybody did the same."

I turned with loathing from the woman who could **utter** so **unfeeling** a speech to a person just saved, on the very edge of death; but I felt **languid** and unable to reflect on all that had passed. The whole series of my life appeared to me as a dream; I sometimes doubted if indeed it were all true, for it never presented itself to my mind with the force of reality.

As the images that floated before me became more distinct, I grew feverish; a darkness pressed around me; no one was near me who **soothed** me with the gentle voice of love; no dear hand supported me. The physician came and prescribed medicines, and the old woman prepared them for me; but utter carelessness was visible in the first, and the expression of

---

utter [ʌ́tər] v.
말하다, 표현하다
unfeeling [ʌnfíːliŋ] adj.
느낌이 없는; 무정한, 냉혹한
languid [lǽŋgwid] adj.
맥없는, 나른한, 노곤한

soothe [suːð] v.
달래다, 진정시키다

brutality was strongly marked in the **visage** of the second. Who could be interested in the fate of a murderer but the **hangman** who would gain his fee?

These were my first reflections, but I soon learned that Mr. Kirwin had shown me extreme kindness. He had caused the best room in the prison to be prepared for me (wretched indeed was the best); and it was he who had provided a physician and a nurse. It is true, he seldom came to see me, for although he ardently desired to relieve the sufferings of every human creature, he did not wish to be present at the agonies and miserable ravings of a murderer. He came, therefore, sometimes to see that I was not neglected, but his visits were short and with long intervals.

One day, while I was gradually recovering, I was seated in a chair, my eyes half open and my cheeks **livid** like those in death. I was overcome by gloom and misery and often reflected I had better seek death than desire to remain in a world which to me was **replete** with wretchedness. At one time I considered whether I should not declare myself guilty and suffer the penalty of the law, less innocent than poor Justine had been. Such were my thoughts when the door of my apartment was opened and Mr. Kirwin entered. His countenance expressed sympathy and compassion; he drew a chair close to mine and addressed me in French,

"I fear that this place is very shocking to you; can I do anything to make you more comfortable?"

"I thank you, but all that you mention is nothing to me; on the whole earth there is no comfort which I am capable of receiving."

"I know that the sympathy of a stranger can be but of little relief to one borne down as you are by so strange a misfortune. But you will, I hope, soon quit this melancholy **abode**, for doubtless evidence can easily be brought to free you from the criminal charge."

"That is my least concern; I am, by a course of strange events, become the most miserable of mortals. Persecuted and tortured as I am and have been, can death be any evil to me?"

"Nothing indeed could be more unfortunate and agonising than the strange chances that have lately occurred. You were thrown, by some surprising accident, on this shore, **renowned** for its **hospitality**, seized immediately, and charged with murder. The first sight that was presented to your eyes was the body of your friend, murdered in so **unaccountable** a manner and placed, as it were, by some fiend across your path."

As Mr. Kirwin said this, notwithstanding

---

abode [əbóud] n.
주거, 거처

renowned [rináund] adj.
유명한, 명성이 있는
hospitality [hàspitǽləti / hɔ̀spi-] n.
환대, 후한 대접
unaccountable [ʌ̀nəkáuntəbəl]
adj. 설명할 수 없는, 영문 모를

retrospect [rétrəspèkt] n.
회고, 회상
relation [riléiʃ-ən] n.
친척, 친족, 혈연

the agitation I endured on this **retrospect** of my sufferings, I also felt considerable surprise at the knowledge he seemed to possess concerning me. I suppose some astonishment was exhibited in my countenance, for Mr. Kirwin hastened to say, "Immediately upon your being taken ill, all the papers that were on your person were brought me, and I examined them that I might discover some trace by which I could send to your **relations** an account of your misfortune and illness. I found several letters, and, among others, one which I discovered from its commencement to be from your father. I instantly wrote to Geneva; nearly two months have elapsed since the departure of my letter. But you are ill; even now you tremble; you are unfit for agitation of any kind."

"This suspense is a thousand times worse than the most horrible event; tell me what new scene of death has been acted, and whose murder I am now to lament?"

"Your family is perfectly well," said Mr. Kirwin with gentleness; "and someone, a friend, is come to visit you."

mock [mɑk / mɔ(:)k] v.
조롱하다, 놀리다
taunt [tɔːnt, tɑːnt] v.
비웃다, 조롱하다
incitement [insáitmənt] n.
고무, 선동, 자극

I know not by what chain of thought the idea presented itself, but it instantly darted into my mind that the murderer had come to **mock** at my misery and **taunt** me with the death of Clerval, as a new **incitement** for me to comply with his hellish desires. I put my hand before my eyes, and cried out in agony, "Oh! Take him away! I cannot see him; for God's sake, do not let him enter!"

Mr. Kirwin regarded me with a troubled countenance. He could not help regarding my exclamation as a presumption of my guilt and said in rather a severe tone, "I should have thought, young man, that the presence of your father would have been welcome instead of inspiring such violent **repugnance**."

"My father!" cried I, while every feature and every muscle was relaxed from anguish to pleasure. "Is my father indeed come? How kind, how very kind! But where is he, why does he not hasten to me?"

My change of manner surprised and pleased the magistrate; perhaps he thought that my former exclamation was a momentary return of **delirium**, and now he instantly resumed his former benevolence. He rose and quitted the room with my nurse, and in a moment my father entered it.

Nothing, at this moment, could have given me greater pleasure than the arrival of my father. I stretched out my hand to him and cried, "Are you then safe — and Elizabeth — and Ernest?"

My father calmed me with assurances of

repugnance [ripʌ́gnəns] n.
질색, 강한 반감

delirium [dilíriəm] n.
환영, 섬망, 열광

dwell on:
깊이 생각하다, 상세히 말하다
fatality [feitǽləti, fət-] n.
(죽음을 초래하는) 재해, 재난, 불행

converse [kənvə́:rs] v.
대화하다
precarious [prikéəriəs] adj.
불확실한, 불안정한, 위험한

their welfare and endeavoured, by **dwelling on** these subjects so interesting to my heart, to raise my desponding spirits; but he soon felt that a prison cannot be the abode of cheerfulness. "What a place is this that you inhabit, my son!" said he, looking mournfully at the barred windows and wretched appearance of the room. "You travelled to seek happiness, but a **fatality** seems to pursue you. And poor Clerval —"

The name of my unfortunate and murdered friend was an agitation too great to be endured in my weak state; I shed tears.

"Alas! Yes, my father," replied I; "some destiny of the most horrible kind hangs over me, and I must live to fulfil it, or surely I should have died on the coffin of Henry."

We were not allowed to **converse** for any length of time, for the **precarious** state of my health rendered every precaution necessary that could ensure tranquillity. Mr. Kirwin came in and insisted that my strength should not be exhausted by too much exertion. But the appearance of my father was to me like that of my good angel, and I gradually recovered my health.

As my sickness quitted me, I was absorbed by a gloomy and black melancholy that nothing could dissipate. The image of Clerval was for ever before me, ghastly and murdered. More than once the agitation into which these reflections threw me made my friends dread a dangerous **relapse**. Alas! Why did they preserve so miserable and detested a life? It was surely that I might fulfil my destiny, which is now drawing to a close. Soon, oh, very soon, will death extinguish these throbbings and relieve me from the mighty weight of anguish that bears me to the dust; and, in executing the award of justice, I shall also sink to rest. Then the appearance of death was distant, although the wish was ever present to my thoughts; and I often sat for hours motionless and speechless, wishing for some mighty revolution that might bury me and my destroyer in its ruins.

The season of the **assizes** approached. I had already been three months in prison, and although I was still weak and in continual danger of a relapse, I was obliged to travel nearly a hundred miles to the country town where the court was held. Mr. Kirwin charged himself with every care of collecting witnesses and arranging my defence. I was spared the disgrace of appearing publicly as a criminal, as the case was not brought before the court that decides on life and death. The grand jury rejected the bill, on its being proved that I was on the Orkney Islands at the hour the body of my friend was found; and a fortnight after my removal I was liberated from prison.

My father was **enraptured** on finding me freed from the **vexations** of a criminal charge, that I was again allowed to breathe the fresh atmosphere and permitted to return to my native country. I did not participate in these feelings, for to me the walls of a dungeon or a palace were alike hateful. The cup of life was poisoned for ever, and although the sun shone upon me, as upon the happy and gay of heart, I saw around me nothing but a dense and frightful darkness, penetrated by no light but the glimmer of two eyes that glared upon me. Sometimes they were the expressive eyes of Henry, languishing in death, the dark orbs nearly covered by the lids and the long black lashes that fringed them; sometimes it was the watery, clouded eyes of the monster, as I first saw them in my chamber at Ingolstadt.

My father tried to awaken in me the feelings of affection. He talked of Geneva, which I should soon visit, of Elizabeth and Ernest; but these words only drew deep groans from me. Sometimes, indeed, I felt a wish for happiness and thought with melancholy delight of my beloved cousin or longed, with a devouring *maladie du pays*, to see once more the blue lake and rapid Rhone, that had been so dear to me in early childhood; but my general state of feeling was a **torpor** in which a prison was as welcome a residence as the divinest scene in nature; and these fits were seldom interrupted but by paroxysms of anguish and despair. At these moments I often endeavoured to put an end to the existence I loathed, and it required **unceasing** attendance and vigilance to restrain me from committing some dreadful act of violence.

Yet one duty remained to me, the recollection of which finally triumphed over my selfish despair. It was necessary that I should return without delay to Geneva, there to watch over the lives of those I so fondly loved and to lie in wait for the murderer, that if any chance led me to the place of his concealment, or if he dared again to **blast** me by his presence, I might, with unfailing aim, put an end to the existence of the monstrous image which I had **endued** with the **mockery** of a soul still more monstrous. My father still desired to delay our departure, fearful that I could not sustain the fatigues of a journey, for I was a shattered wreck — the shadow of a human being. My strength was gone. I was a mere skeleton, and fever night and day preyed upon my wasted frame.

Still, as I urged our leaving Ireland with such **inquietude** and impatience, my father

repass [ri:pǽs, -pάːs] v.
다시 지나가다, 되돌아가다
reside [rizáid] v.
살다, 거주하다

thought it best to yield. We took our passage on board a vessel bound for Havre-de-Grâce and sailed with a fair wind from the Irish shores. It was midnight. I lay on the deck looking at the stars and listening to the dashing of the waves. I hailed the darkness that shut Ireland from my sight, and my pulse beat with a feverish joy when I reflected that I should soon see Geneva. The past appeared to me in the light of a frightful dream; yet the vessel in which I was, the wind that blew me from the detested shore of Ireland, and the sea which surrounded me, told me too forcibly that I was deceived by no vision and that Clerval, my friend and dearest companion, had fallen a victim to me and the monster of my creation. I **repassed**, in my memory, my whole life; my quiet happiness while **residing** with my family in Geneva, the death of my mother, and my departure for Ingolstadt. I remembered, shuddering, the mad enthusiasm that hurried me on to the creation of my hideous enemy, and I called to mind the night in which he first lived. I was unable to pursue the train of thought; a thousand feelings pressed upon me, and I wept bitterly.

Ever since my recovery from the fever, I had been in the custom of taking every night a small quantity of **laudanum**, for it was by

laudanum [lɔ́ːd-ənəm] n.
아편제

preservation [prèzərvéiʃən] n.
보존, 보호
respite [réspit] n.
연기, 유예, 휴식
truce [tru:s] n.
정전, 휴전, 일시적 중지
impart [impá:rt] v.
주다, 전하다
susceptible [səséptəbəl] adj.
느끼기 쉬운, 걸리기 쉬운, 영향받기 쉬운

means of this drug only that I was enabled to gain the rest necessary for the **preservation** of life. Oppressed by the recollection of my various misfortunes, I now swallowed double my usual quantity and soon slept profoundly. But sleep did not afford me **respite** from thought and misery; my dreams presented a thousand objects that scared me. Towards morning I was possessed by a kind of nightmare; I felt the fiend's grasp in my neck and could not free myself from it; groans and cries rang in my ears. My father, who was watching over me, perceiving my restlessness, awoke me; the dashing waves were around, the cloudy sky above, the fiend was not here: a sense of security, a feeling that a truce was established between the present hour and the irresistible, disastrous future **imparted** to me a kind of calm forgetfulness, of which the human mind is by its structure peculiarly **susceptible**.

Chapter 22

overtax [òuvərtǽks] v.
과중한 짐을 지우다, 혹사하다
indefatigable [ìndifǽtigəbəl]
adj. 지칠 줄 모르는, 끈기있는
origin [ɔ́:rədʒin, árə- / ɔ́ri-] n.
기원, 발단, 원인
remedy [rémədi] v.
고치다, 치료하다
incurable [inkjúərəbəl] adj.
낫지 않는, 불치의
society [səsáiəti] n.
교제, (남과의) 동석
celestial [səléstʃəl] adj.
하늘의, 천국의, 거룩한
mechanism [mékənìz-əm] n.
기구, 구조, 짜임새
unchain [ʌntʃéin] v.
사슬에서 풀어 주다, 속박을 풀다, 해방하다

The voyage came to an end. We landed, and proceeded to Paris. I soon found that I had **overtaxed** my strength and that I must repose before I could continue my journey. My father's care and attentions were **indefatigable**, but he did not know the **origin** of my sufferings and sought erroneous methods to **remedy** the **incurable** ill. He wished me to seek amusement in **society**. I abhorred the face of man. Oh, not abhorred! They were my brethren, my fellow beings, and I felt attracted even to the most repulsive among them, as to creatures of an angelic nature and **celestial mechanism**. But I felt that I had no right to share their intercourse. I had **unchained** an enemy among them whose joy it was to shed their blood and to revel in their groans. How they would, each and all, abhor me and hunt me from the world, did they know my **unhallowed** acts and the crimes which had their source in me!

My father yielded at length to my desire to avoid society and strove by various arguments to banish my despair. Sometimes he thought that I felt deeply the **degradation** of being obliged to answer a charge of murder, and he endeavoured to prove to me the **futility** of pride.

"Alas! My father," said I, "how little do you know me. Human beings, their feelings and passions, would indeed be degraded if such a wretch as I felt pride. Justine, poor unhappy Justine, was as innocent as I, and she suffered the same charge; she died for it; and I am the cause of this — I murdered her. William, Justine, and Henry — they all died by my hands."

My father had often, during my imprisonment, heard me make the same **assertion**; when I thus accused myself, he sometimes seemed to desire an explanation, and at others he appeared to consider it as the **offspring** of delirium, and that, during my illness, some idea of this kind had presented itself to my imagination, the remembrance of which I preserved in my **convalescence**. I avoided

consternation [kɑ̀nstərnéiʃən / kɔ̀n-] n.
경악, 대경실색

inmate [ínmèit] n.
주거인, 동거인

unbounded [ʌnbáundid] adj.
한정되지 않은, 무한한

infatuation [infæ̀tʃuéiʃən] n.
열중함, 심취

explanation and maintained a continual silence concerning the wretch I had created. I had a persuasion that I should be supposed mad, and this in itself would for ever have chained my tongue. But, besides, I could not bring myself to disclose a secret which would fill my hearer with **consternation** and make fear and unnatural horror the **inmates** of his breast. I checked, therefore, my impatient thirst for sympathy and was silent when I would have given the world to have confided the fatal secret. Yet still, words like those I have recorded would burst uncontrollably from me. I could offer no explanation of them, but their truth in part relieved the burden of my mysterious woe.

Upon this occasion my father said, with an expression of **unbounded** wonder, "My dearest Victor, what **infatuation** is this? My dear son, I entreat you never to make such an assertion again."

"I am not mad," I cried energetically; "the sun and the heavens, who have viewed my operations, can bear witness of my truth. I am the assassin of those most innocent victims; they died by my machinations. A thousand times would I have shed my own blood, drop by drop, to have saved their lives; but I could not, my father, indeed I could not sacrifice the whole human race."

deranged [diréindʒd] adj.
혼란된, 미친
obliterate [əblítərèit] v.
없애다

incoherent [ìnkouhíərənt, -hér-] adj.
앞뒤가 맞지 않는, 지리멸렬한
curb [kə:rb] v.
억제하다, 구속하다
imperious [impíəriəs] adj.
오만한, 고압적인, 도도한

The conclusion of this speech convinced my father that my ideas were **deranged**, and he instantly changed the subject of our conversation and endeavoured to alter the course of my thoughts. He wished as much as possible to **obliterate** the memory of the scenes that had taken place in Ireland and never alluded to them or suffered me to speak of my misfortunes.

As time passed away I became more calm; misery had her dwelling in my heart, but I no longer talked in the same **incoherent** manner of my own crimes; sufficient for me was the consciousness of them. By the utmost self-violence I **curbed** the **imperious** voice of wretchedness, which sometimes desired to declare itself to the whole world, and my manners were calmer and more composed than they had ever been since my journey to the sea of ice.

A few days before we left Paris on our way to Switzerland, I received the following letter from Elizabeth:

"My dear Friend,

"It gave me the greatest pleasure to receive a letter from my uncle dated at Paris; you are no longer at a formidable distance, and I may hope to see you in less than a fortnight. My poor cousin, how much you must have suffered! I

void [vɔid] adj.
없는, 결핍한

augment [ɔ:gmént] v.
늘리다, 증대하다

expect to see you looking even more ill than when you quitted Geneva. This winter has been passed most miserably, tortured as I have been by anxious suspense; yet I hope to see peace in your countenance and to find that your heart is not totally **void** of comfort and tranquillity.

"Yet I fear that the same feelings now exist that made you so miserable a year ago, even perhaps **augmented** by time. I would not disturb you at this period, when so many misfortunes weigh upon you, but a conversation that I had with my uncle previous to his departure renders some explanation necessary before we meet.

"Explanation! You may possibly say, What can Elizabeth have to explain? If you really say this, my questions are answered and all my doubts satisfied. But you are distant from me, and it is possible that you may dread and yet be pleased with this explanation; and in a probability of this being the case, I dare not any longer postpone writing what, during your absence, I have often wished to express to you but have never had the courage to begin.

"You well know, Victor, that our union had been the favourite plan of your parents ever since our infancy. We were told this when young, and taught to look forward to it as an event that would certainly take place. We were affectionate playfellows during childhood, and, I believe, dear and valued friends to one another as we grew older. But as brother and sister often entertain a lively affection towards each other without desiring a more intimate union, may not such also be our case? Tell me, dearest Victor. Answer me, I **conjure** you by our mutual happiness, with simple truth — Do you not love another?

"You have travelled; you have spent several years of your life at Ingolstadt; and I confess to you, my friend, that when I saw you last autumn so unhappy, flying to solitude from the society of every creature, I could not help supposing that you might regret our connection and believe yourself bound in honour to fulfil the wishes of your parents, although they opposed themselves to your **inclinations**. But this is false reasoning. I confess to you, my friend, that I love you and that in my airy dreams of **futurity** you have been my constant friend and companion. But it is your happiness I desire as well as my own when I declare to you that our marriage would render me eternally miserable unless it were the **dictate** of your own free choice. Even now I weep to think that, borne down as you are by the cruellest misfortunes, you may **stifle**, by the word 'honour', all hope of that love and happiness which

---

conjure [kʌ́ndʒər, kʌ́n-] v.
간청하다, 탄원하다, 부탁하다

inclination [inklənéiʃən] n.
좋아함, 기호, 의향
futurity [fjuːtjúrəti, -tʃúr- / -tjúəri-] n.
미래, 장래, 후세
dictate [díkteit] n.
(양심, 이성 따위의) 명령, 지령, 지시
stifle [stáif-əl] v.
억누르다, 억제하다

would alone restore you to yourself. I, who have so **disinterested** an affection for you, may increase your miseries tenfold by being an obstacle to your wishes. Ah! Victor, be assured that your cousin and playmate has too sincere a love for you not to be made miserable by this **supposition**. Be happy, my friend; and if you obey me in this one request, remain satisfied that nothing on earth will have the power to interrupt my tranquillity.

"Do not let this letter **disturb** you; do not answer tomorrow, or the next day, or even until you come, if it will give you pain. My uncle will send me news of your health, and if I see but one smile on your lips when we meet, occasioned by this or any other exertion of mine, I shall need no other happiness.

Elizabeth Lavenza.

Geneva, May 18th, 17—

This letter **revived** in my memory what I had before forgotten, the threat of the fiend — *"I will be with you on your wedding-night!"* Such was my **sentence**, and on that night would the daemon employ every art to destroy me and tear me from the glimpse of happiness which promised partly to console my sufferings. On that night he had determined to **consummate** his crimes by my death. Well, be it so; a deadly struggle would then assuredly take place, in which if he were victorious I should be at peace and his power over me be at an end. If he were **vanquished**, I should be a free man. Alas! What freedom? Such as the peasant enjoys when his family have been massacred before his eyes, his cottage burnt, his lands laid waste, and he is turned **adrift**, homeless, penniless, and alone, but free. Such would be my liberty except that in my Elizabeth I possessed a treasure, alas, balanced by those horrors of remorse and guilt which would pursue me until death.

Sweet and beloved Elizabeth! I read and reread her letter, and some softened feelings stole into my heart and dared to whisper **paradisiacal** dreams of love and joy; but the apple was already eaten, and the angel's arm **bared** to drive me from all hope. Yet I would die to make her happy. If the monster executed his threat, death was **inevitable**; yet, again, I considered whether my marriage would hasten my fate. My destruction might indeed arrive a few months sooner, but if my torturer should suspect that I postponed it, influenced by his **menaces**, he would surely find other and perhaps more dreadful means of revenge. He had vowed *to be with me on my wedding-night*, yet he did not consider that threat as binding him to peace in the meantime, for as if to show me

enunciation [inʌnsieiʃən] n.
공표, 선언, 언명
conduce [kəndjúːs] v.
도움이 되다, 이바지하다, (어떤 결과로) 이끌다
retard [ritáːrrd] v.
늦추다, 더디게 하다

consecrate [kánsəkrèit / kɔ́n-] v.
바치다, 정진하다
confide [kənfáid] v.
(비밀 등을) 털어놓다

that he was not yet satiated with blood, he had murdered Clerval immediately after the **enunciation** of his threats. I resolved, therefore, that if my immediate union with my cousin would **conduce** either to hers or my father's happiness, my adversary's designs against my life should not **retard** it a single hour.

In this state of mind I wrote to Elizabeth. My letter was calm and affectionate. "I fear, my beloved girl," I said, "little happiness remains for us on earth; yet all that I may one day enjoy is centred in you. Chase away your idle fears; to you alone do I **consecrate** my life and my endeavours for contentment. I have one secret, Elizabeth, a dreadful one; when revealed to you, it will chill your frame with horror, and then, far from being surprised at my misery, you will only wonder that I survive what I have endured. I will **confide** this tale of misery and terror to you the day after our marriage shall take place, for, my sweet cousin, there must be perfect confidence between us. But until then, I conjure you, do not mention or allude to it. This I most earnestly entreat, and I know you will comply."

In about a week after the arrival of Elizabeth's letter we returned to Geneva. The sweet girl welcomed me with warm affection, yet tears were in her eyes as she beheld my emaciated frame and feverish cheeks. I saw a change in her also. She was thinner and had lost much of that heavenly **vivacity** that had before charmed me; but her gentleness and soft looks of compassion made her a more fit companion for one blasted and miserable as I was.

The tranquillity which I now enjoyed did not endure. Memory brought madness with it, and when I thought of what had passed, a real insanity possessed me; sometimes I was furious and burnt with rage, sometimes low and **despondent**. I neither spoke nor looked at anyone, but sat motionless, bewildered by the multitude of miseries that overcame me.

Elizabeth alone had the power to draw me from these fits; her gentle voice would soothe me when transported by passion and inspire me with human feelings when sunk in **torpor**. She wept with me and for me. When reason returned, she would **remonstrate** and endeavour to inspire me with **resignation**. Ah! It is well for the unfortunate to be resigned, but for the guilty there is no peace. The agonies of remorse poison the luxury there is otherwise sometimes found in indulging the excess of grief.

Soon after my arrival my father spoke of my immediate marriage with Elizabeth. I remained silent.

"Have you, then, some other **attachment**?"

"None on earth. I love Elizabeth and look forward to our union with delight. Let the day therefore be fixed; and on it I will consecrate myself, in life or death, to the happiness of my cousin."

"My dear Victor, do not speak thus. Heavy misfortunes have befallen us, but let us only cling closer to what remains and transfer our love for those whom we have lost to those who yet live. Our circle will be small but bound close by the ties of affection and mutual misfortune. And when time shall have softened your despair, new and dear objects of care will be born to replace those of whom we have been so cruelly deprived."

Such were the lessons of my father. But to me the remembrance of the threat returned; nor can you wonder that, omnipotent as the fiend had yet been in his deeds of blood, I should almost regard him as **invincible**, and that when he had pronounced the words *"I shall be with you on your wedding-night,"* I should regard the threatened fate as **unavoidable**. But death was no evil to me if the loss of Elizabeth were balanced with it, and I therefore, with a contented and even cheerful countenance, agreed with my father that if my cousin would consent, the ceremony should take place in ten days, and thus put, as I imagined, the seal to my fate.

Great God! If for one instant I had thought what might be the hellish intention of my fiendish **adversary**, I would rather have banished myself for ever from my native country and wandered a friendless **outcast** over the earth than have consented to this miserable marriage. But, as if possessed of magic powers, the monster had blinded me to his real intentions; and when I thought that I had prepared only my own death, I hastened that of a far dearer victim.

As the period fixed for our marriage drew nearer, whether from **cowardice** or a **prophetic** feeling, I felt my heart sink within me. But I concealed my feelings by an appearance of hilarity that brought smiles and joy to the countenance of my father, but hardly deceived the ever-watchful and nicer eye of Elizabeth. She looked forward to our union with placid contentment, not unmingled with a little fear, which past misfortunes had impressed, that what now appeared certain and tangible happiness might soon dissipate into an airy dream and leave no trace but deep and everlasting regret.

Preparations were made for the event, congratulatory visits were received, and all wore

adversary [ǽdvərsèri / -səri] n.
적, 상대
outcast [áutkæ̀st / -kɑ̀:st] n.
버림받은 사람, 추방자

cowardice [káuərdis] n.
겁, 소심, 비겁
prophetic [prəfétik] adj.
예언의, 예언적인

a smiling appearance. I shut up, as well as I could, in my own heart the anxiety that preyed there and entered with seeming earnestness into the plans of my father, although they might only serve as the decorations of my tragedy. Through my father's exertions a part of the inheritance of Elizabeth had been restored to her by the Austrian government. A small possession on the shores of Como belonged to her. It was agreed that, immediately after our union, we should proceed to Villa Lavenza and spend our first days of happiness beside the beautiful lake near which it stood.

In the meantime I took every **precaution** to defend my person in case the fiend should openly attack me. I carried pistols and a dagger constantly about me and was ever on the watch to prevent **artifice**, and by these means gained a greater degree of tranquillity. Indeed, as the period approached, the threat appeared more as a **delusion**, not to be regarded as worthy to disturb my peace, while the happiness I hoped for in my marriage wore a greater appearance of certainty as the day fixed for its **solemnisation** drew nearer and I heard it continually spoken of as an occurrence which no accident could possibly prevent.

Elizabeth seemed happy; my tranquil demeanour contributed greatly to calm her mind.

---

precaution [prikɔ́:ʃən] n. 조심, 경계
artifice [ɑ́:rtəfis] n. 계략, 교묘한 수단
delusion [dilú:ʒən] n. 망상
solemnization [sɑ̀ləmnizéiʃən / sɔ̀ləm-] n. 식을 올림, 예식 거행

presentiment [prizéntəmənt] n. 예감, 육감
diffidence [dífidəns] n. 자신 없음, 망설임, 사양

nuptial [nʌpʃ-əl, -tʃ-əl] adj. 결혼의, 결혼식의

emulate [émjəlèit] v. 우열을 다투다, 겨루다

But on the day that was to fulfil my wishes and my destiny, she was melancholy, and a **presentiment** of evil pervaded her; and perhaps also she thought of the dreadful secret which I had promised to reveal to her on the following day. My father was in the meantime overjoyed, and, in the bustle of preparation, only recognised in the melancholy of his niece the **diffidence** of a bride.

After the ceremony was performed a large party assembled at my father's, but it was agreed that Elizabeth and I should commence our journey by water, sleeping that night at Evian and continuing our voyage on the following day. The day was fair, the wind favourable; all smiled on our **nuptial** embarkation.

Those were the last moments of my life during which I enjoyed the feeling of happiness. We passed rapidly along; the sun was hot, but we were sheltered from its rays by a kind of canopy while we enjoyed the beauty of the scene, sometimes on one side of the lake, where we saw Mont Salêve, the pleasant banks of Montalègre, and at a distance, surmounting all, the beautiful Mont Blanc, and the assemblage of snowy mountains that in vain endeavour to **emulate** her; sometimes coasting the opposite banks, we saw the mighty Jura opposing its dark side to the ambition that would quit its native country, and an almost insurmountable barrier to the invader who should wish to enslave it.

I took the hand of Elizabeth. "You are sorrowful, my love. Ah! If you knew what I have suffered and what I may yet endure, you would endeavour to let me taste the quiet and freedom from despair that this one day at least permits me to enjoy."

"Be happy, my dear Victor," replied Elizabeth; "there is, I hope, nothing to distress you; and be assured that if a lively joy is not painted in my face, my heart is contented. Something whispers to me not to depend too much on the prospect that is opened before us, but I will not listen to such a sinister voice. Observe how fast we move along and how the clouds, which sometimes obscure and sometimes rise above the dome of Mont Blanc, render this scene of beauty still more interesting. Look also at the innumerable fish that are swimming in the clear waters, where we can distinguish every pebble that lies at the bottom. What a divine day! How happy and serene all nature appears!"

Thus Elizabeth endeavoured to **divert** her thoughts and mine from all reflection upon melancholy subjects. But her **temper** was **fluctuating**; joy for a few instants shone in her eyes,

divert [divə́:rt, dai-] v.
전환시키다, 돌리다
temper [témpə:r] n.
기분, 기질, 성향
fluctuate [flʌ́ktʃuèit] v.
오르내리다, 변동하다

distraction [distrǽkʃən] n.
정신이 흐트러짐, 주의 산만

chasm [kǽzəm] n.
깊게 갈라진 틈; 작은 협곡
glen [glen] n.
골짜기
amphitheater [ǽmfəθὶːətər / -fiθὶə-] n.
원형 경기장
spire [spaiə:r] n.
뾰족탑, 뾰족한 꼭대기

waft [wɑːft, wæft] v.
감돌게 하다, 가볍게 나르다

but it continually gave place to **distraction** and reverie.

The sun sank lower in the heavens; we passed the river Drance and observed its path through the **chasms** of the higher and the **glens** of the lower hills. The Alps here come closer to the lake, and we approached the **amphitheatre** of mountains which forms its eastern boundary. The **spire** of Evian shone under the woods that surrounded it and the range of mountain above mountain by which it was overhung.

The wind, which had hitherto carried us along with amazing rapidity, sank at sunset to a light breeze; the soft air just ruffled the water and caused a pleasant motion among the trees as we approached the shore, from which it **wafted** the most delightful scent of flowers and hay. The sun sank beneath the horizon as we landed, and as I touched the shore I felt those cares and fears revive which soon were to clasp me and cling to me for ever.

Chapter 23

It was eight o'clock when we landed; we walked for a short time on the shore, enjoying the transitory light, and then retired to the inn and contemplated the lovely scene of waters, woods, and mountains, obscured in darkness, yet still displaying their black outlines.

The wind, which had fallen in the south, now rose with great violence in the west. The moon had reached her summit in the heavens and was beginning to descend; the clouds swept across it swifter than the flight of the vulture and dimmed her rays, while the lake reflected the scene of the busy heavens, rendered still busier by the restless waves that were beginning to rise. Suddenly a heavy storm of rain descended.

I had been calm during the day, but so soon as night obscured the shapes of objects, a thousand fears arose in my mind. I was anxious and watchful, while my right hand grasped a pistol which was hidden in my bosom; every sound terrified me, but I resolved that I would sell my life dearly and not shrink from the conflict until my own life or that of my **adversary** was **extinguished**.

Elizabeth observed my agitation for some time in timid and fearful silence, but there was something in my glance which **communicated** terror to her, and trembling, she asked, "What is it that agitates you, my dear Victor? What is it you fear?"

"Oh! Peace, peace, my love," replied I; "this night, and all will be safe; but this night is dreadful, very dreadful."

I passed an hour in this state of mind, when suddenly I reflected how fearful the combat which I momentarily expected would be to my wife, and I earnestly entreated her to retire, resolving not to join her until I had obtained some knowledge as to the situation of my enemy.

She left me, and I continued some time walking up and down the passages of the house and inspecting every corner that might afford a

---

adversary [ǽdvərsèri / -səri] n.
적, 상대
extinguish [ikstíŋgwiʃ] v.
없애다, 소멸시키다

communicate [kəmjú:nəkèit] v.
전하다, 옮기다

retreat [ritríːt] n.
은신처, 피난처

retreat to my adversary. But I discovered no trace of him and was beginning to conjecture that some fortunate chance had intervened to prevent the execution of his menaces when suddenly I heard a shrill and dreadful scream. It came from the room into which Elizabeth had retired. As I heard it, the whole truth rushed into my mind, my arms dropped, the motion of every muscle and fibre was suspended; I could feel the blood trickling in my veins and tingling in the extremities of my limbs. This state lasted but for an instant; the scream was repeated, and I rushed into the room.

expire [ikspáiər] v.
끝나다, 종료되다; 숨을 거두다
obstinate [ábstənit / ɔ́b-] adj.
완고한, 완강한, 집요한

Great God! Why did I not then **expire**! Why am I here to relate the destruction of the best hope and the purest creature on earth? She was there, lifeless and inanimate, thrown across the bed, her head hanging down and her pale and distorted features half covered by her hair. Everywhere I turn I see the same figure — her bloodless arms and relaxed form flung by the murderer on its bridal bier. Could I behold this and live? Alas! Life is **obstinate** and clings closest where it is most hated. For a moment only did I lose recollection; I fell senseless on the ground.

When I recovered I found myself surrounded by the people of the inn; their countenances expressed a breathless terror, but the horror of others appeared only as a mockery, a shadow of the feelings that oppressed me. I escaped from them to the room where lay the body of Elizabeth, my love, my wife, so lately living, so dear, so worthy. She had been moved from the posture in which I had first beheld her, and now, as she lay, her head upon her arm and a handkerchief thrown across her face and neck, I might have supposed her asleep. I rushed towards her and embraced her with ardour, but the deadly languor and coldness of the limbs told me that what I now held in my arms had ceased to be the Elizabeth whom I had loved and cherished. The murderous mark of the fiend's grasp was on her neck, and the breath had ceased to issue from her lips.

While I still hung over her in the agony of despair, I happened to look up. The windows of the room had before been darkened, and I felt a kind of panic on seeing the pale yellow light of the moon illuminate the chamber. The shutters had been thrown back, and with a sensation of horror not to be described, I saw at the open window a figure the most hideous and abhorred. A grin was on the face of the monster; he seemed to jeer, as with his fiendish finger he pointed towards the corpse of my wife. I rushed towards the window, and drawing a pistol from my bosom, fired; but he eluded me,

report [ripɔ́:rt] n.
총성, 포성, 폭발음

I rushed towards the window, and drawing a pistol from my bosom, fired; but he eluded me ...

leaped from his station, and running with the swiftness of lightning, plunged into the lake.

The **report** of the pistol brought a crowd into the room. I pointed to the spot where he had disappeared, and we followed the track with boats; nets were cast, but in vain. After passing several hours, we returned hopeless, most of my companions believing it to have been a form conjured up by my fancy. After having landed, they proceeded to search the country, parties going in different directions among the woods and vines.

I attempted to accompany them and proceeded a short distance from the house, but my head whirled round, my steps were like those of a drunken man, I fell at last in a state of utter exhaustion; a film covered my eyes, and my skin was parched with the heat of fever. In this state I was carried back and placed on a bed, hardly conscious of what had happened; my eyes wandered round the room as if to seek something that I had lost.

After an interval I arose, and as if by instinct, crawled into the room where the corpse of my beloved lay. There were women weeping around; I hung over it and joined my sad tears to theirs; all this time no distinct idea presented itself to my mind, but my thoughts rambled to various subjects, reflecting confusedly on my misfortunes and their cause. I was bewildered, in a cloud of wonder and horror. The death of William, the execution of Justine, the murder of Clerval, and lastly of my wife; even at that moment I knew not that my only remaining friends were safe from the malignity of the fiend; my father even now might be writhing under his grasp, and Ernest might be dead at his feet. This idea made me shudder and recalled me to action. I started up and resolved to return to Geneva with all possible speed.

There were no horses to be procured, and I must return by the lake; but the wind was unfavourable, and the rain fell in torrents. However, it was hardly morning, and I might reasonably hope to arrive by night. I hired men to row and took an oar myself, for I had always experienced relief from mental torment in bodily exercise. But the overflowing misery I now felt, and the excess of agitation that I endured rendered me incapable of any exertion. I threw down the oar, and leaning my head upon my hands, gave way to every gloomy idea that arose. If I looked up, I saw scenes which were familiar to me in my happier time and which I had contemplated but the day before in the company of her who was now but a shadow and a recollection. Tears streamed from my eyes. The rain had ceased for a moment, and

I saw the fish play in the waters as they had done a few hours before; they had then been observed by Elizabeth. Nothing is so painful to the human mind as a great and sudden change. The sun might shine or the clouds might lower, but nothing could appear to me as it had done the day before. A fiend had snatched from me every hope of future happiness; no creature had ever been so miserable as I was; so frightful an event is single in the history of man.

But why should I dwell upon the incidents that followed this last overwhelming event? Mine has been a tale of horrors; I have reached their **acme**, and what I must now relate can but be **tedious** to you. Know that, one by one, my friends were snatched away; I was left desolate. My own strength is exhausted, and I must tell, in a few words, what remains of my hideous narration.

I arrived at Geneva. My father and Ernest yet lived, but the former sunk under the **tidings** that I bore. I see him now, excellent and **venerable** old man! His eyes wandered in vacancy, for they had lost their charm and their delight — his Elizabeth, his more than daughter, whom he **doted** on with all that affection which a man feels, who in the decline of life, having few affections, clings more earnestly to those that remain. Cursed, cursed be the fiend that

---

acme [ǽkmi] n.
절정, 정점
tedious [tíːdiəs, -dʒəs] adj.
지루한, 싫증나는, 장황한

tiding [taidiŋ] n.
소식, 정보, 뉴스
venerable [vénərəbəl] adj.
존경할 만한
dote [dout] v.
맹목적으로 사랑하다

brought misery on his grey hairs and doomed him to waste in wretchedness! He could not live under the horrors that were accumulated around him; the **springs** of existence suddenly **gave way**; he was unable to rise from his bed, and in a few days he died in my arms.

What then became of me? I know not; I lost sensation, and chains and darkness were the only objects that pressed upon me. Sometimes, indeed, I dreamt that I wandered in flowery meadows and pleasant **vales** with the friends of my youth, but I awoke and found myself in a dungeon. Melancholy followed, but by degrees I gained a clear conception of my miseries and situation and was then released from my prison. For they had called me mad, and during many months, as I understood, a solitary cell had been my habitation.

Liberty, however, had been a useless gift to me, had I not, as I awakened to reason, at the same time awakened to revenge. As the memory of past misfortunes pressed upon me, I began to reflect on their cause — the monster whom I had created, the miserable daemon whom I had sent abroad into the world for my destruction. I was possessed by a maddening rage when I thought of him, and desired and ardently prayed that I might have him within my grasp to wreak a great and **signal** revenge on his

---

spring [spriŋ] n.
원천, 근원
give way:
무너지다, 부서지다

vale [veil] n.
골짜기, 계곡

signal [sígn-əl] adj.
두드러진, 현저한, 주목할 만한

repair [ripéə:r] v.
가다, 자주 다니다
exert [igzə́:rt] v.
(힘, 능력 등을) 내다, 쓰다, 노력하다
apprehension [æprihénʃən] n.
체포, 구금

deposition [dèpəzíʃən, dì:p-] n.
(법정 등에서의) 증언
deviate [dí:vièit] v.
벗어나다, 빗나가다
invective [invéktiv] n.
욕설, 악담, 독설

cursed head.

Nor did my hate long confine itself to useless wishes; I began to reflect on the best means of securing him; and for this purpose, about a month after my release, I **repaired** to a criminal judge in the town and told him that I had an accusation to make, that I knew the destroyer of my family, and that I required him to **exert** his whole authority for the **apprehension** of the murderer.

The magistrate listened to me with attention and kindness. "Be assured, sir," said he, "no pains or exertions on my part shall be spared to discover the villain."

"I thank you," replied I; "listen, therefore, to the **deposition** that I have to make. It is indeed a tale so strange that I should fear you would not credit it were there not something in truth which, however wonderful, forces conviction. The story is too connected to be mistaken for a dream, and I have no motive for falsehood." My manner as I thus addressed him was impressive but calm; I had formed in my own heart a resolution to pursue my destroyer to death, and this purpose quieted my agony and for an interval reconciled me to life. I now related my history briefly but with firmness and precision, marking the dates with accuracy and never **deviating** into **invective** or exclamation.

The magistrate appeared at first perfectly incredulous, but as I continued he became more attentive and interested; I saw him sometimes shudder with horror; at others a lively surprise, unmingled with disbelief, was painted on his countenance.

When I had concluded my narration, I said, "This is the being whom I accuse and for whose **seizure** and punishment I call upon you to exert your whole power. It is your duty as a magistrate, and I believe and hope that your feelings as a man will not **revolt** from the execution of those functions on this occasion."

This address caused a considerable change in the **physiognomy** of my own **auditor**. He had heard my story with that half kind of belief that is given to a tale of spirits and supernatural events; but when he was called upon to act officially in consequence, the whole tide of his incredulity returned. He, however, answered mildly, "I would willingly afford you every aid in your pursuit, but the creature of whom you speak appears to have powers which would put all my exertions to defiance. Who can follow an animal which can traverse the sea of ice and inhabit caves and dens where no man would venture to intrude? Besides,

---

seizure [síːʒəːr] n.
잡기, 체포
revolt [rivóult] v.
거슬리다, 반감을 품다

physiognomy [fiziágnəmi / -ɔ́n-] n.
얼굴, 얼굴 생김새, 인상
auditor [ɔ́ːditər] n.
듣는 사람, 방청자

commission [kəmíʃən] n.
(과실을) 범하기, 저지름, 범행

hover [hʌ́vər, hɑ́v] v.
떠다니다, 맴돌다, 배회하다
chamois [ʃǽmi / ʃǽmwɑ:] n.
샤무아(알프스 영양)
desert [dizə́:rt] n.
응분의 상 또는 벌, 당연한 대가

proportionate [prəpɔ́:rʃənit] adj. 균형잡힌, 어울리는
impracticable [imprǽktikəbəl] adj.
실행 불가능한

moment [móumənt] n.
중요성, 중대사
turn loose:
해방하다, 자유롭게 하다

some months have elapsed since the **commission** of his crimes, and no one can conjecture to what place he has wandered or what region he may now inhabit."

"I do not doubt that he **hovers** near the spot which I inhabit, and if he has indeed taken refuge in the Alps, he may be hunted like the **chamois** and destroyed as a beast of prey. But I perceive your thoughts; you do not credit my narrative and do not intend to pursue my enemy with the punishment which is his **desert**."

As I spoke, rage sparkled in my eyes; the magistrate was intimidated.

"You are mistaken," said he. "I will exert myself, and if it is in my power to seize the monster, be assured that he shall suffer punishment **proportionate** to his crimes. But I fear, from what you have yourself described to be his properties, that this will prove **impracticable**; and thus, while every proper measure is pursued, you should make up your mind to disappointment."

"That cannot be; but all that I can say will be of little avail. My revenge is of no **moment** to you; yet, while I allow it to be a vice, I confess that it is the devouring and only passion of my soul. My rage is unspeakable when I reflect that the murderer, whom I have **turned loose** upon society, still exists. You refuse my just demand; I have but one resource, and I devote myself, either in my life or death, to his destruction."

I trembled with excess of agitation as I said this; there was a **frenzy** in my manner, and something, I doubt not, of that **haughty fierceness** which the **martyrs** of old are said to have possessed. But to a Genevan magistrate, whose mind was occupied by far other ideas than those of devotion and heroism, this elevation of mind had much the appearance of madness. He endeavoured to soothe me as a nurse does a child and reverted to my tale as the effects of delirium.

"Man," I cried, "how ignorant art thou in thy pride of wisdom! Cease; you know not what it is you say."

I broke from the house angry and disturbed and retired to meditate on some other **mode** of action.

---

frenzy [frénzi] n.
열광, 광란, 격분
haughty [hɔ́:ti] adj.
도도한, 오만한, 불손한
fierceness [fiərsnis] n.
거침, 난폭함, 맹렬함
martyr [mά:rtər] n.
순교자

mode [moud] n.
양식, 형식, 방법

Chapter 24

My present situation was one in which all voluntary thought was swallowed up and lost. I was hurried away by fury; revenge alone endowed me with strength and composure; it moulded my feelings and allowed me to be calculating and calm at periods when otherwise delirium or death would have been my **portion**.

My first resolution was to quit Geneva for ever; my country, which, when I was happy and beloved, was dear to me, now, in my **adversity**, became hateful. I provided myself with a sum of money, together with a few jewels which had belonged to my mother, and departed.

And now my wanderings began which are

---

portion [pɔ́:rʃən] n.
운명, 운

adversity [ædvə́:rsəti, əd-] n.
역경, 불행, 불운

to cease but with life. I have traversed a vast portion of the earth and have endured all the hardships which travellers in deserts and barbarous countries are **wont** to meet. How I have lived I hardly know; many times have I stretched my **failing** limbs upon the sandy plain and prayed for death. But revenge kept me alive; I dared not die and leave my adversary in being.

When I quitted Geneva my first labour was to gain some **clue** by which I might **trace** the steps of my fiendish enemy. But my plan was unsettled, and I wandered many hours round the **confines** of the town, uncertain what path I should pursue. As night approached I found myself at the entrance of the cemetery where William, Elizabeth, and my father reposed. I entered it and approached the tomb which marked their graves. Everything was silent except the leaves of the trees, which were gently agitated by the wind; the night was nearly dark, and the scene would have been solemn and **affecting** even to an uninterested observer. The spirits of the departed seemed to **flit** around and to cast a shadow, which was felt but not seen, around the head of the mourner.

The deep grief which this scene had at first excited quickly gave way to rage and despair. They were dead, and I lived; their murderer

preside [prizáid] v.
통할하다, 관장하다
pursue [pərsú: / -sjú:] v.
뒤쫓다, 추적하다
perish [périʃ] v.
죽다, 소멸하다
preserve [prizə́:rv] v.
보전하다, 유지하다
call on:
요구하다, 부탁하다
minister [mínistər] n.
대리인, 대행자

adjuration [æ̀dʒəréiʃən] n.
선서, 서약

also lived, and to destroy him I must drag out my weary existence. I knelt on the grass and kissed the earth and with quivering lips exclaimed, "By the sacred earth on which I kneel, by the shades that wander near me, by the deep and eternal grief that I feel, I swear; and by thee, O Night, and the spirits that **preside** over thee, to **pursue** the daemon who caused this misery, until he or I shall **perish** in mortal conflict. For this purpose I will **preserve** my life; to execute this dear revenge will I again behold the sun and tread the green herbage of earth, which otherwise should vanish from my eyes for ever. And I **call on** you, spirits of the dead, and on you, wandering **ministers** of vengeance, to aid and conduct me in my work. Let the cursed and hellish monster drink deep of agony; let him feel the despair that now torments me."

I had begun my **adjuration** with solemnity and an awe which almost assured me that the shades of my murdered friends heard and approved my devotion, but the furies possessed me as I concluded, and rage choked my utterance.

I was answered through the stillness of night by a loud and fiendish laugh. It rang on my ears long and heavily; the mountains re-echoed it, and I felt as if all hell surrounded me with mockery and laughter. Surely in that moment

I should have been possessed by frenzy and have destroyed my miserable existence but that my vow was heard and that I was reserved for vengeance. The laughter died away, when a well-known and abhorred voice, apparently close to my ear, addressed me in an audible whisper, "I am satisfied, miserable wretch! You have determined to live, and I am satisfied."

I darted towards the spot from which the sound proceeded, but the devil eluded my grasp. Suddenly the broad disk of the moon arose and shone full upon his ghastly and distorted shape as he fled with more than mortal speed.

I pursued him, and for many months this has been my task. Guided by a slight clue, I followed the windings of the Rhône, but vainly. The blue Mediterranean appeared, and by a strange chance, I saw the fiend enter by night and hide himself in a vessel bound for the Black Sea. I took my passage in the same ship, but he escaped, I know not how.

Amidst the wilds of Tartary and Russia, although he still evaded me, I have ever followed in his track. Sometimes the peasants, scared by this **horrid apparition**, informed me of his path; sometimes he himself, who feared that if I lost all trace of him I should despair and die, left some mark to guide me. The snows descended on my head, and I saw the print of

extricate [ékstrəkèit] v.
풀다, 구출하다, 해방하다
insurmountable [ìnsər-máuntəbəl] adj.
극복할 수 없는, 넘을 수 없는
repast [ripǽst, -pá:st] n.
식사, 음식
invoke [invóuk] v.
기원하다, 호소하다
bedim [bidím] v.
흐리게 하다

subsist [səbsíst] v.
살아가다

his huge step on the white plain. To you first entering on life, to whom care is new and agony unknown, how can you understand what I have felt and still feel? Cold, want, and fatigue were the least pains which I was destined to endure; I was cursed by some devil and carried about with me my eternal hell; yet still a spirit of good followed and directed my steps and when I most murmured would suddenly **extricate** me from seemingly **insurmountable** difficulties. Sometimes, when nature, overcome by hunger, sank under the exhaustion, a **repast** was prepared for me in the desert that restored and inspirited me. The fare was, indeed, coarse, such as the peasants of the country ate, but I will not doubt that it was set there by the spirits that I had **invoked** to aid me. Often, when all was dry, the heavens cloudless, and I was parched by thirst, a slight cloud would **bedim** the sky, shed the few drops that revived me, and vanish.

 I followed, when I could, the courses of the rivers; but the daemon generally avoided these, as it was here that the population of the country chiefly collected. In other places human beings were seldom seen, and I generally **subsisted** on the wild animals that crossed my path. I had money with me and gained the friendship of the villagers by distributing it; or I brought with me some food that I had killed, which, after taking a small part, I always presented to those who had provided me with fire and utensils for cooking.

My life, as it passed thus, was indeed hateful to me, and it was during sleep alone that I could taste joy. O blessed sleep! Often, when most miserable, I sank to repose, and my dreams lulled me even to rapture. The spirits that guarded me had provided these moments, or rather hours, of happiness that I might **retain** strength to fulfil my **pilgrimage**. Deprived of this **respite**, I should have sunk under my hardships. During the day I was sustained and inspirited by the hope of night, for in sleep I saw my friends, my wife, and my beloved country; again I saw the **benevolent** countenance of my father, heard the silver tones of my Elizabeth's voice, and beheld Clerval enjoying health and youth. Often, when wearied by a **toilsome** march, I persuaded myself that I was dreaming until night should come and that I should then enjoy reality in the arms of my dearest friends. What agonising fondness did I feel for them! How did I cling to their dear forms, as sometimes they haunted even my waking hours, and persuade myself that they still lived! At such moments vengeance, that burned within me, died in my heart, and I

---

retain [ritéin] v.
보유하다, 유지하다
pilgrimage [pílgrimidʒ] n.
긴 여행
respite [réspit] n.
연기, 유예, 휴식
benevolent [bənévələnt] adj.
호의적인, 친절한, 인정 많은
toilsome [tɔ́ilsəm] adj.
고생스러운, 고달픈, 힘든

enjoin [endʒɔ́in] v.
이르다, 명하다, 요구하다

instigate [ínstəgèit] v.
부추기다, 선동하다
reign [rein] n.
치세, 통치, 지배
legible [lédʒəb-əl] adj.
읽을 수 있는, 판별 가능한
impassive [impǽsiv] adj.
고통을 느끼지 않는, 무감각한
tardily [tá:rdəli] adv.
느리게, 늦게, 더디게
period [píəriəd] n.
말기, 종결, 종지부

perish [périʃ] v.
죽다, 소멸하다
tedious [tí:diəs, -dʒəs] adj.
지루한, 싫증나는, 장황한

pursued my path towards the destruction of the daemon more as a task **enjoined** by heaven, as the mechanical impulse of some power of which I was unconscious, than as the ardent desire of my soul.

What his feelings were whom I pursued I cannot know. Sometimes, indeed, he left marks in writing on the barks of the trees or cut in stone that guided me and **instigated** my fury. "My **reign** is not yet over" — these words were **legible** in one of these inscriptions — "you live, and my power is complete. Follow me; I seek the everlasting ices of the north, where you will feel the misery of cold and frost, to which I am **impassive**. You will find near this place, if you follow not too **tardily**, a dead hare; eat and be refreshed. Come on, my enemy; we have yet to wrestle for our lives, but many hard and miserable hours must you endure until that **period** shall arrive."

Scoffing devil! Again do I vow vengeance; again do I devote thee, miserable fiend, to torture and death. Never will I give up my search until he or I **perish**; and then with what ecstasy shall I join my Elizabeth and my departed friends, who even now prepare for me the reward of my **tedious** toil and horrible pilgrimage!

As I still pursued my journey to the

> "Come on, my enemy; we have yet to wrestle for our lives, but many hard and miserable hours must you endure until that period shall arrive."

northward, the snows thickened and the cold increased in a degree almost too severe to support. The peasants were shut up in their hovels, and only a few of the most hardy ventured forth to seize the animals whom starvation had forced from their hiding-places to seek for prey. The rivers were covered with ice, and no fish could be procured; and thus I was cut off from my chief article of maintenance.

The triumph of my enemy increased with the difficulty of my labours. One inscription that he left was in these words: "Prepare! Your toils only begin; wrap yourself in furs and provide food, for we shall soon enter upon a journey where your sufferings will satisfy my everlasting hatred."

My courage and **perseverance** were **invigorated** by these scoffing words; I resolved not to fail in my purpose, and calling on Heaven to support me, I continued with **unabated fervour** to traverse immense deserts, until the ocean appeared at a distance and formed the utmost boundary of the horizon. Oh! How unlike it was to the blue seasons of the south! Covered with ice, it was only to be distinguished from land by its superior wildness and ruggedness. The Greeks wept for joy when they beheld the Mediterranean from the hills of Asia, and hailed with rapture the boundary of

---

perseverance [pə̀ːrsəvíːrəns] n.
인내, 끈기, 버팀
invigorate [invígərèit] v.
원기를 돋구다, 북돋다
unabated [ʌ̀nəbéitid] adj.
줄지 않는, 약해지지 않는
fervor / fervour [fə́ːrvər] n.
열렬, 진지, 열정

notwithstanding [nàtwiðstǽndiŋ, -wiθ- / nɔ̀t-] prep. ~에도 불구하고
gibe, jibe [ʤaib] n. 조롱, 비웃음, 헐뜯음
grapple [grǽpəl] v. 맞잡고 겨루다, 해결하려고 고심하다
inconceivable [ìnkənsí:vəbəl] adj. 상상도 할 수 없는, 믿을 수 없는
lose ground: 지다, 밀리다, 뒤쳐지다
hamlet [hǽmlit] n. 작은 마을
drove [drouv] n. 가축떼

their toils. I did not weep, but I knelt down and with a full heart thanked my guiding spirit for conducting me in safety to the place where I hoped, **notwithstanding** my adversary's **gibe**, to meet and **grapple** with him.

Some weeks before this period I had procured a sledge and dogs and thus traversed the snows with **inconceivable** speed. I know not whether the fiend possessed the same advantages, but I found that, as before I had daily **lost ground** in the pursuit, I now gained on him, so much so that when I first saw the ocean he was but one day's journey in advance, and I hoped to intercept him before he should reach the beach. With new courage, therefore, I pressed on, and in two days arrived at a wretched **hamlet** on the seashore. I inquired of the inhabitants concerning the fiend and gained accurate information. A gigantic monster, they said, had arrived the night before, armed with a gun and many pistols, putting to flight the inhabitants of a solitary cottage through fear of his terrific appearance. He had carried off their store of winter food, and placing it in a sledge, to draw which he had seized on a numerous **drove** of trained dogs, he had harnessed them, and the same night, to the joy of the horror-struck villagers, had pursued his journey across the sea in a direction that led to no land; and they conjectured that he must speedily be destroyed by the breaking of the ice or frozen by the eternal frosts.

On hearing this information I suffered a temporary **access** of despair. He had escaped me, and I must commence a destructive and almost endless journey across the mountainous ices of the ocean, amidst cold that few of the inhabitants could long endure and which I, the native of a genial and sunny climate, could not hope to survive. Yet at the idea that the fiend should live and be **triumphant**, my rage and vengeance returned, and like a mighty tide, overwhelmed every other feeling. After a slight repose, during which the spirits of the dead hovered round and **instigated** me to toil and revenge, I prepared for my journey.

I exchanged my land-sledge for one fashioned for the **inequalities** of the Frozen Ocean, and purchasing a plentiful stock of **provisions**, I departed from land.

I cannot guess how many days have passed since then, but I have endured misery which nothing but the eternal sentiment of a just **retribution** burning within my heart could have enabled me to support. Immense and rugged mountains of ice often **barred** up my passage, and I often heard the thunder of the **ground sea**, which threatened my destruction.

protraction [proutrǽkʃən] n.
오래 끌기, 연장
expanse [ikspǽns] n.
광활한 공간, 넓디넓은 장소

But again the frost came and made the paths of the sea secure.

By the quantity of provision which I had consumed, I should guess that I had passed three weeks in this journey; and the continual **protraction** of hope, returning back upon the heart, often wrung bitter drops of despondency and grief from my eyes. Despair had indeed almost secured her prey, and I should soon have sunk beneath this misery. Once, after the poor animals that conveyed me had with incredible toil gained the summit of a sloping ice mountain, and one, sinking under his fatigue, died, I viewed the **expanse** before me with anguish, when suddenly my eye caught a dark speck upon the dusky plain. I strained my sight to discover what it could be and uttered a wild cry of ecstasy when I distinguished a sledge and the distorted proportions of a well-known form within. Oh! With what a burning gush did hope revisit my heart! Warm tears filled my eyes, which I hastily wiped away, that they might not intercept the view I had of the daemon; but still my sight was dimmed by the burning drops, until, giving way to the emotions that oppressed me, I wept aloud.

disencumber [dìsenkʌ́mbər] v.
장애물을 제거하다

But this was not the time for delay; I **disencumbered** the dogs of their dead companion, gave them a plentiful portion of food, and after an hour's rest, which was absolutely necessary, and yet which was bitterly irksome to me, I continued my route. The sledge was still visible, nor did I again lose sight of it except at the moments when for a short time some ice-rock concealed it with its intervening **crags**. I indeed perceptibly gained on it, and when, after nearly two days' journey, I beheld my enemy at no more than a mile distant, my heart bounded within me.

But now, when I appeared almost within grasp of my foe, my hopes were suddenly extinguished, and I lost all trace of him more utterly than I had ever done before. A ground sea was heard; the thunder of its progress, as the waters rolled and swelled beneath me, became every moment more **ominous** and terrific. I pressed on, but in vain. The wind arose; the sea roared; and, as with the mighty shock of an earthquake, it split and cracked with a tremendous and overwhelming sound. The work was soon finished; in a few minutes a tumultuous sea rolled between me and my enemy, and I was left drifting on a scattered piece of ice that was continually lessening and thus preparing for me a hideous death.

In this manner many appalling hours passed; several of my dogs died, and I myself was about to sink under the accumulation of distress

---

crag [kræg] n.
우뚝 솟은 험한 바위

ominous [ámənəs / ɔ́m-] adj.
불길한

Oh! With what a burning gush did hope revisit my heart! Warm tears filled my eyes, which I hastily wiped away, that they might not intercept the view I had of the daemon

succor [sʌ́kər] n.
구조, 원조
induce [indjúːs] v.
설득하다, 유발하다
grant [grænt, grɑːnt] v.
주다, 부여하다, 허가하다
vigor [vígər] n.
활기, 체력, 힘

in a few minutes a tumultuous sea rolled between me and my enemy, and I was left drifting on a scattered piece of ice that was continually lessening and thus preparing for me a hideous death.

when I saw your vessel riding at anchor and holding forth to me hopes of **succour** and life. I had no conception that vessels ever came so far north and was astounded at the sight. I quickly destroyed part of my sledge to construct oars, and by these means was enabled, with infinite fatigue, to move my ice raft in the direction of your ship. I had determined, if you were going southwards, still to trust myself to the mercy of the seas rather than abandon my purpose. I hoped to **induce** you to **grant** me a boat with which I could pursue my enemy. But your direction was northwards. You took me on board when my **vigour** was exhausted, and I should soon have sunk under my multiplied hardships into a death which I still dread, for my task is unfulfilled.

Oh! When will my guiding spirit, in conducting me to the daemon, allow me the rest I so much desire; or must I die, and he yet live? If I do, swear to me, Walton, that he shall not escape, that you will seek him and satisfy my vengeance in his death. And do I dare to ask of you to undertake my pilgrimage, to endure the hardships that I have undergone? No; I am not so selfish. Yet, when I am dead, if he should appear, if the ministers of vengeance should conduct him to you, swear that he shall not live — swear that he shall not triumph over my accumulated woes and survive to add to the list of his dark crimes. He is **eloquent** and **persuasive**, and once his words had even power over my heart; but trust him not. His soul is as hellish as his form, full of **treachery** and fiend-like **malice**. Hear him not; call on the names of William, Justine, Clerval, Elizabeth, my father, and of the wretched Victor, and thrust your sword into his heart. I will hover near and direct the steel aright.

Walton, *in continuation.*

August 26th, 17—.

You have read this strange and terrific story, Margaret; and do you not feel your blood congeal with horror, like that which even now **curdles** mine? Sometimes, seized with sudden agony, he could not continue his tale; at others, his voice broken, yet piercing, uttered with difficulty the words so **replete** with anguish. His fine and lovely eyes were now lighted up with **indignation**, now subdued to **downcast** sorrow and quenched in infinite wretchedness. Sometimes he commanded his countenance and tones and related the most horrible incidents with a tranquil voice, suppressing every mark of agitation; then, like a volcano bursting forth, his face would suddenly change to an

imprecation [imprikeiʃən] n.
(사람 등에게 재앙이 내리라고) 빌기, 저주하기
connected [kənéktid] adj.
결합된, 맥락이 있는, 일관성 있는
own [oun] v.
인정하다, 자인하다
asseveration [əsevəreiʃən] n.
단언, 언명, 주장
impenetrable [impénətrəbəl] adj. 완고한, 받아들이지 않는

whither [hwíðə:r] adv.
어디로

posterity [pɑstérəti / pɔs-] n.
자손, 후세, 후대

expression of the wildest rage as he shrieked out **imprecations** on his persecutor.

His tale is **connected** and told with an appearance of the simplest truth, yet I **own** to you that the letters of Felix and Safie, which he showed me, and the apparition of the monster seen from our ship, brought to me a greater conviction of the truth of his narrative than his **asseverations**, however earnest and connected. Such a monster has, then, really existence! I cannot doubt it, yet I am lost in surprise and admiration. Sometimes I endeavoured to gain from Frankenstein the particulars of his creature's formation, but on this point he was **impenetrable**.

"Are you mad, my friend?" said he. "Or **whither** does your senseless curiosity lead you? Would you also create for yourself and the world a demoniacal enemy? Peace, peace! Learn my miseries and do not seek to increase your own."

Frankenstein discovered that I made notes concerning his history; he asked to see them and then himself corrected and augmented them in many places, but principally in giving the life and spirit to the conversations he held with his enemy. "Since you have preserved my narration," said he, "I would not that a mutilated one should go down to **posterity**."

> destitute [déstətjùːt] adj.
> 가지지 않은, ~이 없는
> converse [kánvəːrs / kɔ́n-] n.
> 담화, 환담
> communion [kəmjúːnjən] n.
> 교제, 친교, 교감

Thus has a week passed away, while I have listened to the strangest tale that ever imagination formed. My thoughts and every feeling of my soul have been drunk up by the interest for my guest which this tale and his own elevated and gentle manners have created. I wish to soothe him, yet can I counsel one so infinitely miserable, so **destitute** of every hope of consolation, to live? Oh, no! The only joy that he can now know will be when he composes his shattered spirit to peace and death. Yet he enjoys one comfort, the offspring of solitude and delirium; he believes that when in dreams he holds **converse** with his friends and derives from that **communion** consolation for his miseries or excitements to his vengeance, that they are not the creations of his fancy, but the beings themselves who visit him from the regions of a remote world. This faith gives a solemnity to his reveries that render them to me almost as imposing and interesting as truth.

> "Or whither does your senseless curiosity lead you? Would you also create for yourself and the world a demoniacal enemy?

Our conversations are not always confined to his own history and misfortunes. On every point of general literature he displays unbounded knowledge and a quick and piercing **apprehension**. His **eloquence** is forcible and touching; nor can I hear him, when he relates a pathetic incident or endeavours to move the passions of pity or love, without tears. What

> apprehension [æ̀prihénʃən] n.
> 이해, 터득
> eloquence [éləkwəns] n.
> 웅변, 능변

a glorious creature must he have been in the days of his prosperity, when he is thus noble and godlike in ruin! He seems to feel his own worth and the greatness of his fall.

"When younger," said he, "I believed myself destined for some great enterprise. My feelings are profound, but I possessed a coolness of judgment that fitted me for **illustrious** achievements. This sentiment of the worth of my nature supported me when others would have been oppressed, for I deemed it criminal to throw away in useless grief those talents that might be useful to my fellow creatures. When I reflected on the work I had completed, no less a one than the creation of a sensitive and rational animal, I could not rank myself with the herd of common projectors. But this thought, which supported me in the commencement of my career, now serves only to plunge me lower in the dust. All my speculations and hopes are as nothing, and like the archangel who **aspired** to **omnipotence**, I am chained in an eternal hell. My imagination was vivid, yet my powers of analysis and application were intense; by the union of these qualities I conceived the idea and executed the creation of a man. Even now I cannot recollect without passion my reveries while the work was incomplete. I trod heaven in my thoughts, now **exulting** in my

---

illustrious [ilʌ́stiəs] adj.
뛰어난, 빛나는
aspire [əspáiər] v.
열망하다, 갈망하다
omnipotence [ɑmnípətəns / ɔm-] n.
전능
exult [igzʌ́lt] v.
기뻐하다

powers, now burning with the idea of their effects. From my infancy I was **imbued** with high hopes and a lofty ambition; but how am I sunk! Oh! My friend, if you had known me as I once was, you would not recognise me in this state of **degradation**. Despondency rarely visited my heart; a high destiny seemed to bear me on, until I fell, never, never again to rise."

Must I then lose this admirable being? I have longed for a friend; I have sought one who would sympathise with and love me. Behold, on these desert seas I have found such a one, but I fear I have gained him only to know his value and lose him. I would reconcile him to life, but he repulses the idea.

"I thank you, Walton," he said, "for your kind intentions towards so miserable a wretch; but when you speak of new ties and fresh affections, think you that any can replace those who are gone? Can any man be to me as Clerval was, or any woman another Elizabeth? Even where the affections are not strongly moved by any superior excellence, the companions of our childhood always possess a certain power over our minds which hardly any later friend can obtain. They know our **infantine dispositions**, which, however they may be afterwards modified, are never **eradicated**; and they can judge of our actions with more certain conclusions

undertaking [ʌ̀ndərtéikiŋ] n.
일, 사업
fraught [frɔːt] adj.
~을 내포한, ~으로 가득 찬
utility [juːtíləti] n.
쓸모가 있음, 유용, 유익, 실리
lot [lɑt / lɔt] n.
운, 운명

as to the integrity of our motives. A sister or a brother can never, unless indeed such symptoms have been shown early, suspect the other of fraud or false dealing, when another friend, however strongly he may be attached, may, in spite of himself, be contemplated with suspicion. But I enjoyed friends, dear not only through habit and association, but from their own merits; and wherever I am, the soothing voice of my Elizabeth and the conversation of Clerval will be ever whispered in my ear. They are dead, and but one feeling in such a solitude can persuade me to preserve my life. If I were engaged in any high **undertaking** or design, **fraught** with extensive **utility** to my fellow creatures, then could I live to fulfil it. But such is not my destiny; I must pursue and destroy the being to whom I gave existence; then my **lot** on earth will be fulfilled and I may die."

encompass [inkʌ́mpəs] v.
둘러싸다, 에워싸다, 포위하다
peril [pérəl] n.
위험, 위기

My beloved Sister,   September 2nd.

I write to you, **encompassed** by **peril** and ignorant whether I am ever doomed to see again dear England and the dearer friends that inhabit it. I am surrounded by mountains of ice which admit of no escape and threaten every moment to crush my vessel. The brave fellows whom I have persuaded to be my companions look towards me for aid, but I have none to bestow. There is something terribly appalling in our situation, yet my courage and hopes do not desert me. Yet it is terrible to reflect that the lives of all these men are endangered through me. If we are lost, my mad schemes are the cause.

And what, Margaret, will be the state of your mind? You will not hear of my destruction, and you will anxiously await my return. Years will pass, and you will have visitings of despair and yet be tortured by hope. Oh! My beloved sister, the sickening failing of your heart-felt expectations is, in prospect, more terrible to me than my own death. But you have a husband and lovely children; you may be happy. Heaven bless you and make you so!

My unfortunate guest regards me with the tenderest compassion. He endeavours to fill me with hope and talks as if life were a possession which he valued. He reminds me how often the same accidents have happened to other navigators who have attempted this sea, and in spite of myself, he fills me with cheerful **auguries**. Even the sailors feel the power of his eloquence; when he speaks, they no longer despair; he rouses their energies, and while they hear his voice they believe these vast mountains of ice are **molehills** which will vanish before the **resolutions** of man. These

---

augury [ɔ́:gjəri] n.
전조, 조짐
molehill [móulhìl] n.
두더지가 파 놓은 흙두둑, 하찮은 일, 사소한 장애
cf) make a mountain out of a molehill — 침소봉대하다
resolution [rèzəlúːʃ-ən] n.
결심, 단호함, 의지

transitory [trǽnsətɔ̀:ri, -zə- / -t-əri] adj.
일시적인, 덧없는, 무상한
mutiny [mjú:t-əni] n.
반란, 폭동

imminent [ímənənt] adj.
임박한, 곧 일어날 듯한

wan [wɑn / wɔn] adj.
창백한
deputation [dèpjətéiʃən] n.
대표, 대표단
requisition [rèkwəzíʃ-ən] n.
요구, 청구

feelings are **transitory**; each day of expectation delayed fills them with fear, and I almost dread a **mutiny** caused by this despair.

September 5th.

A scene has just passed of such uncommon interest that, although it is highly probable that these papers may never reach you, yet I cannot forbear recording it.

We are still surrounded by mountains of ice, still in **imminent** danger of being crushed in their conflict. The cold is excessive, and many of my unfortunate comrades have already found a grave amidst this scene of desolation. Frankenstein has daily declined in health; a feverish fire still glimmers in his eyes, but he is exhausted, and when suddenly roused to any exertion, he speedily sinks again into apparent lifelessness.

I mentioned in my last letter the fears I entertained of a mutiny. This morning, as I sat watching the **wan** countenance of my friend — his eyes half closed and his limbs hanging listlessly—I was roused by half a dozen of the sailors, who demanded admission into the cabin. They entered, and their leader addressed me. He told me that he and his companions had been chosen by the other sailors to come in **deputation** to me to make me a **requisition** which, in justice, I could not refuse. We were **immured** in ice and should probably never escape, but they feared that if, as was possible, the ice should dissipate and a free passage be opened, I should be rash enough to continue my voyage and lead them into fresh dangers, after they might happily have surmounted this. They insisted, therefore, that I should engage with a solemn promise that if the vessel should be freed I would instantly direct my course southwards.

This speech troubled me. I had not despaired, nor had I yet conceived the idea of returning if set free. Yet could I, in justice, or even in possibility, refuse this demand? I hesitated before I answered, when Frankenstein, who had at first been silent, and indeed appeared hardly to have force enough to attend, now roused himself; his eyes sparkled, and his cheeks flushed with momentary vigour. Turning towards the men, he said,

"What do you mean? What do you demand of your captain? Are you, then, so easily turned from your design? Did you not call this a glorious **expedition**? And **wherefore** was it glorious? Not because the way was smooth and **placid** as a southern sea, but because it was full of dangers and terror, because at every new incident your **fortitude** was to be **called**

---

immure [imjúər] v.
감금하다, 가두다

expedition [èkspədíʃən] n.
(집단, 단체의) 모험, 원정
wherefore [hwéə:rfɔ̀:r] adv.
(의문사) 무엇 때문에, 왜
placid [plǽsid] adj.
조용한, 평온한
fortitude [fɔ́:rtətjù:d] n.
용기, 불굴의 정신, 인내
call forth:
(용기 따위를) 불러일으키다, 끌어내다

brave [breiv] v.
무릅쓰다, 용감하게 맞서다
hand down:
(판결을) 언도하다, 판정하다, 공언하다
mutable [mjú:təb-əl] adj.
변하기 쉬운, 변덕스러운
stigma [stíɡmə] n.
치욕, 오명, 불명예

And wherefore was it glorious? Not because the way was smooth and placid as a southern sea, but because it was full of dangers and terror, ...

forth and your courage exhibited, because danger and death surrounded it, and these you were to **brave** and overcome. For this was it a glorious, for this was it an honourable undertaking. You were hereafter to be hailed as the benefactors of your species, your names adored as belonging to brave men who encountered death for honour and the benefit of mankind. And now, behold, with the first imagination of danger, or, if you will, the first mighty and terrific trial of your courage, you shrink away and are content to be **handed down** as men who had not strength enough to endure cold and peril; and so, poor souls, they were chilly and returned to their warm firesides. Why, that requires not this preparation; ye need not have come thus far and dragged your captain to the shame of a defeat merely to prove yourselves cowards. Oh! Be men, or be more than men. Be steady to your purposes and firm as a rock. This ice is not made of such stuff as your hearts may be; it is **mutable** and cannot withstand you if you say that it shall not. Do not return to your families with the **stigma** of disgrace marked on your brows. Return as heroes who have fought and conquered and who know not what it is to turn their backs on the foe."

He spoke this with a voice so modulated to the different feelings expressed in his speech, with an eye so full of lofty design and heroism, that can you wonder that these men were moved? They looked at one another and were unable to reply. I spoke; I told them to retire and consider of what had been said, that I would not lead them farther north if they strenuously desired the contrary, but that I hoped that, with reflection, their courage would return.

They retired and I turned towards my friend, but he was sunk in **languor** and almost deprived of life.

How all this will terminate, I know not, but I had rather die than return shamefully, my purpose unfulfilled. Yet I fear such will be my fate; the men, unsupported by ideas of glory and honour, can never willingly continue to endure their present hardships.

September 7th.

The die is cast; I have consented to return if we are not destroyed. Thus are my hopes blasted by cowardice and indecision; I come back ignorant and disappointed. It requires more **philosophy** than I possess to bear this injustice with patience.

September 12th.

It is past; I am returning to England. I have lost my hopes of utility and glory; I have lost my friend. But I will endeavour to detail these bitter circumstances to you, my dear sister; and while I am wafted towards England and towards you, I will not despond.

September 9th, the ice began to move, and roarings like thunder were heard at a distance as the islands split and cracked in every direction. We were in the most imminent peril, but as we could only remain passive, my chief attention was occupied by my unfortunate guest whose illness increased in such a degree that he was entirely confined to his bed. The ice cracked behind us and was driven with force towards the north; a breeze sprang from the west, and on the 11th the passage towards the south became perfectly free. When the sailors saw this and that their return to their native country was apparently assured, a shout of tumultuous joy broke from them, loud and long-continued. Frankenstein, who was dozing, awoke and asked the cause of the tumult. "They shout," I said, "because they will soon return to England."

"Do you, then, really return?"

"Alas! Yes; I cannot **withstand** their demands. I cannot lead them unwillingly to danger, and I must return."

"Do so, if you will; but I will not. You may give up your purpose, but mine is assigned to

withstand [wiðstǽnd, wiə-] v.
견디다, 저항하다, 거역하다

me by Heaven, and I dare not. I am weak, but surely the spirits who assist my vengeance will endow me with sufficient strength." Saying this, he endeavoured to spring from the bed, but the exertion was too great for him; he fell back and fainted.

It was long before he was restored, and I often thought that life was entirely extinct. At length he opened his eyes; he breathed with difficulty and was unable to speak. The surgeon gave him a composing **draught** and ordered us to leave him undisturbed. In the meantime he told me that my friend had certainly not many hours to live.

His **sentence** was **pronounced**, and I could only grieve and be patient. I sat by his bed, watching him; his eyes were closed, and I thought he slept; but presently he called to me in a feeble voice, and bidding me come near, said, "Alas! The strength I relied on is gone; I feel that I shall soon die, and he, my enemy and **persecutor**, may still be in being. Think not, Walton, that in the last moments of my existence I feel that burning hatred and ardent desire of revenge I once expressed; but I feel myself justified in desiring the death of my adversary. During these last days I have been occupied in examining my past conduct; nor do I find it blameable. In a fit of enthusiastic madness I created a rational creature and was bound towards him to assure, as far as was in my power, his happiness and well-being. This was my duty, but there was another still **paramount** to that. My duties towards the beings of my own species had greater claims to my attention because they included a greater proportion of happiness or misery. Urged by this view, I refused, and I did right in refusing, to create a companion for the first creature. He showed **unparalleled malignity** and selfishness in evil; he destroyed my friends; he devoted to destruction beings who possessed exquisite sensations, happiness, and wisdom; nor do I know where this thirst for vengeance may end. Miserable himself that he may render no other wretched, he ought to die. The task of his destruction was mine, but I have failed. When actuated by selfish and vicious motives, I asked you to undertake my unfinished work, and I renew this request now, when I am only induced by reason and virtue.

"Yet I cannot ask you to **renounce** your country and friends to fulfil this task; and now that you are returning to England, you will have little chance of meeting with him. But the consideration of these points, and the well balancing of what you may esteem your duties, I leave to you; my judgment and ideas are already disturbed by the near approach of death. I dare not ask you to do what I think right, for I may still be **misled** by passion.

"That he should live to be an **instrument** of **mischief disturbs** me; in other respects, this hour, when I **momentarily** expect my **release**, is the only happy one which I have enjoyed for several years. The forms of the beloved dead flit before me, and I hasten to their arms. Farewell, Walton! Seek happiness in tranquillity and avoid ambition, even if it be only the apparently innocent one of **distinguishing** yourself in science and discoveries. Yet why do I say this? I have myself been **blasted** in these hopes, yet another may succeed."

His voice became fainter as he spoke, and at length, exhausted by his effort, he sank into silence. About half an hour afterwards he attempted again to speak but was unable; he pressed my hand feebly, and his eyes closed for ever, while the irradiation of a gentle smile passed away from his lips.

Margaret, what comment can I make on the **untimely extinction** of this glorious spirit? What can I say that will enable you to understand the depth of my sorrow? All that I should express would be inadequate and feeble. My tears flow; my mind is overshadowed by a cloud of disappointment. But I journey towards

---

mislead [mislí:d] v.
그릇 인도하다, 판단을 그르치게 하다, 현혹시키다

instrument [ínstrəmənt] n.
도구, 수단, 방편
mischief [místʃif] n.
손해, 재해, 악영향
disturb [distə́:rb] v.
마음을 어지럽게 하다, 불안하게 하다
momentarily [móuuməntèrili / -təri] adv.
곧, 즉각, 즉시
release [rilí:s] n.
해방, 구출, 면제
distinguish [distíŋgwiʃ] v.
눈에 띄게 하다, 두드러지게 하다, 유명하게 하다
blast [blæst, blɑ:st] v.
망치다, 파괴하다, 파멸시키다

untimely [ʌntáimli] adj.
때아닌, 너무 이른
extinction [ikstíŋkʃən] n.
사멸, 절멸, 폐절

portend [pɔːrténd] v.
~의 전조가 되다, ~을 미리 알리다

"That he should live to be an instrument of mischief disturbs me; ..."

uncouth [ʌnkúːθ] adj.
괴상한, 기묘한

England, and I may there find consolation.

I am interrupted. What do these sounds **portend**? It is midnight; the breeze blows fairly, and the watch on deck scarcely stir. Again there is a sound as of a human voice, but hoarser; it comes from the cabin where the remains of Frankenstein still lie. I must arise and examine. Good night, my sister.

Great God! What a scene has just taken place! I am yet dizzy with the remembrance of it. I hardly know whether I shall have the power to detail it; yet the tale which I have recorded would be incomplete without this final and wonderful catastrophe.

I entered the cabin where lay the remains of my ill-fated and admirable friend. Over him hung a form which I cannot find words to describe — gigantic in stature, yet **uncouth** and distorted in its proportions. As he hung over the coffin, his face was concealed by long locks of ragged hair; but one vast hand was extended, in colour and apparent texture like that of a mummy. When he heard the sound of my approach, he ceased to utter exclamations of grief and horror and sprung towards the window. Never did I behold a vision so horrible as his face, of such loathsome yet appalling hideousness. I shut my eyes involuntarily and endeavoured to recollect what were my duties with regard to this destroyer. I called on him to stay.

He paused, looking on me with wonder, and again turning towards the lifeless form of his creator, he seemed to forget my presence, and every feature and gesture seemed instigated by the wildest rage of some uncontrollable passion.

"That is also my victim!" he exclaimed. "In his murder my crimes are consummated; the miserable series of my being is wound to its close! Oh, Frankenstein! Generous and self-devoted being! What does it avail that I now ask thee to pardon me? I, who irretrievably destroyed thee by destroying all thou lovedst. Alas! He is cold, he cannot answer me."

His voice seemed suffocated, and my first impulses, which had suggested to me the duty of obeying the dying request of my friend in destroying his enemy, were now suspended by a mixture of curiosity and compassion. I approached this tremendous being; I dared not again raise my eyes to his face, there was something so scaring and **unearthly** in his ugliness. I attempted to speak, but the words died away on my lips. The monster continued to utter wild and incoherent self-reproaches. At length I gathered resolution to address him in a pause of the **tempest** of his passion.

"Your **repentance**," I said, "is now **superfluous**. If you had listened to the voice of

---

unearthly [ʌnə́:rəli] adj.
이 세상의 것이 아닌, 초자연적인, 괴상한
tempest [témpist] n.
사나운 비바람, 폭풍우; 대소동, 대혼란

repentance [ripéntəns] n.
후회, 참회
superfluous [su:pə́:rfluəs] adj.
불필요한, 쓸데없는

heed [hi:d] v.
주의하다, 조심하다
remorse [rimɔ́:rs] n.
후회, 양심의 가책
extremity [ikstréməti] n.
막다름, 궁지
dead [ded] adj.
죽은 듯한, 무감각한, 느끼지 못하는

author [ɔ́:θər] n.
창조자, 장본인

conscience and **heeded** the stings of **remorse** before you had urged your diabolical vengeance to this **extremity**, Frankenstein would yet have lived."

"And do you dream?" said the daemon. "Do you think that I was then **dead** to agony and remorse? He," he continued, pointing to the corpse, "he suffered not in the consummation of the deed. Oh! Not the ten-thousandth portion of the anguish that was mine during the lingering detail of its execution. A frightful selfishness hurried me on, while my heart was poisoned with remorse. Think you that the groans of Clerval were music to my ears? My heart was fashioned to be susceptible of love and sympathy, and when wrenched by misery to vice and hatred, it did not endure the violence of the change without torture such as you cannot even imagine.

"After the murder of Clerval I returned to Switzerland, heart-broken and overcome. I pitied Frankenstein; my pity amounted to horror; I abhorred myself. But when I discovered that he, the **author** at once of my existence and of its unspeakable torments, dared to hope for happiness, that while he accumulated wretchedness and despair upon me he sought his own enjoyment in feelings and passions from the indulgence of which I was for ever barred, then impotent envy and bitter indignation filled me with an insatiable thirst for vengeance. I recollected my threat and resolved that it should be accomplished. I knew that I was preparing for myself a deadly torture, but I was the slave, not the master, of an impulse which I detested yet could not disobey. Yet when she died! Nay, then I was not miserable. I had cast off all feeling, subdued all anguish, to riot in the excess of my despair. Evil thenceforth became my good. Urged thus far, I had no choice but to adapt my nature to an element which I had willingly chosen. The completion of my demoniacal design became an insatiable passion. And now it is ended; there is my last victim!"

I was at first touched by the expressions of his misery; yet, when I called to mind what Frankenstein had said of his powers of eloquence and persuasion, and when I again cast my eyes on the lifeless form of my friend, indignation was rekindled within me. "Wretch!" I said. "It is well that you come here to whine over the desolation that you have made. You throw a torch into a pile of buildings, and when they are consumed, you sit among the ruins and **lament** the fall. **Hypocritical** fiend! If he whom you mourn still lived, still would he be the object, again would he become the prey, of

---

lament [ləmént] v.
슬퍼하다, 비탄하다, 애도하다
hypocritical [hìpəkrítikəl] adj.
위선의, 위선적인

accursed [əkə́:rsid] adj.
저주받은, 가증스런
malignity [məlígnəti] n.
악의, 원한

purport [pərpɔ́:rt, pə́:rpɔ:rt] n.
의미, 의도
opprobrium [əpróubriəm] n.
불명예, 비난
pardon [pá:rdn] v.
용서하다, 관대히 봐주다
unfold [ʌnfóuld] v.
펼치다, 드러내다, 밝히다
degrade [digréid] v.
강등시키다, 떨어뜨리다, 타락시키다

your **accursed** vengeance. It is not pity that you feel; you lament only because the victim of your **malignity** is withdrawn from your power."

"Oh, it is not thus — not thus," interrupted the being. "Yet such must be the impression conveyed to you by what appears to be the **purport** of my actions. Yet I seek not a fellow feeling in my misery. No sympathy may I ever find. When I first sought it, it was the love of virtue, the feelings of happiness and affection with which my whole being overflowed, that I wished to be participated. But now that virtue has become to me a shadow, and that happiness and affection are turned into bitter and loathing despair, in what should I seek for sympathy? I am content to suffer alone while my sufferings shall endure; when I die, I am well satisfied that abhorrence and **opprobrium** should load my memory. Once my fancy was soothed with dreams of virtue, of fame, and of enjoyment. Once I falsely hoped to meet with beings who, **pardoning** my outward form, would love me for the excellent qualities which I was capable of **unfolding**. I was nourished with high thoughts of honour and devotion. But now crime has **degraded** me beneath the meanest animal. No guilt, no mischief, no malignity, no misery, can be found comparable to mine. When

run over:
훑어보다, 검토하다

contumely [kəntjúːməli, kántjumə̀ːli / kɔ́n-] n.
오만, 무례
execrate [éksikrèit] v.
통렬히 비난하다, 혐오하다, 저주하다
rustic [rʌ́stik] n.
시골 사람, 농부
virtuous [vɔ́ːrtʃuəs] adj.
덕이 높은, 고결한, 정숙한
immaculate [imǽkjəlit] adj.
깨끗한, 청순한, 순결한
abortion [əbɔ́ːrʃən] n.
미숙아, 불구, 기형적인 사람(것)

I **run over** the frightful catalogue of my sins, I cannot believe that I am the same creature whose thoughts were once filled with sublime and transcendent visions of the beauty and the majesty of goodness. But it is even so; the fallen angel becomes a malignant devil. Yet even that enemy of God and man had friends and associates in his desolation; I am alone.

"You, who call Frankenstein your friend, seem to have a knowledge of my crimes and his misfortunes. But in the detail which he gave you of them he could not sum up the hours and months of misery which I endured wasting in impotent passions. For while I destroyed his hopes, I did not satisfy my own desires. They were for ever ardent and craving; still I desired love and fellowship, and I was still spurned. Was there no injustice in this? Am I to be thought the only criminal, when all humankind sinned against me? Why do you not hate Felix, who drove his friend from his door with **contumely**? Why do you not **execrate** the **rustic** who sought to destroy the saviour of his child? Nay, these are **virtuous** and **immaculate** beings! I, the miserable and the abandoned, am an **abortion**, to be spurned at, and kicked, and trampled on. Even now my blood boils at the recollection of this injustice.

"But it is true that I am a wretch. I have

select [silékt] adj.
가려낸, 정선한, 최고의
specimen [spésəmən] n.
견본, 표본, 샘플
irremediable [ìrimí:diəbəl] adj. 고칠 수 없는, 돌이킬 수 없는

consummate [kánsəmèit / kón-] v.
성취하다, 완성하다
thither [θíðə:r, ðíð-] adv.
그쪽으로, 저쪽으로
consume [kənsú:m] v.
없애다, 파괴하다, 소멸시키다
unhallowed [ʌnhǽloud] adj.
사악한, 죄가 많은

murdered the lovely and the helpless; I have strangled the innocent as they slept and grasped to death his throat who never injured me or any other living thing. I have devoted my creator, the **select specimen** of all that is worthy of love and admiration among men, to misery; I have pursued him even to that **irremediable** ruin. There he lies, white and cold in death. You hate me, but your abhorrence cannot equal that with which I regard myself. I look on the hands which executed the deed; I think on the heart in which the imagination of it was conceived and long for the moment when these hands will meet my eyes, when that imagination will haunt my thoughts no more.

"Fear not that I shall be the instrument of future mischief. My work is nearly complete. Neither yours nor any man's death is needed to **consummate** the series of my being and accomplish that which must be done, but it requires my own. Do not think that I shall be slow to perform this sacrifice. I shall quit your vessel on the ice raft which brought me **thither** and shall seek the most northern extremity of the globe; I shall collect my funeral pile and **consume** to ashes this miserable frame, that its remains may afford no light to any curious and **unhallowed** wretch who would create such another as I have been. I shall die. I shall no longer feel the agonies which now consume me or be the prey of feelings unsatisfied, yet unquenched. He is dead who called me into being; and when I shall be no more, the very remembrance of us both will speedily vanish. I shall no longer see the sun or stars or feel the winds play on my cheeks. Light, feeling, and sense will pass away; and in this condition must I find my happiness. Some years ago, when the images which this world affords first opened upon me, when I felt the cheering warmth of summer and heard the rustling of the leaves and the warbling of the birds, and these were all to me, I should have wept to die; now it is my only consolation. Polluted by crimes and torn by the bitterest remorse, where can I find rest but in death?

"Farewell! I leave you, and in you the last of humankind whom these eyes will ever behold. Farewell, Frankenstein! If thou wert yet alive and yet cherished a desire of revenge against me, it would be better satiated in my life than in my destruction. But it was not so; thou didst seek my extinction, that I might not cause greater wretchedness; and if yet, in some mode unknown to me, thou hadst not ceased to think and feel, thou wouldst not desire against me a vengeance greater than that which I feel. Blasted as thou wert, my agony was still

"... Polluted by crimes and torn by the bitterest remorse, where can I find rest but in death?

rankle [rǽŋk-əl] v.
욱신거리다, 쑤시다

extinct [ikstíŋkt] adj.
사멸한, 없어진

conflagration [kɑ̀nfləgréiʃən / kɔ̀n-] n.
큰불, 대화재

superior to thine, for the bitter sting of remorse will not cease to **rankle** in my wounds until death shall close them for ever.

"But soon," he cried with sad and solemn enthusiasm, "I shall die, and what I now feel be no longer felt. Soon these burning miseries will be **extinct**. I shall ascend my funeral pile triumphantly and exult in the agony of the torturing flames. The light of that **conflagration** will fade away; my ashes will be swept into the sea by the winds. My spirit will sleep in peace, or if it thinks, it will not surely think thus. Farewell."

He sprang from the cabin-window as he said this, upon the ice raft which lay close to the vessel. He was soon borne away by the waves and lost in darkness and distance.

"The light of that conflagration will fade away; my ashes will be swept into the sea by the winds. My spirit will sleep in peace, or if it thinks, it will not surely think thus. Farewell."